My Father – Reith of the BBC

I dedicate this book to Murray, and to our family,
Mark, Iona, Martha and Kirsty,
who give back more than they will ever know.

My Father – Reith of the BBC

MARISTA LEISHMAN

Foreword by Sir Michael Checkland

SAINT ANDREW PRESS
Edinburgh

First published in 2006 by
SAINT ANDREW PRESS
121 George Street, Edinburgh EH2 4YN

10-digit ISBN 0 7152 0834 9 (Hardback)
13-digit ISBN 978 0 7152 0834 2 (Hardback)

British Library Cataloguing in Publication Data
A catalogue record for this book is available from the British Library.

Typeset in 12/14 Plantin and 13/15 Perpetua by Waverley Typesetters
Printed and bound in Germany by Bercker GmbH

CONTENTS

LIST OF ILLUSTRATIONS

14. With Christopher and Marista.
15. Harrias House, Beaconsfield. Marista with her father and mother.
16. Harrias House, Beaconsfield, and adjoining farm.
17. Still towering above everyone.
18. *The Birth of Broadcasting.* At a reception given by Oxford University Press and the BBC to mark the publication of *The Birth of Broadcasting* by Professor Asa Briggs. The picture shows (L to R) Mr John Brown (OUP), Professor Asa Briggs, Captain Peter Eckersley, Lord Reith, Mr Hugh Carleton Greene. © BBC
19. Dressed for the General Assembly of the Church of Scotland, 1967.
20. With Malcolm Muggeridge, in Kelvingrove Park, Glasgow.
21. As Lord High Commissioner in the uniform of the Royal Company of Archers, the Queen's Bodyguard in Scotland, at the General Assembly, 1967. Image courtesy of *The Herald & Evening Times* picture archive.
22. *Lord Reith Looks Back*: 1967. With Malcolm Muggeridge during the filming of *Lord Reith Looks Back*. © BBC
23. *Lord Reith Looks Back*: 1967. © BBC
24. Marista.
25. Murray Leishman.
26. Portrait of John Reith. This painting, by Sir Gerald Kelly, is now on show as part of a permanent exhibition in the South Atrium of the Media Centre, Wood Lane, London. © BBC
27. Photograph by Simon Jones: Marista Leishman standing in front of 'John Reith, 1st Baron Reith of Stonehaven' by Sir Oswald Birley. With grateful thanks to the Scottish National Portrait Gallery.

FOREWORD

THE MORNING after I was selected as the eleventh Director General of the BBC, I went into a crowded press conference in the Council Chamber of Broadcasting House. It was pointed out that I was not a programme-maker. Turning round in my chair, I looked up to the large portrait of Lord Reith behind me and replied: 'Neither was he'. I was asked no more questions like that. His outstanding contribution to the establishment, independence, purpose and ethos of the BBC was known to all.

What was not known was a different portrait – that of John Reith as a father, husband and family man. I had invited Marista, Reith's daughter, to a promenade concert at the Royal Albert Hall. I had heard of her love of music. I also knew a little about the difficult relationship she had had with her father, but I had no notion of the length, breadth and depth of that estrangement, which this book so honestly exposes. There are recollections of her childhood, descriptions of life at home, trips to America and family holidays – but also the revelation that her husband Murray was on her father's list of the seven men he most hated. Even to have such a list is, in itself, so illuminating. The public achievement of the father is set against a background of profound human frailty at home.

Marista describes her father as 'a soloist, free of political constraint, the restrictions of democracy and the agendas of consensus systems'. He was a Director General who forged the independence of the BBC, to which it has clung throughout its history. It was clear, wrote Reith, 'that the Government should leave the BBC alone and trust to me'. He needed the comfort of monopoly in broadcasting, and later defended it in the House of Lords in the 1950s when the introduction of commercial television was being debated. He deployed a breathtaking arrogance of power. This was hardly surprising when he was right at the centre of political and royal events, as the emerging influence of radio broadcasting began to be understood. Alongside this, his protestations of his own mediocrity ring false. He saw 'the Almighty there in my appointment to the job and there in the execution of it'. His search for honours and recognition was unceasing, and descriptions of his later over-elaborate deputising for the Queen at Holyrood are revealing.

Would the John Reith described in this book have adapted to the many developments in broadcasting since he left the BBC in 1938? His unhappiness with the idea of a modest staff association is a long way from the organised broadcasting trade unions which flexed their muscles in the 1970s and 1980s. His visionary deployment of wireless was based on the power of the Word which he had experienced in the manse and the pulpit. It was not matched by any sense of the potential of television. In programming, he wished to be ahead – not in step with the public. Nothing could be further from the focus groups and sophisticated audience research and measurement of the twenty-first century. His personality and style thrived on monopoly. The multi-channel competitive world of radio and television, the development of non-broadcast technologies in new media, the joint ventures, the co-productions – none of this would have suited such a powerful individualist, whose inability to work with others blocked so many opportunities for him after he left the BBC.

As long as he had independent command, such as he had enjoyed at the BBC, his energetic leadership and great organisational ability were demonstrated in all his work after leaving. They were clear in town-planning, or in preparations for D-Day and civil aviation. So was his inability to collaborate with others, which Churchill saw so clearly in refusing his many requests for various appointments and which led Reith so bitterly to complain to him 'As someone whom you broke and whose life you ruined'. Reith inhabited a world of triumphs and insults.

This book again emphasises the importance to the BBC of the relationships between the Director General, the Chairman and the Board of Governors. When too much emotional effort goes into dealing with tensions with the Governors, such as the disaffection between Reith and Lady Snowden, the organisation invariably suffers and staff become unsettled. Reith's solution to Ramsay MacDonald of suggesting that he himself should become Chairman was an unlikely prospect. Instead, the appointment of the wise conciliator John Whitley, a former Speaker of the House of Commons, brought an immediate change in the demeanour of the Director General. As Reith wrote in his diary, 'It seemed that a raging storm had been suddenly hushed to calm. In fact he brought, immediately, by his very coming, peace. Free from internal strife, suspicion and distrust, one was able, undistracted, to get on with the job.' Many future Director Generals would have liked such a Chairman during their period of office. How would Reith have coped with today's Board of Governors with their separate premises, a staff of thirty-five and the use of external consultants to regulate and measure the performance of the Director General and his Board of Management?

Reith had talked as early as 1928 of leaving the BBC, and later dreamed of a recall as the continual frustration of later jobs proved so unrewarding to him. Inevitably, he had the fault of all Director Generals of seeing their successors fail compared with their own achievements as seen by themselves. His daughter saw that 'His other occupations, with however much of his own spirit he imbued them, he always experienced as intervals after which he might return to his vocation in the BBC'.

Like many after him, Reith did find his only true vocation in the BBC. As Director General, he shaped and occupied what is still today the most challenging and rewarding creative job in the country. The BBC, which he started, is still based on broadcasting as a public service by a public corporation under Royal Charter, with the obligation to educate, inform and entertain. For all his many faults as a father, as seen through the eyes of his daughter and set out so painfully in this book, John Reith remains one of the commanding figures of the twentieth century and the creator of one of its greatest institutions.

SIR MICHAEL CHECKLAND
Director General of the BBC, 1987–92

A NOTE FROM THE AUTHOR

THIS BOOK tells a story. It is told as a story is told – not as a rigid chronological timeline. While chronological telling has the advantage of simple authority, it can lack the flexibility to develop themes and character. Sometimes a characteristic can be described best by moving forwards a few years to some incident. Of course, it is not always easy to say whether a particular thing happened when I was six or four or eight years old. Hindsight joins up the anecdotes and the observations; following a rigid timeline would dilute the impact.

The story is about me and my relationship with my father. As our lives were intertwined, it was necessary to bring my voice into the story at an early point. For this reason, a second typeface has been used. One typeface tells, broadly speaking, John Reith's story; the second tells mine. They overlap, interject and interlink, which I think serves as a visual representation of our relationship.

MARISTA LEISHMAN
May 2006

SOME KEY EVENTS

1889   John Charles Walsham Reith born on 20 July in Stonehaven, north-east Scotland. Raised in Glasgow.

1921   Marries Muriel Odhams near Brighton in southern England.

1922   On 30 December, John becomes general manager of the new British Broadcasting Company in London.

1926   The BBC becomes a Corporation with a board of governors. John is its first Director General, and is knighted.

1932   Marista Muriel Reith born on 10 April in Beaconsfield near London. Educated at home until age 14.

1938   John leaves the BBC to manage Imperial Airways.

1940   John becomes an MP, serves for two years in wartime cabinet as Minister for Information, then Transport, then Works, and is raised to the peerage as the 1st Baron of Stonehaven.

1943   and 1944: John organises logistics for D-Day invasion of occupied France.

1945   onwards: John holds numerous post-war chairmanships.

1946   Marista attends boarding school from age 14.

1949   John's autobiography, *Into the Wind*, is published.

1951   Marista attends University of St Andrews, studies English and Philosophy, and meets Murray Leishman.

1960   They marry on 3 December and have four children over the following years.

1967   and 1968: John serves as Lord High Commissioner at the week-long General Assembly of the Church of Scotland.

1970   John and Muriel move from London to Edinburgh, where he is awarded the Order of the Thistle.

1971   John dies on 16 June. His ashes are buried at Rothie-murchus.

PROLOGUE

*T*HE BACKGROUND – if not the foreground – to my childhood was the BBC. As my sibling, it occupied a place of such importance in my father's experience that it rendered meagre indeed any attempts of mine to signify – especially as, in the context in which I was attempting to grow up, everything was very large. So bizarre an upbringing with so dominant a figure at the centre was not, however, without its stimulus.

We grew up together, the BBC and I. The elder by ten years, it was – in my father's eyes – the favoured child in whom huge energies were invested. I, on the other hand, coming along later, was ornamental by comparison.

The BBC and I scarcely knew each other. Occasionally, I would hear mention of my sibling's initials; but it was some time before I knew what they stood for. This only occurred after my father had walked away from his eldest child, at which point he had two things to say about the BBC: that he regretted ever having left it, and that he regretted ever having had anything to do with it. Although these two statements together made little sense, there was something to be learned: that, while part of my father's life was ordered and controlled to the point of obsession – from the storage of his pencils to the drafting of nationally important management proposals – his attitude to the issues and institutions in which he had invested emotionally was often one conspicuously without clarity, logic or order.

Years later, when he had poured a concentration of effort and attachment into my approaching adulthood, he was to find, as with the BBC, that he could only experience the other's autonomy as an insult. In response to my increasing independence, he had first to fulminate and then, again, to walk away, regretting that he had had anything to do with me.

Nevertheless, after more than eighty years, for good or ill, the BBC is seldom out of the news. The tall ghost of its creator seems still to stalk the corridors of Broadcasting House, brooding dolefully on its daily outpourings. His name, meanwhile, has passed into the language – and 'Reithian standards' have become a benchmark for today.

Malcolm Muggeridge, journalist, wit and television personality, in his 1967 television interviews, said of Reith that he was the stuff of legend. But, since he was my father and the background to an eventful childhood, I prefer to look behind the legend, leave some of it intact and consider *why* he seemed to believe that the world was made for him. His narcissistic extremes propelled him nearly to the top of the tree before abandoning him to inevitable downfall.

This is an account of growing up in John Reith's household. It is the story of a father who is more interested in his children for what they can do to assist his image than for who they are in their own right.

Here is a child having to do without the luxury of mediocrity while managing the expectation of exceptional intelligence and capability. Here is the man who, having placed a particular stamp on the BBC – those same Reithian values, in fact – permits himself an irregular lifestyle and, claiming a special alliance with the Almighty, finds the practices and attitudes of Christianity not to his taste. Here also is the man behind whose grim image lies an engaging eccentric; who, rather than squeeze himself into an Austin 7, rides along on the bonnet, umbrella opened out to the sunshine.

My story is of Reith as an actor playing the only part he could: that of himself, for which he also supplied stage, plot and audience; the man who – drawing on the role model of his grandfather and his pioneering mission to open up the River Clyde to navigation, shipbuilding and commerce – himself unlocked the ether to communication, education and entertainment.

My story is also that of surviving Reith and discovering that my aims never did include living out his frustrations for him. And, too, that there is still much about him to be celebrated.

In 1930, the Postmaster General, H. B. Lees Smith, was appointing the new BBC Chairman. The BBC had been in business for eight years – the last four as a public corporation – and John Whitley was chosen to be its second Chairman. Both wise and experienced, he was nonetheless startled, as he began his term of office, to be told the PMG's view of the BBC's Director General. 'I doubt if you will be seeing all that much of Reith,' said Mr Lees Smith. 'We fear he's off his head and won't be at the BBC all that much longer.'

Nowadays, an image which many retain of John Reith is as an old man taking part in a televised interview with John Freeman. The latter's celebrated television series *Face to Face* included in-depth interviews with Bertrand Russell, Carl Gustav Jung and Dame Edith Sitwell. Reith's patriarchal profile fills the screen; his conspicuous features have become more pronounced, the scar that crosses his cheek in a ferocious diagonal the more shocking. In fact, he seems almost to enjoy the intruding camera and certainly does not object to its probing eye's familiarity. Suddenly he offers a wild ghoulish smile, as inconsequential as it is fake. Another camera catches the gimlet glare boring into his questioner. For the more discerning, here is the old rogue easily manipulating a large viewing audience so that they respond according to his plan, caught like rabbits in the glare, fascinated. They will marvel at his presence: a phenomenon of which they once knew, now enigmatically returned from another planet, and the feeling never far away that, in his view anyway, the universe has been made for him. Because he also needs to be pitied, he is piteous; and they will hate him for that too. It is with the same Machiavellian guile that he surprises and wrong-foots his well-known interviewer. He flatters him by staging a laboured search for an answer; and then, with as many rolled *R*s as amount to a rock-fall, he is responding with a fresh challenge: 'Do I make myself entir-r-rely clear-r-r, Mr Fr-r-reeman?' He uses his eyebrows in the manner of a conductor with his baton before a large orchestra; the agile and articulate Mr Freeman is, as intended, disconcerted. 'Yes, yes, oh yes. Perfectly clear, Lord Reith.' He hurries on: 'What you've said is excellent'. He struggles to retain his foothold, experienced campaigner though he is. Meanwhile, also as intended, Reith's viewing public and all but his most hardened critics are filled with distress at the shabby ways in which he has been treated throughout his public life – only to be carried in on a tide of astonishment at his capacities and achievements, of which, with an air of displaced courtesy, he would make out that he is practically unaware, receiving new information with feigned surprise and preferring to celebrate his failures.

Now innocence, like an area of melt in a frozen Highland burn, spreads across Reith's face. He is malleable and eager to please, and speaks in a bedside voice. He is signalling his total readiness to respond as well and as fast as he can to anything that may be required of him. This time, he is a child looking for love; now his concerns are discarded to make way for the questioner's whim. Freeman moves fast, trying to come level with this latest climate change. 'He is splendidly cast as himself,' writes Malcolm Muggeridge, 'and puts on as fine a performance in this role now as ever he did in his life's long run.'[1]

But, when the Postmaster General made his arresting remark about Reith to the new Chairman, it was because he had noticed something about Reith that was to permeate the BBC as long as he was in charge: that same furious current, which was to power a BBC beyond anyone's imaginings, had a destructive – or self-destructive – capacity, so that, within its own white-water turbulence, Reith, who could have gone on to pour his singular leadership and organisational capacities into the war effort and into post-war reconstruction, was left destabilised, fulminating on the sidelines. One reviewer remarked on the benefits that might have followed had Churchill attached to his war initiatives the dynamo called Reith. 'Though this be madness,' said Polonius of Hamlet, 'yet there is method in it.'[2]

The BBC Governors, when on occasion they assemble in the Council Chamber of Broadcasting House, are still not entirely distanced from the portrait above them and the penetrating glare of John Reith. From the canvas, something of the sitter's controlling energy surges forward – a restless presence urgent to join in the exchange and impose on it the dynamic of his lofty ideals, arguing for the larger view. Thus it was that the British Broadcasting Company in its early days was already looking to an Empire Service; its *Radio Times*, launched in its second year, had quickly gained a readership of 900,000. Reith's fame travelled the world, the BBC regularly made headlines, and prime ministers and archbishops were astonished by the airwaves, bold to make use of them, and ever ready to further the BBC's influence.

Four years into its life, in 1926, the roller-coaster ride of the BBC as a company changed. With the coming of Corporation status and a Board of Governors in its train, the triumphs and the miseries of its Director General, as he now was – and of the Corporation itself – gave way to one another in graceless exchange. The number of people that Reith perceived to be bad figures around him exceeded the good as his injured and tumescent ego responded to them with rage or ugly triumph. And then the fateful stirrings to achieve – which, as a youth, he had experienced on the summit of Cairngorm in the Scottish Highlands in the days when only the ptarmigan birds were there to make a crowd – were marvellously realised with the coming of the new Chairman in 1930. John Whitley came, dispensing wisdom and understanding, and won for himself his Director General's affection and gratitude. Reith worked as freely and as happily as he ever did, and, having grown himself an exorbitant ego, was discovering that he did not need it all the time. Whitley, who had a reputation for being quick on the uptake, took pleasure in Reith being twice as quick as he.

In this period, public-service broadcasting was at its most fully consolidated, and Reith had most freedom to be his considerable and effective self. These years of growth and stability constituted 'the lucid intervals and happy pauses'[3] of his life and of the BBC's life. Reith was like de Gaulle: tall and tragi-comic, except that de Gaulle was far too worldly-conscious to make such a parade of his zones of torment. Anyhow, Reith was always short on satisfaction, even when orchestrating the death of a king, the abdication of another or the coronation of a third. No matter how well the task was accomplished or how great the plaudits, the personal letters inundating his office and the headlines on every news-stand, his gratification evaporated fast. He still strained after his personal Everest, that accomplishment through which he would finally stand supreme.

But, in the same way that climbers in the Cairngorm mountains have been disconcerted by a fearsome form moving in the mist among the peaks and crags – a phenomenon of the weather producing the illusion of a giant figure whom they named the Gray Man of Ben Macdui – so Reith entertained his own fantasies of power and position. They were mirages of his own making, results of what one journalist has called 'that peculiarly Scottish ethic which produces a super ego of terrifying proportions and a view of human experience as an endless assault course'.

Thus, when broadcasting fell into his lap to cultivate, it had, for Reith, to be free of competition. Without its monopoly, the BBC might have had to play for safety, prosecute the obviously popular lines, count its clients, study and meet their reactions, curry favour and, finally, subordinate itself to the vote. He used 'the brute force of monopoly to stamp Christian morality on the British people, a dictatorship of broadcasting – as though Milton hadn't made the case for unlicensed utterance',[4] as the historian A. J. P. Taylor wrote. Or, in Reith's words: 'The Government should leave the BBC alone and trust to me'.

When he left the BBC in 1938, no-one was clear, least of all Reith himself, why he had done so. If rumours of war, like distant thunder, began to rumble and he saw a role for himself, other theories contradicted this: for instance, as far as the Governors were concerned, his time was up. Perhaps he even feared his own invention. It had, after all, at sixteen years old, become adolescent. But still these theories did not exhaust the other forces at work. One was Winston Churchill, whose singular processes during crises Reith curiously understood and whose warlike spirit his own resembled. There could not be room for them both; and, after it was all over, he wrote to Churchill as 'someone whom you broke and whose life you ruined'. 'Old Wuthering Heights', Churchill called him, thus capturing the rugged, ferocious look of a prophet of doom. Reith thought Churchill a 'horrid fellow' who had kept him off the air for eight years – and, in his turn, Reith took a self-destructive pleasure in annoying the prime minister and giving him ample justification for his view that 'Reith was difficult to work with'. Along with Malcolm Muggeridge, one might have asked: 'How can this man continue to convey an impression of greatness despite so many intimations of littleness?'

As a child in Reith's household – I was only six when he left the BBC – I was conscious of something like greatness, except that for me it meant largeness. Everything about him was very large: the size of the print which regularly proclaimed his name from newspaper headlines; the house in which we lived; the car in which he rode; the desk at which he sat; and the rages into which he flew. The dictionaries and reference books which surrounded his desk, and the gold fountain pen which lay across it like a telegraph pole: these were huge and imposing, as were his portrait on the wall and the titles and positions of all the people with whom he consorted. Those in his vicinity seemed to be looking up to him, as did I – since, being small, I had to regard him in the kneecap. I was experiencing him in ways very similar to all those other people who read of him in their newspapers – as a large and distant fantasy of sorts.

For me, this was because the household was run on the departmental lines characteristic of the day. The servants were in their territories inside and outside, and the nursery and its ancillary rooms were in their wing of the house well distanced from its principal area, which was public and formal. There did not seem to be a neutral zone in which the parents consorted with the children: my father because he could not think what to say either to them or to the nurse, and my mother because she seldom found a way of getting past the nurse to reach the children, except occasionally on the nurse's half-day off. This became, for me, a small festival. Otherwise, nursery visits were formal and occasional, like a state visit, and mostly amounted to singing hymns with great awkwardness at bedtime. My parents did not so much converse as exchange conversational fragments, she responding with 'Oh!' or 'Really?' or 'Oh dear!' – hardly the stuff of stimulating exchange. Seated at Sunday lunch, the silences were punctuated by his unconnected observations. They must have emerged from his thought processes at the time, and bore no relation to anyone else's; and, as such, they stood about like tree stumps snapped off in a gale, spaced out across a blasted landscape.

But the remarks did, I noticed, contain recurring references or names. For instance, it became clear that something somewhere had been retrieved from a letterbox. There was a place called Rothiemurchus, and it was incomparably beautiful. Somewhere, too, a tollhouse figured large – and a man known as the village wheelwright.

And then there were names that I began to recognise, as, surfacing occasionally like dolphins out of a sea of preoccupation, they were spiked with venom before again sliding below the waves. To 'Bowser' was apparently attached 'Jezebel'. There was 'Mrs Snowden': her name sounded with more regularity than anyone else's and was apparently as detestable as 'That Dreadful Sister of Mine' was disgraceful. 'My Brother Douglas' was always 'Deceased', from which I picked up something apparently to his credit, while 'My Father' and 'My Mother' had clearly attained a status of saintly perfection. I thought that possibly my own mother would not quite share this view.

As for us, my older brother Christopher and I were to carry out great things that my father had not achieved, like being prime minister and head of the Women's Royal Naval Service. But Christopher did not enjoy politics, and I had no wish to be Head Wren – a large form, encased in a shapeless uniform, giving orders. John Reith found it hard to love his children for their own sake.

Meantime, I experienced my father having more than usually powerful associations with his own childhood. His family life was very present to him, since he regularly referred to the manse in Glasgow, his elderly parents' dedication to the church, and his six brothers and sisters, mostly immersed in their own affairs, he himself the youngest by ten years.

The household that he went on to dominate and in which I grew up was characterised by oddity and unconformity; and while, like most young people, at times I was often lonely and perplexed, I was seldom bored. Stimulus, after all, comes from the most unexpected sources.

Now I have begun to try to find out what lay behind all those random intimations and upheavals of his, and to discover the connecting story. I have drawn on the rich source of information which is to be found in Ian

McIntyre's biography, *The Expense of Glory* (HarperCollins, 1993), and on Professor Asa Briggs' authoritative *The History of Broadcasting in the United Kingdom* (Oxford University Press, 1961). I am grateful to the BBC through its Written Archivist, Jacqueline Kavanagh, for its unconditional agreement both to the use of those quotations from Prof. Briggs over which it retains rights, and to the use of quotations from *The Reith Diaries*, both the manuscript and the enclosure volumes. I am also grateful for the use of quotations from Reith's autobiography, *Into the Wind*, reproduced by kind permission of Hodder & Stoughton Limited.

I have also had the opportunity afforded by a different view of things. Murray, my husband, having begun his professional life as a minister of the Church of Scotland, went on to train and practise as a psychoanalytical psychotherapist. This gave us a new broad perspective – one by no means unfamiliar to my father, who had read Freud and Jung. It made us better placed to deflect the brickbats which regularly came our way, especially when we were engaged and newly married. Of course, we made mistakes – people under pressure usually do – but, through some of the insights of the psychodynamic process, we were able to walk away from much that was unkindly meant as someone else's agenda. Some of the following pages reflect what I have learned of this approach. My father had taken to himself a hurt that was much greater than the one he would inflict on us; his studies in the field had failed to save him from himself.

NOTES

1. *Muggeridge TV Interviews, Introduction: The Listener 30.11.67,* by permission of David Higham Associates.
2. Shakespeare, *Hamlet,* Act II, Scene 2, line 211.
3. Francis Bacon, *History of Henry VII.*
4. A. J. P. Taylor, *English History 1914–1945,* The Oxford History of England series (2001), by permission of Oxford University Press.

1

The Manse in Glasgow

M Y FATHER was brought up in the austere atmosphere of a
Scottish manse. This chapter traces, in narrative form, the
stormy relationships in his family against the background of
solemn piety. Such things may well have led to the inconsistencies in my
father's character in which undoubted greatness was yet hung about with
so many littlenesses (to echo Muggeridge).

An elderly man sits at his desk, bent over in deep absorption. One
side of his face is in heavy shadow; but, as in a Raeburn portrait,
his distinguished features and thick curly hair are caught in the
beam of the nearby gas lamp. His desk-top has been extended with
the help of several extra tables, mostly disordered and of different
heights but with the idea of accommodating the paraphernalia of
his labours. Leaning intently over one of several open tomes, he
is making pencilled notes onto sheets of paper, resting on more
sheets in dog-eared disarray. Behind them are toppling towers of
volumes; some just lie about the floor. More papers stuffed into
a heavy chest beside him stick out in a desultory way and prevent

1

some drawers from shutting; but he is not bothered about these things. In the quiet, the pewter clock ticks comfortably above the fireplace; the fire is languid, however, because it is needing attention, and the old man has not noticed.

Drawn up to one side of the fire is an armchair in which he often sits. It is faded into no particular colour at all, the upholstered plush of the armrests worn through and several crumpled cushions pushed between the uprights. The chair opposite, not quite so worn and low, is favoured for visitors. Since this minister of a West End church in Glasgow is both well known and well liked, plenty of his parishioners call on him. Some must make do with the upright balloon-backed chairs, beloved of Victorians, as uncomfortable as they are ergonomically unsound. One of them has disappeared under the minister's black gown and cassock, his academic hood flung down in the careless haste of scholarly preoccupations. A coal shifts in the fireplace and a brief flame sprouts into life, setting up a responsive winking from among the thick links of the minister's gold watch-chain. Scattered along the dusty mantelpiece is a throng of family photographs: from them, the minister's wife looks out severely, her five sons and two daughters arranged around in unsmiling concentration. One of the sons is a schoolboy but almost as tall as his adult siblings.

Horses' hooves sound from the foot of Lynedoch Street; as they grow louder, it is clear that the animal is labouring to draw a heavy carrier's cart up the long hill. The wheels on the cobbles rattle as they pass the manse window and carry on by the College Church. The sound dies away into the precincts of Park Circus Place. Other sounds penetrate the minister's study but, for a little while longer, are unnoticed: the maid carrying the coal up the stairs dumps the scuttle noisily at the door of one of the bedrooms, and, by knocking, she draws a grunt from the occupant. She takes in the coal, her exertions unacknowledged, and emerges to draw breath on the landing. But then the doorbell rings two floors below, and she starts down the stair again. She does not swear – you do not swear in Dr Reith's manse – but there is a sharp clicking of the tongue. The minister hears the bell and sighs – it is probably a parishioner's call, and he is keen not to be disturbed.

Suddenly, there is a new sound which no-one can ignore: hammering is followed by the sound of something hefty being dragged across the floor. Then a man's voice is raised angrily, followed by a shriek and verbal flow, which the minister recognises as coming from his daughter Jean. She is most often at the centre of family rows; none of his family responds to the peaceful ways that he urges. His face twitches, and he sighs deeply. The rapping at his door is sudden and imperious – and there they are, Jean and her older brother Robert, pushing their way in before he can answer. Small, sharp, waspish and with her mother's looks, Jean protests the innocence of her case. 'What is the point of having electric light in the house if I can't have it in my room?' She speaks rapidly to crowd out her brother. 'I must have it in my room. I spend more time there than anywhere else in the house. I have to go to my room to get away from the others.' Robert must now override her with his louder voice. There is something about their father's otherworldliness which, while generating adoration from his congregation, acts like an electric charge on his children's fury. Robert addresses his father. 'I cannot understand', he says, 'why you and mother let her get away with it. All on her own, she's gone off and made arrangements with the electrician to suit herself – that when he's working downstairs in the hall and dining room and in here' – he waves his arm as though to encircle the study about to be bathed in this forthcoming effulgence – 'he puts a wire through the ceiling from below and into her room.' Jean's verbal cataract does not amount to a sentence, and Robert carries on over the top of it.

The study door is still open as they argue, half in, half out of the room. 'I thought I saw her in the electrician's shop in Woodlands Road the other day, and I thought she'd be up to no good', Robert says. 'Sneaking down there to lay on something for herself, and never, I'll be bound, having asked you or mother. Did you?' He wheels round and stares at Jean. 'Did you ask before creeping off to the shop?' Dr Reith searches for diversionary tactics, but the son's exasperation seems to be about to translate into blows. He never was much good at facing up to the devious ways in which his children arrange things for themselves. 'Just because you haven't got what it takes to get things done, you can't blame me.' Jean pauses to search for the matter of a new volley, allowing the minister to intervene with a diplomatic issue which they have not considered. Archie's and Beta's rooms are on the same landing; have they discussed this with them? Jean brushes this aside, and now, a little lamely, says that with her poor eyesight she cannot be expected to carry on with that hopeless gas light; and anyway the electrician has already started in her room. Sure enough, the sounds of drilling and more furniture-shifting come unmistakably from her room. Robert, in challenging tones, hopes that his father, with mother, will reconsider in the light of what Jean has done and instruct the man to do the other rooms on the landing also. Skilfully, he redirects the fire towards his father.

As though judging her moment, a maid is climbing the stair to tell the minister that there is indeed a member of the congregation hoping to see him and that she is waiting in the sitting room. It is not lost on the three that their exchange, carried out at the stairhead, has probably been listened to by the servants in the stairwell below and that the visitor, too, has heard a lot. Dr Reith, heavily preoccupied, goes downstairs and is relieved to find the sitting-room door now closed so that, as he enters, he can greet his parishioner a little more easily. He shakes hands gravely and invites her to come up to his study, closing the door firmly behind him.

The front doorbell rings again, and this time, when the maid opens the door, she finds John, the youngest in the family by ten years. In 1905, he looks older than his sixteen years: he is over six foot tall, and his wrists stick out well below the sleeves of his blue Glasgow Academy blazer. His mother has decided that they can save the cost of a new school outfit because he is almost certainly leaving the Academy and going to boarding school next session. She and Dr Reith had had a terrible shock when the Academy had put it to them that it could no longer allow his unruly behaviour in its midst. They did not quite say 'expel', but that is what they meant. Boarding school, well away from home, was the only solution.

John had a poor academic record; and, between long spells when he was apparently uninterested in what was going on around him, his temper would suddenly get the better of him and flare up into near-violence. He had never taken kindly to his father's promptings to work harder at school and to try to control his anger. The two spoke in different languages, the father's mostly biblical. Now he launches himself gracelessly into the hall with never a nod to the maid. He climbs the stairs two at a time and, scarcely pausing to knock, bursts into his mother's sitting room, only to wheel round and out again, slamming the door. As usual, she is out visiting in the parish when he comes home, and his father is nowhere to be seen either. He is the soul of dislocated adolescence.

John always longed to get his mother to himself; he was experienced by the brothers and sister as an interloper and a further drain on the rare commodity of their parents' attention. Under the smooth and godly appearance of the manse of the prosperous Glasgow church, there seethed the rivalries and hatreds of the many siblings. But the Rev. Dr and Mrs Reith perhaps felt that the reverence generated by their prayers and labours among the congregation would reach and influence for the good the lives of their children. On account of their selfish preoccupation with the Gospel, they could not understand the evidence mounting up before them that their children were needy, hungering for love and attention that were of a more practical and demonstrative kind. The awkward little ceremony when the family and servants gathered daily together under the good Doctor and pretended to pray was not an answer to their children's needs. As soon as the prayer was over, they tore into one another with their furies and frustrations. Dr Reith was more than ever perplexed by the particular commotion which was his youngest son. When the older brothers talked their father into sending him away to boarding school 'to knock some sense into him' and then into signing him on for a five-year engineering apprenticeship, John experienced the many faces of rejection and decided somewhere within himself that, if they did not love him as he was, he would relaunch himself, assume an exaggerated character and find achievement on his own terms. He cultivated a warlike exterior, supported by his height and pronounced features. Later, this was helped on by his war wound. He liked to practise 'the language of vituperation', a habit which never quite deserted him.

A manse, or minister's residence, in the Free Church of Scotland, in which John Reith was struggling to grow up, was going to be more than usually evangelical and otherworldly, as well as being part of a prosperous congregation of successful people. The Free Church itself had been formed through a dramatic split from its parent Church of Scotland (thereafter known as the Auld Kirk). Pursued by the evangelically minded, it sought spiritual independence from civil interference and much greater freedom in the appointment of ministers to congregations. The old system, with its state connection, was failing, in the opinion of many reformist minds, to meet the spiritual needs of the people. Thus, at the 1843 meeting of the General Assembly of the Church of Scotland, one third of those present, ministers and elders, rose and left the Assembly in St Andrew's Church in George Street, Edinburgh, and, in long and solemn march, wound their way down the hill to the Tanfield Hall in Canonmills in north Edinburgh. This was the Disruption, and its purpose was to replace the Established Church and set up rival congregations and schools in every parish. Five hundred Free Churches were established within two years.

It was regularly referred to by John Reith, always with passion: 'The Disruption', he said, 'was the most magnificent bid for freedom made from within the Church of Scotland'. Undeterred by any bothersome clutter of facts, he told about those fiercely independent men who walked out of charge and manse to form the Free Church of Scotland, a new body that could offer no assurance of either. 'Dr Thomas Chalmers was their leader', he said. 'One day, I shall write a piece for *Blackwood's Magazine* telling of his life and achievements, and of my father's admiration for him.' This, when his public life had quite fallen away, he did. But, as page mounted upon typed page, and the long-suffering Jo Stanley, his faithful secretary from the early BBC days, retyped yet again, so the pain and grief which it caused him grew: his article, to be

6

restricted in length to meet the space capacity of the magazine, grew like a mammoth on the run, and John Reith found himself no more able than any others graciously to abide by the editorial pen. His conviction about his calling as a writer did not always remain strong. Nor did his article enlarge on the nature of the theology to which the Free Church subscribed and on the evangelical – as opposed to the moderate – beliefs in which he himself had been brought up, with their conservative view of biblical truth. He did not go in for analytical or comparative thinking, even retrospectively. What was, was – and that was enough for anyone.

One of the Free Church leaders had been the Rev. Dr George Reith, John's father. He had been persuaded into the ministry by his own father, George Reith, general manager of the Clyde Navigation Trust. Dr Reith's church, the Free College Church, was built in 1857 out of the Disruption, in association with the new theological college of the Free Church persuasion, on one of Glasgow's most commanding sites. It looked across on one side to the gantries of the Clyde and on the other to Kelvingrove Park. It was of this congregation that the Rev. George Reith, then aged 24, became colleague to the minister in post and then his successor in 1866, the start of his fifty-three-year ministry there.

Despite its piety, the manse of the College Free Church was the austere setting for all the contumacious relationships within John Reith's family; and they all seemed to have taken so tenacious a hold on his mind as to stay around and about him all his days. Truly, it might be said that, in him, the generations of the Reiths lived on, and few of them were to his advantage.

Or, indeed, to mine either. These people perpetuated themselves in ways that did little to ease matters between my father and me as I grew up. It was as though, feeling himself let down by his own early experiences, he was caught up in a horrid continuity, and the family that succeeded his own first family was going to let him down in the same way. Thus programmed, the second family punctiliously delivered its disappointment to him.

John Reith held his father in some awe: a man whom he described as being of presence and dignity, and possessed of great eloquence in the pulpit. As an able student at Marischal College, Aberdeen, George Reith had won prizes and scholarships; but his youngest son felt himself to be, by comparison, an intellectual and moral failure. This perception started John's lifelong drive to justify himself to his father, both in his father's lifetime and beyond it. John saw his father as saintly; but he was clearly as irascible as his own father, George Reith, before him had been. He, who could preach a fine moral outrage at the social injustices of the day – and leave few unmoved by his exhortations – could also spontaneously combust into indignation of a kind more personal and immediate than his pulpit eloquence. One day, he was walking in the Speyside hills with the Rev. William Forrester when they were met by a gamekeeper. The gamekeeper regarded them as trespassers and remonstrated with them, only to be countered by Dr Reith's vehement interrogation: 'Do you know who I am?' There was no mistaking the command in the voice of the large man with the arresting look. He went on: 'Do you not know that there is no law of trespass in Scotland?' Professor Forrester was to remark, years later: 'What was left of that gamekeeper was not worth taking away in a wheelbarrow' – a demolition job characteristic of each generation of these Reiths with powerful and inflamed minds.

Most years, Dr and Mrs Reith spent two months of the summer in the manse at Rothiemurchus on Speyside in Inverness-shire. By exchanging pulpits with the incumbent there, Dr Reith was spared the cost of accommodating his large family. It was an arrangement that suited them all. John was to describe these as 'halcyon days' and the place as being one 'of incomparable beauty'.

Back in the summer of 1905, the quiet lanes of Rothiemurchus are banked with yellow bedstraw and the fairy bluebell of Scotland. As a buzzard circles over nearby Loch an Eilean uttering its plaintive cry, the old pines' dark gnarled clusters give sweet resin scent to hushed breezes. Footfall on the peaty track circling the loch makes a hollow thud until it lands on the hard and twisted network of exposed pine roots. Down at Aviemore station, the train from Glasgow is about to arrive. Three open carriages are lined up out on the forecourt. When the train draws in, the horses, accustomed to the commotion, are undisturbed. On the platform, all the porters are queuing with their barrows at the luggage van and then wrestling with massive trunks, hampers and portmanteaux. Dr Reith, a tall figure with grey curly hair and prominent chin, holds firmly on to his valise: he plans uninterrupted writing on his two-month break. He counts the items as they are unloaded, and addresses the men courteously, their names prefixed with 'Mr'. A regular visitor, he even remembers some of their family members by name. They respond in turn with that truly Highland combination of courtesy, respect and ease – there could be no class distinction up here. Out on the forecourt, the third carriage is for luggage alone – the driver looks anxious as it sits lower and lower onto its springs. Dr Reith notices it, and they arrange for a piece each to be loaded into the other two cabs. Mrs Reith is already seated in the first, along with two of her family, Jean and Ernest. Douglas climbs into the second, and the two maids follow. 'Where's John?' Douglas sounds impatient, climbs out and runs back onto the platform, looking up and down. One of the porters sees him and points to a lone figure at the far end of the platform, beyond the point where the last carriage is drawn up. 'I think that's him, Sir. He's enjoying the view.' Douglas calls to John, but his voice is drowned out by the sudden and severe hissing of steam escaping from the great locomotive in the green livery of the Highland Railways line. Next comes the imperious whistle for departure, followed by the measured thuds of the great pistons at work. The gentle forward glide gathers speed, and the sound-bursts assume their own rhythm – *one*, two, three, four, *one*, two, three, four.

Two figures are standing side by side on the last stretch of the by now empty platform, well beyond the black and white canopy and the last tub of geraniums. Naturally, at first John does not hear his brother's call; then he does not want to; and so he continues to stare into the distance. But, by now, Douglas is finding that a compassion has overtaken his impatience. This youth, his junior by ten years, seems never to have had it easy; he has never been able to make friends or enjoy himself. Douglas stands beside him, sharing the view and managing not to say anything as they hear first one carriage, and then a second, leave and scrunch their way across the gravel. The plain of Rothiemurchus stretches before them, studded with pines and giving way to the panorama of the Cairngorm mountains. 'Carn Eilrig, Cairn Toul, Braeriach, Cairn Gorm, Ben Macdui – the Lairig Ghru.' John is talking out loud as though to himself but wanting Douglas to hear. And then, explosively: 'God's country'. He wheels round and stalks off down the platform, Douglas following patiently behind. They climb into the carriage, and John sits down heavily in his own corner, reserving the right to silence all the way.

Leaving Aviemore, they take the rough road to Loch Morlich and stop at Inverdruie. Douglas has seen the blacksmith, Mr MacKenzie, at work and calls out to him. The blacksmith's premises look curiously cobbled together, a blackened chimney poking crookedly through a hole in the soot-laden roof but nevertheless channelling a plume of heavy furnace smoke into the air. The school next door is quiet now for the holidays, but from this industrious corner come the sounds of the new shoe hammered home and the stamping of waiting horses tethered under the big beech tree across the way. Mr MacKenzie straightens up slowly, dropping the hefty hind leg he was filing prior to shoeing. He recognises Douglas and comes across, all smiles, rubbing his right hand on his leather apron. He holds it out, still blackened, to Douglas, who grasps it warmly. 'Aye, Mr Douglas, it's good to see ye. And Mr John, too. How are ye?' Mr John stirs himself, smiles awkwardly, but takes the outstretched hand, touched at the warmth and the welcome.

On they go another mile; the twisting lane is shaded with birch and oak. And then, at the monument in the fork of this side road, they turn to the left. Encouraged by the blacksmith's greeting, John has found his voice again and is asking Douglas about this monument. He replies: 'It's to a Professor James Martineau, a philosopher, who stayed every year with his family at the house next to ours, the Polchar. He kept up a campaign to overthrow the rights which some landlords assumed for themselves to keep the public off their land. He would emerge from the Polchar after dark to remove No Entry notices and wire fittings. Oddly, he himself escaped arrest, and they put up this monument to him after his death, quite recently, in 1900. His three daughters contribute generously to the community.'

But, by now, John is watching a small burn in a hurry running close by and almost on a level with the road. Perhaps he is charmed by the green of the short grass beside the limpid stream and the white-barked birch, its gentle form sustaining the drooping habit of its branches so that they resemble a shower of rain. Then they stop, and the driver climbs down to lead his horse onto the narrow track that runs past the Polchar, with its diamond-paned windows, and onwards to the Old Manse of Rothiemurchus, where the family regularly stays. The track can just about take the carriage, and they draw up before the 'low-browed manse of Rothiemurchus', as Dr Hugh Macmillan called it. Fortunately, the other carriages have unloaded and left; even so, there is scarcely turning space, and the driver encourages his horse round gently.

Douglas and John help with the back-breaking task of distributing the luggage around the house. They will share a room, as will Jean and Beta, while Ernest has his own; he is restless at night. Now he is already looking lost. He picks up a pile of rugs tied together, hesitates, then carries them into the sitting room, gripped by a great anxiety. 'My violin! My violin!' he calls out. 'Where is it?' 'Here you are, Ernest, I looked after it specially for you. I was afraid you might forget it.' Jean has, indeed, taken care of it for her brother, and this sudden gentleness springs from concern for his troubled state and the love of music that they share. Ernest seizes the scarred case and clasps it to himself. 'Don't say I wasn't looking after your interests', says Jean, carrying the bundle of rugs out again to drop one in each bedroom.

As well as his writing and his studies of St John's Gospel, Dr Reith, in exchanging manses, will assume essential duties for the minister of Rothiemurchus, preaching every Sunday and taking on urgent pastoral care. This year, Douglas will preach for him twice before leaving for the Indian mission field. Occasionally,

11

he accompanies his father on his climbs in the Cairngorms. The old man is an experienced climber, with occasional trips to Switzerland for his sport, but, now in his mid-sixties, no longer has the energy for the high tops and is happy with his own company on his less ambitious walks. Dear Ernest, after all, is so withdrawn – except when playing his violin – and, when Dr Reith is with John, he feels ill at ease and lost to know what to talk about beyond urging him to work hard at school and trying to introduce a little reality to those grandiose ideas of his about running a railway company. It is all very well this great admiration of his for his grandfather and his achievements as a young man as manager of the then newly opened Aberdeen-to-Forfar railway, but he forgets that Grandfather George first served his apprenticeship as a wheelwright. John, too, should learn some sort of trade. His academic record, after all, is nothing to be proud of; and university, even if Dr Reith could afford it – which he knows he certainly cannot – is not for him.

And so John, also, takes to striding over the hills on his own – self-absorbed, but, somewhere within himself, deeply responsive to the Highland scene. This was never more grand than among the hills, burns and pine trees of Rothiemurchus and the distant Cairn Gorm mountain with its perpetually snow-filled corrie, known to locals as Snowgoose. One day, returning from a day's hike, John descends Creag Dhubh and then crosses over the shoulder of Carn Eilrig, his route taking him along the shore of Loch an Eilean and finally past a crofter's house. He pauses at its view across the loch to the island and its tumbledown castle, where once an osprey famously nested. Then he glances at the little stone house itself, full of aged charm despite the occupier's lack of urgency about tidying up round about. There must be a better way of disposing of disused implements than abandoning them to the nettles, John thinks. A woman comes out and starts to hang out her washing; she sees the passer-by and then, on a second look, recognises him. 'Is that you, Mr John?' she calls, leaving her basket to come down the garden path. She holds out her hand, and he gravely returns the greeting. She has a fresh batch of scones, she says – no doubt he can smell the baking – and she would be pleased if he would like to come in and try them. John hesitates. 'And the milk is fresh from the cow, and there is my own home-made raspberry jam.' Not to press him too hard, she enlarges on the abundance of juicy raspberries growing all around, wild for the taking. Not a fruit-and-veg man himself, John nods polite agreement; but, with the smell of the scones, he becomes aware of just how hungry he is. Such warmth and kindness are not to be passed up, and he gets himself into the kitchen, managing with her warnings not to bang his head on the door frame. He folds down into a wooden chair at the table, and she notices that he is carrying a bunch of heather, now in full bloom, which he puts down carefully in front of himself. 'Now, help yourself', she says. He looks up at her with his mumbled thanks, and she is touched. 'Poor lad,' she thinks, 'they don't seem to have much time for him up at the manse.'

In return for this sudden attention, he allows himself to be questioned. 'Your brother, Archie, now, we haven't seen him here for a while. They say he's in England in a church down there?' Anyone a little less absorbed in himself and in the next scone would have been curious to discover how she had learned about their family squabble; but, released by the comfort of it all, John obligingly explains that his parents had been unhappy about Archie leaving the Church of Scotland in favour of an Anglican charge – and he goes on to divulge that he, John, is now at a boarding school called Gresham's near Holt in Norfolk, near where Archie for the present is working as a curate. Oh well. And is he happy there? 'No, not at all', comes the booming reply. In fact, he had run – or rather, bicycled – away to escape the new headmaster, who was beastly to him and would certainly never hear what he had to say. What a shame, she thinks. Lonely at school as well, and probably misunderstood too. 'But you'll not have much longer there, and you'll be able to choose what you do next.' He considers enlarging, but a further scone claims his attention, and he glares ferociously at it as though in some remembered guise of self-protection. His sister, Beta, he says in response to some further prompting, is coming up next weekend for a few days. She is a nurse in Edinburgh. He is glad about this. In fact, struck by a sudden thought, he would cycle over and meet her at Aviemore station – she had written to say when she was coming and had asked if they could order a cab for her. He had another sister? Yes – Jean. He makes a face. 'But she's a fine pianist, I've heard', pursues his interlocutor, taking the grimace as a reply. 'So I've heard, too', he says, grimly. 'But she doesn't care to play in front of anyone, so what's the good of that?' 'Now, Ernest. He will play for you, I expect?' Well, she knows that Ernest is not himself. John winces, and she feels she has gone too far. 'No, Robert isn't here', he answers, as she hastens onto safer ground. 'He's trying to be a marine engineer in Newcastle.' He speaks ungraciously. She moves over to the window. 'You know, we miss the ospreys that used to nest on the castle. No-one has seen them for a while.' She rattles on because she can sense him starting to go. 'We last had a nest in 1899: there were three chicks, they said, but only one survived. They made a grand sight diving into the water and coming up with a fish. Mind you, the fishermen didn't care for them one bit.' By now on his feet, John collects up his heather and gives her a stiff little speech of thanks, clearly rehearsed. Despite her warnings, he does not bend enough to avoid the low beam, and cracks his head most painfully. His thanks get tangled up in his assurance that it is nothing; and, speaking between gritted teeth, he leaves hurriedly. The crofter, surveying the last of her scones and the crumbs and bits of heather all around, feels sad.

She might have felt even more sad had she witnessed the next years of the young man's life. When he left boarding school in 1906 at the age of 17, he was sure of only one thing: 'I was not going to be a mediocrity'. He would have liked to have stayed on another year and then tried for Oxford or Cambridge entrance – Glasgow he probably considered beneath him. Instead, his family, who apparently were all involved in deciding what to do about John, concluded that he should take an engineering apprenticeship. This decision, conflicting with his own inner insistence about a special destiny, amounted to torment. John, it seems, was not consulted. The bitterness of what was done to him stayed with him all his days.

Forty years later, in 1946, the recollections remained as clear as the previous day's. Sir William Haley, the BBC's new Director General, and his wife were visiting us at Harrias House, Beaconsfield, where my brother and I were brought up. John passionately told them: 'I knew that I was not meant to be a mediocrity'. Everybody said: 'No, no, of course not' very quickly; but they were left in no doubt that he had been burdened at the time with the conviction that his were exceptional talents. He would have to endure huge frustration at having been ruthlessly channelled by his family into an occupation for which he was ill suited. 'It was an awful prostitution of my intellectual ability', he told them, with feeling. 'It was an affront to one's intelligence and intellect. Even today, I can feel indignant', he said – and no-one doubted him.

His brother Archie, eighteen years his senior, supported the decision because, John heard, 'it would knock the nonsense out of me. And Robert' – he spoke of this brother with even more palpable dislike – 'said that steam was the basis of all power. He was some sort of a marine engineer at the time.' If Sir William noticed that this was a piece of irony on the part of the said Robert, he kept it well hidden. But, as I sat quietly by, I noticed that John never referred to his brother Douglas, whose concern for his youngest brother was seldom graciously received. On the question of university for John, Douglas had written to him from his missionary posting in India to assure him that, in seeing him primarily as a man of action, he was in no way undervaluing his exceptional intelligence. Nor did John divulge how hurtful his father could be. He had responded harshly to his son's final and desperate attempt to escape the five-year apprenticeship at the Hyde Park Locomotive Works in Glasgow's Springburn, coupled with evening classes at the technical college. He had, he told his father, found himself an opening in the Caledonian Railway, something which would lead to a managerial position. He had thought that a railway job would win his father's approval, since his own father had started his distinguished career that way. But the response was bruising. 'Yes,' the old man had said, 'and be a railway clerk for the rest of your life.'

Despite the bitter prospect of five long, weary years in locomotive shops, experience with bits and pieces of machinery, the ghastly hours and squalid circumstances, 'I decided', John said, abruptly, 'somehow to go through with it'. 'How did you find the men with whom you were working?' asked Lady Haley. 'Presumably your background was very different from theirs. Did you get on?' John shot her a penetrating look, recognising a sensible question. 'One of my brothers', he said in reply, 'spoke with some relish before I started about what would happen to a "gentleman apprentice" at the hands of his fellows. And so, to show him that I was entirely able to stand up for myself, I acquired an engineer's skip cap, and I wore it at an angle. Also, I got hold of the rough cloth muffler which the men wore instead of a collar. And then I adopted a ferocious scowl. I had been practising that.' In due course, he dropped the cap and the muffler; but the scowl was there to stay. He also remained awkward and aloof; his father, as ever careless about these things, remarked that 'his social graces were such that he would be better living on a desert island'.

Lady Haley persisted with her question. 'Did you find yourself accepted by the others,' she said, 'or did they regard you as different and therefore odd?' He replied: 'I began, to my surprise, to find that I was getting to be quite liked. I seemed to attract a certain amount of notice, not all of which was by any means unfavourable. Mark you, I was now in my fourth year at the works, with another year to go. I used to argue for socialism – in fact, rather asserted myself – but nobody seemed to mind. Furthermore, the general manager approved of me and had me shifted around from one department to another – from the template shop to the iron foundry, the drawing office and the smithy. No-one', he said, by way of a proclamation, 'can talk to me about hours and conditions.' But sitting there, silently taking it all in, I wondered that, after nearly forty years, there seemed to be no recognition that things might have changed in the interval. 'I had a most tremendous admiration for my father', John said. 'But I had been thrust into the most brainless profession imaginable.' The old hurt was very apparent.

Sir William, however, had picked up an earlier point, and he spoke out of a well-stored mind. 'Would I be right in thinking that this was in the time of the Red Clydesiders?' he said. 'Did you go to hear Jimmy

Maxton speak; John Wheatley, if I'm remembering right? These men seem to have had an enormous effect on Glasgow and the west of Scotland just before the war. I have never thought of you as being among their number. And yet here you are saying that you were arguing for them among the locomotive men – who, I am sure, would not have been slow to argue either.' In the general election of 1922, Glasgow returned ten Labour members out of fifteen constituencies. Maxton and Wheatley were among the group of loved radicals who spoke for the manual workers, disrupting Westminster.

Although John would not have chosen to be drawn on the subject of politics, he replied convincingly enough. 'I was always susceptible to oratory,' he said, 'and suspected that I might one day be able to move many to my point of view.' Sir William was nodding; my mother was waiting passively behind the teapot, not expecting to join in. 'I was more moved by Maxton's powers of persuasion than by the questions on which he was persuasive. Although' – he went on hurriedly – 'I was by no means unfamiliar with the questions of social injustice on which I regularly heard my father preach.' He emphasised the words 'my father' by suddenly withdrawing the pressured utterance and speaking in a voice that retreated into something gentler, far away.

Sir William changed the subject. 'What did you emerge as?' he asked. 'I was a Journeyman Locomotive Fitter', John said proudly. 'I also', he said, not wanting the moment to pass too soon, 'had excellent references. The chief executive wrote that I had made the very best use of my time, and my foreman prepared a mock testimonial which was, as I recall, to 'wee Jock Reith ... this able loafer ... who is very good at doing a job after it is finished'. Wee Jock was as gratified by this testimonial as by any other. It must have been, I thought, at the North British Locomotive Works that he learned not only to be a fitter but also how to get alongside all sorts and conditions of men.

As for me, I was entirely used to being an audience as my father held forth. Aged 14 in 1946, it would have been more appropriate for me to have experienced a good-going resentment; this might have been possible, had I had more experience of other families and their dynamics at work.

My boredom would, however, suddenly be interrupted by a targeted question, detonated in such a way as to leave no doubt that my answer might throw good light on the questioner.

But, since my father had had little experience of being listened to in a loving way in his youth, it was unlikely that he had that capacity in turn. Not for the first time, the parents' unrecognised problems were dumped on the children.

2

An Irretrievable Loss

OHN REITH's passionate friendship with a young man seven years his junior lasted many years. Following a nearly fatal First World War wound, John was posted to the USA. There, he cast himself in a heroic mould, attracting to himself a certain following. But, on his return home, he had to face the loss of his friend's affection. He got himself a wife instead and looked for work.

A young man, and a lonely one, John Reith at last found a friend in Charlie Bowser – DCB, as he was known. The Bowser family lived near the manse of the College Church in Lynedoch Street in Glasgow's West End. One day in May 1912, John and Charlie first met and had a long conversation in the manse garden. John was 23 and Charlie 16. 'Very nice little chap', John noted from his great height. 'I like him.' Next, he was 'very good looking and had awfully pretty eyes'; they met more and more often. John chided himself for being so fond of the boy: 'It's quite ridiculous', he said, and did not mean it. But his family did mean it, and were bothered as John's feelings flooded into infatuation. 'The David and Jonathan business looks like thirty cents compared with what Charlie and I have', he announced, a few years later, to his still-bewildered father. In John's mind was the story of David weeping over the death of Saul and of Jonathan his son: 'I am distressed for thee my brother Jonathan; very pleasant hast thou been unto me; thy love was wonderful, passing the love of women' (2 Samuel 1:26). He had found love and understanding at last, experiencing happiness as never before. When the Bowser family announced their removal to London, John was desolate. Charlie and he had an intense farewell visit to Comrie in Perthshire, carving their initials on the seat on Monument Hill. And then another, this time recording their visit on an obliging tree. Whenever Charlie made return visits from London, John was overwhelmed with excitement.

Then came the First World War, and John joined the 5th Scottish Rifles. He became transport officer and was soon posted to France. The parting with Charlie, before finally crossing the Channel, was more than usually soulful. Charlie, like John, had come from an intensely religious background – Charlie's in the Baptist Church – and to fervent prayers were this time attached presents and a ring.

Returning unexpectedly from France for a weekend's leave, John took the opportunity to stage his own entry to the College Church and its Sunday morning service. This service was always a weighty event, with earnest prayers and preaching and the metrical psalms sung to their named and stately tunes: Stracathro, Glasgow, Crimond, the Old Hundredth. Now John timed it so that the church was already full and the whispers dying away in expectation of the minister's entry. Instead, from the back of the church came a measured tread of an emphatic kind, carrying with it a distinctively metallic rattle. Up the aisle, on his way to the family pew at the very front, strode the youngest Reith, a man of six foot six inches, dressed in full battle rig. Heads spun round and then reverted for urgent whispers; on he went, all eyes following his progress, the rattle of his spurs accompanying him to his place. No-one could know that he had adjusted his spurs – he had enlarged the holes housing the ratchets – so that they agitated the more insistently as he walked. Seconds later, in came the minister.

At the Front, John soon became conspicuous, and not just to his own side. Whatever the setting – and this one could scarcely be more unlikely – he felt that he had to put on a performance. He would walk about in full view of the German trenches; and, on one occasion, he made use of the No Man's Land between the two sides when caught short. The Germans were only a few hundred yards away.

My father's sense of his having a special assignation in life, for which he was provided with an assured indemnity of some kind, was already developed to an absurd degree. The only difference when I knew him was that, in attempting to live out his destiny, he found himself spectacularly to have failed. It was always about failure and never about success that he spoke. Sitting with my mother and me on either side of him at the dining-room table in our home at Beaconsfield, he spoke, as it were, to himself. 'My golly,' he said, fiercely regarding the salt and pepper so that you almost saw them reduced to a small heap of dust, 'my golly. Nobody knows how far I've failed.' I waited for the next bit; I had heard it before. 'What I was capable of compared with what I've achieved is pitiable.' And the pressured silence that built up was like that which precedes the monstrous clap of thunder overhead. My mother's timorous comment seemed to act as a detonator to release Jove's thunder. 'But surely the BBC was a great achievement?' 'The Bee ... Bee ... Cee ...' – and he banged on the table so that his cufflinks rattled and the silver tableware hopped about. 'The BBC is going to the dogs. All that I laid down is being systematically disregarded; given priority treatment to be dismantled; the standards that I set rubbished in favour of pandering to what the people – the people, forsooth – want.' Spoken in this way, the reference was given an extra coating of contumely. 'I ought never to have bothered. A failure. A ghastly failure.' My mother gave him a decent interval to contemplate the ruins of his life before starting to clear the dishes onto the trolley. I got up too and gingerly took away his plate from before him. I wondered if I pitied him. He certainly was piteous; but I knew that, while I was seldom afraid of him, many people were, and that he despised them for being so. He just went on sitting there hunched in despondency, looking nowhere particularly other than inwardly at those malignant figures of his. I swept away the crumbs with the brush and crumb-tray nevertheless.

Now, before the German trenches, it was this same sense of destiny, and therefore of invulnerability, which usefully supported exhibitionism – so that, when he walked about between the lines, hideously over-exposed, he was a target that no sniper could resist, and part of his face was blown away by the inevitable bullet. He then went on to use the resulting ghastly scar as proof positive of a singular guarantee. He never had any difficulty in being photographed from that side, and went on repetitiously to tell how, as he lay there looking up at the blue sky, he lamented that he would be spoiling his new uniform; and then how, on a scrap of paper, he wrote to his mother: 'I'm all right'. Otherwise, he never spoke of the trenches.

He was in Millbank Hospital in London for nearly a month, going on to win a Ministry of Munitions appointment based in the USA. This came about as a result of his developing sense of the need to fight his own corner and burst through the restrictions faced in his youth. Even though he might describe his father as 'saintly', there is no doubt that he experienced Dr George Reith as amply destructive of his career plans. The more the young man spoke of seeking his fortune in London, the more he would be crushingly told that he would return with his tail between his legs. To defend himself against this parental undermining, allied to an acute sense of his own capabilities, he learned to spot men of influence who would notice him and help him to realise his ambitions.

One such person was E. W. Moir, a hard man who had nevertheless agreed to take the young man into Pearsons, the big civil-engineering firm, straight after his five years with North British Locomotives. Although that appointment was aborted at the outbreak of the First World War, E. W. Moir was to reappear as John's strong advocate in 1917, so that as a consequence John won the appointment with the Ministry of Munitions to take charge of the inspection of small-arms contracts in the USA. The weapons were to be despatched from the Remington Arms factory in Philadelphia to the UK.

He and Charlie parted as elaborately as ever in February 1916 on the platform at Paddington Station in London, where there would have been a display of plenty of the sentimentality that he was so regularly to show in later years. John was to be away for eighteen months. On arrival in Philadelphia, he found he had a gratifyingly smart office. For living, he set himself up in an agreeable little house for rent in the Philadelphia suburb of Swarthmore. It was not long before he was making waves as an engineer in management, meeting leading industrialists and attracting the notice of the oil magnate and philanthropist John D. Rockefeller in the same way as he had done that of E. W. Moir. This was the start of a continuing friendship with branches of the Rockefeller family all his days. He found that he could thrive in this country, where trains, cars and commerce all worked rather than breaking down, and where intelligence was equated with comradeship, zest and enthusiasm. 'The North American world blinds us with its energy',[1] wrote Carlos Fuentes, the Mexican writer. But, if John's energy was making him into a celebrity at work, it was as a public speaker that he attracted the greatest attention. On the platform for the Presbyterian Social Union of Philadelphia, there could be no doubt about the effect that he had on his audience.

He preferred to leave the impression that his performances were spontaneous. As he uncovered his powers and judged his audience exactly, they, gripped by his heroic platform presence, followed him over the Highland hills of Speyside and heard the pibroch sound. But the tall young captain with the ghastly facial scar, the musical voice and the elaborately Scottish speech had a fine cunning too, and, the next moment, they were looking at the stark reality of the trenches, the dead and 'the corner of some foreign field that is forever' – Scotland. John tuned into the American capacity for mixing bitter truths with fluffy illusion, and self-celebration with self-criticism. As one admirer wrote to

23

John's father: 'After so overwhelming a message, the only thing we could do was to sing the Twenty-third Psalm and then go home'.[2]

Dr Reith was no mean preacher; but here was his youngest son constructing a pulpit of his own. John said of himself that he had come upon something within, the existence of which he had been vaguely and vexatiously aware, but which he had never had the opportunity to disclose or develop.[3]

Setting up in rivalry to his father's pulpit one of his own, John was always to attach great weight to his public speaking, often to very great effect. He himself came from an era in which importance was attached to public speaking; and, as well as attending with care to his own performance, he would take it upon himself to see that 'I did not fall short of the family tradition'.

When it came to my turn, I was to carry on what he saw as a tradition, led by his father, practised by John, and then, through his instruction, passing to me. And so, as he coached me in preparation for my boarding-school Sunday service and the lesson to be read, I was aware that my grandfather was the model. Line by line, word by word, we dissected Psalm 139: 'O Lord, thou has searched me and known me'. 'Emphasise the verbs', said my father; and he read it himself. I tried. 'No – not a full stop at the end, but a lift in the voice: "and known me".' I could already detect that here we were getting a rather individual stamp on the Old Testament. I tried again: this was going to take some familiarisation. 'Hmph', he said, and we had a go at verse two. He did it his way, and I tried an imitation. Unsurprisingly, that was by no means good enough. He reread the verse; and, when I had been able to leave behind a schoolgirl giggle about my down-sitting and my uprising, I caught something of the intimacy behind the words and indeed the inscrutable nature of what they told. 'Good', there now exploded from the back pew. 'Such knowledge is too wonderful for me.' I emphasised the 'too', and down he crashed. 'That's not the point. It's the knowledge' – and here he withdrew his voice almost to a whisper so that a mystery moved through the starchy little chapel.

Then we came to verse nine: 'If I take the wings of the morning and dwell in the uttermost parts of the sea' – this he read in a monotone, very slowly. The ensuing pause was so long that I almost wondered if he had been overcome by his own emotional charge. But no; fully in control, he was making way for the solemn entry of the poetic and religious climax: 'Even there shall thy hand lead me and thy right hand shall hold me'.

The next day, the young parson waylaid me. 'You read the lesson like an ordained man', he said. I was not quite sure how pleased I was with the implication of my lowly status as an unordained woman, but the intention was clear and he had been startled. So, for that matter, had I at the experience of having worked very constructively with my father. I knew I had learned a lot, and the individuality of his approach was appealing.

In 1917, in the USA, John began to assert himself politically to the extent that he threw in his lot with a nationwide movement of the churches resisting the Germans' offer of appeasement. In the increasing number of his speaking engagements, John drew attention to atrocities across Europe and offered a picture of his life and circumstances at the Front. It was as though his audiences had never heard anything so dreadful. The British Ambassador asked him to come to Washington to advise him. John became an evangelist for his country and an eloquent claimant on the might of the USA to throw itself in behind Great Britain in the war. He spoke to a Red Cross audience of 5,000 and was much moved by the shaky march-past of thirty veterans of the Civil War. He was bold if not brash, his speaker's powers of persuasion overriding any awareness that he might possibly from time to time be exceeding his remit; he could never be an astute politician. 'He gave us hell', one forbearing host said afterwards, 'but we deserved it.' John was hugely enjoying himself. To the Fellowship of Reconciliation, he said: 'Let us not talk about reconciliation and fellowship as long as there is destruction and desolation in the air, piracy on the high seas and flying murder in the air. If you are going to be in at the death, it is time you set about purchasing a horse.'[4] There is no record of what the FOR made of their speaker's logic here.

One may reasonably speculate, however, that he, like so many survivors of trench warfare, carried fierce scars within himself – the mental ones weighing more heavily than the physical ones, and set to stay with him all his days.

Still in the USA, John's ambitions surged ahead. America was ideal for him, and he still thought that the way ahead for him might be in politics, even though the only thing in the way of his becoming President was that small inconvenience that one must be born a citizen. But John would never be troubled by such mundane considerations as these. Nor did he notice that he had made of the politics of war several useful hand grenades with which to exert great power over any temporary concordat of a gathered audience. He was not the kind of man, as H. L. Mencken said, who 'could sit on the fence and keep both ears to the ground',[5] as any reasonable politician needed to do. What he had was different, and it was not a lot to do with the machinations, minutiae and calculations of the committed politician. As John Mortimer, of 'Rumpole' fame, noted, a politician is like a barrister who must say either what his client wants him to say or what he wants the jury to hear. Likewise, the politician has political masters on one hand and the electorate on the other; he seldom stands up to say: 'This is what I believe'. What John really believed politically was far from clear to himself in any case. He was a romantic, and that gave him permission, in his view anyway, to walk about in the politician's fields. Moreover, he was now making that important discovery about himself: that, while he himself was not a thinker or a searcher after ideas, he possessed and practised the rhetorician's art of persuasion and effect. Although, in later years, his shelves accommodated tomes with lofty names across their spines: Hume, Descartes, Spinoza, Plato, he preferred to make occasional forays into their pages and emerge with a juicy grape of a quotation: 'The starry sky above me and the moral law within me', to which he attached the name Kant like a tail on a kite. Meanwhile, he asked his parents to make sure that the *Glasgow Herald* knew about his doings: Glasgow should not be unaware, he said.

For a time in Swarthmore, John found a new friend. Jimmie Laws was a teenager who reminded him of Charlie. Temporarily, the stream of letters to Charlie dried up as John saw more of Jimmie and, for a while, had him to stay in his digs because Jimmie apparently needed to avoid a measles outbreak at home. Then friendship ripened with Jimmie's older sister Jeanette. John admired Jeanette, pretty and vivacious. He treated her lavishly; but, when she had seriously fallen for him, she had then to learn that theirs could never be more than a warm friendship. She accepted her lot with dignity and, in due course, went on to marry Tom McCabe, head of the Scott Bowater Paper Company.

'I was very, very happy in Swarthmore', John would say in dreamy tones, making by implication an unfavourable comparison with the present. Swarthmore, it seemed, had at that time been filled with wonderful people, including Jeanette McCabe. In his mind's eye, he was meeting all those people again and addressing rapt audiences from high platforms. But what he now spoke about also was the brilliance of the sugar maples – whose name unusually he recalled – and whose blaze in autumn he was trying to describe. Clearly, Buckinghamshire in comparison with all of this was dreadfully dull. But when, as temporary refugees from the Second World War, my mother and brother and I stayed for four long months as guests of 'Aunt Jean' McCabe, I found little to recommend Swarthmore and little love for Aunt Jean.

My father was, as ever, better at enjoying the past than at valuing the present. 'Wouldn't you like to be back in Swarthmore again?' he asked me. And then, completely losing track of his temporary access to what he felt should be my interests, he went on inconsequentially: 'There was old Dr Tuttle. He was a very fine preacher indeed. I enjoyed my visits to Bryn Mawr College immensely. Always made most welcome.' I had no idea what or who he was talking about but was under no pressure to enquire, either from his promptings or from my own. Instead, he suddenly asked: was I happy? Embarrassed, I said: 'Oh yes!'

What I did feel, however, was quite different; and that was about being insistently possessive about the Now rather than the past – and someone else's at that. My possessiveness was undented even by what I was to understand was a deeply unsatisfactory house, garden and part of England. I found these to be rich and exciting. A world, one might say, of one's own.

When John eventually left Swarthmore to return home in late 1917, it was to an emotional reunion with Charlie. The job he went on to find on the south coast near Brighton was one with which even he was satisfied. The Admiralty, in conjunction with the Royal Engineers, were to build a submarine defence barrage to cross the bed of the English Channel to the French coast. Eight colossal floating towers, rising to 170 feet, were to be connected to a substructure at intervals. In the building of these, with 1,800 men and twenty officers under him, John's engineering experience was fully stretched – as were his managerial and strategic powers, which he always knew he had. Charlie was duly installed in a job nearby, and together they set off in the colonel's car with his driver, a Miss Muriel Odhams, at the wheel, both loaned to the two young men for the purpose of house-hunting. That afternoon, they signed on for a rental and arranged more sightings of Miss Odhams. John, pushier than Charlie, claimed more and more of her company but brought along Charlie so that he would not feel left out. Or so he said. For John, after all, since all things were apparently possible, could surely manage the building of giant defensive towers at the same time as friendship with a nice local girl as well as a relationship with the love of his life. He would practise the idea of marriage for the sake of normalcy and the stabilising of that which he and Charlie had. For John, there were no snags attached to his plan.

Charlie, anyway, was co-operating nicely, pronouncing himself 'awfully glad' when John reported that he had embraced Muriel one evening in the garden of the Homestead, at Southwick, where she lived with her parents. Later, John had gone off and bought a ring – yet another one – and had given Muriel a privileged viewing of it, but then had prudently put it away again. You never knew what might happen; he was, perhaps, momentarily in touch with his volatile self. But he explained carefully to a rather surprised Miss Odhams that he had this great love for his mother and father, and that this love had been able to make way for his great love for Charlie. He felt sure, he said, that one day he would be able to love Miss Odhams in the same way very much too. Miss Odhams, a down-to-earth person, found herself swept into a fervent prayer or two and no small embarrassment.

But Muriel's mother did not care for this unmannerly Scot and his strange ways. Learning of the unusual walks that were taking place across the Downs, Muriel on the arms of both men, Mrs Odhams announced – apparently forgetting that her 25-year-old daughter was an independent person who had already lost her first fiancé in the War – that the walks were to stop. Mr Odhams – something of a sleeping partner in his brother's publishing firm – registered a ponderous objection or two. Nevertheless, this jolly farce, a sort of *Così fan tutte*, went on like a specially choreographed dance between John, Muriel and Charlie. It starts with the old story: which of the two men will she marry? The setting is a quiet country lane on a summer evening; the sun is sinking in the west, the blue sea shimmers far away, and, in among the long shadows, all those gnats are just fooling about. In stately *pas-de-trios*, John, Muriel and Charlie are changing places. As John and Charlie quickstep together, they whisper away and bid Muriel move on a little. And so, in a sad and single allemande, she must be alone with her perplexities and the gnats. And then up waltzes John to Muriel, but breaks off to butterfly back to Charlie, who, with a pocket polka, draws forth some morsel and hands it over to John. Still Muriel droops alone. Now, a dashing white sergeant, John pirouettes to her and hands her this thing which, with blushes like the setting sun, she puts on her finger. Lightly they embrace, and a gigue brings them back to Charlie. Expressing themselves 'most awfully glad', they dance a threesome reel – until it dies away into more ardent prayer.

A programme note to this comic caper would read: Charlie loves Muriel; John loves Charlie; Muriel loves Charlie; John wins

Muriel; and they all pray together. But John, in dotty omnipotence, saw himself with Charlie and Muriel in a mystical trio, his love invested in the first, and a sort of regularising role awarded to the second.

But, if the parents ever thought that with engagement would come tranquillity, they found, instead, further troubles. More than once, as they became virtually estranged, Muriel asked John if he would like to call off the engagement. John declined. He had, after all, got the girl and prevented the other from doing so. John would no more have asked Muriel what she felt than he would have realised that this was a bizarre situation of his own making. Meanwhile, Muriel's brothers, attending the same local dances, noticed that Charlie's affection for their sister was conspicuous; they were concerned. John now, at last, found himself, and the others involved, in an emotional mayhem – so much so that he turned for advice elsewhere. His diary[6] notes that, at a meeting at the Pensions Ministry, of all places, presumably in association with his war wound, he was advised to look for psychotherapeutic treatment. But there is no further comment as to whether or not he found it. A little later, he started a substantial collection of books on psychology and psychoanalysis, Freud and Jung among them. His mother and father came to stay for a few days in Southwick. For once, he got his mother's ear as he tried to explain the difficulties he was having with Muriel and her family.

But, in later years, his cousin, Margaret Moffat, was to describe John's mother as 'chilling'. All his life, he had longed for intimacy and affection. He experienced it only fleetingly with Charlie; otherwise, he was experiencing in himself a gap. This, in turn, caused a withdrawn awkwardness, leading, of course, to inhibition in his sexual relationships. He had the words but not the music of relationship. So often, the adult person's life mirrors bonds that were difficult in earlier days. In John's case, born of this experience, what was to be a characteristic of his life's story was already establishing itself: spasms of exceptional brilliance at work played out against a background of emotional crudity.

On this flimsy arrangement, their engagement and then their marriage was based – and, in some sense, held together all their days. From his point of view, it was because she provided a constancy, a warm home and a stabilising influence; but, because he was John, he had also with relentless compulsion to turn that on its head and use it as a trigger for his contempt. Over the years, her womanly devotion towards him probably increased, even in the face of long times in which they were virtually estranged. The fact that I did not expect them finally to fly apart says more about my innocence of the ways of the world than about the force of the bond of mutual dependency which remained between them. As well as his angry criticisms of her – 'Muriel, this smoked salmon is excellent – could you not have provided more? This is not nearly enough' – and her defencelessness, I noticed the way in which the name Bowser would surface. I knew neither why, nor why it always upset them both. As I approached adolescence, I felt that these exchanges recommended home life less and less.

The First World War ended and, with it, John's engineering job on the high towers for the cross-Channel barrage. His father, who had been unwell throughout 1919, died in December. John was devastated, and, to try to assuage his loss, set about enhancing the already idealised picture which he had of him with a new rectitude, moral authority, academic prowess and rhetorical power, all allied to most distinguished looks and a musical voice. By now, the old man's misdeeds had been erased. My father wrote of him in excessive terms, filled with longing. This was one of the versions:

> In magnificence of presence I have not met his equal. His countenance in repose was austere, but his ready smile not just benign – itself a benediction. He was urbane, courteous, cultured; very tall, of great natural dignity, always well dressed. Like his Master he loved children, and they him. To exalt Christ and bring honour to Him in the hearts and lives of all whom he met, and to whom he preached, was his over-mastering and constant passion. He led his hearers into the presence of God. His sense of

grace was apostolic; his sense of righteousness prophetic. When he spoke on social or moral ill, or in defence of one whom he felt to be unjustly assailed, his eyes would flash; the eloquence of his indignation was devastating.[7]

There was no sign here of the years of bitter undermining which the young John had experienced at his father's hand. Sometimes, the pain of injury can to some extent be alleviated by denying its existence and instead elevating the source to some invented or idealised state of righteousness – a state of insubstantial perfection.

After a gap, John started work in Coatbridge, east of Glasgow, with Beardmore's. William Beardmore & Co. were at that time one of the largest engineering concerns in Britain, building ships, locomotives, aircraft and cars at several Scottish locations. John became general manager of their Coatbridge factory, and Charlie was soon on board too. John's habit of taking over another person's life and attempting to manage it for them was a struggle which was to occupy my teenage years. But, for Charlie, it was useful because he was not too good at finding jobs for himself or at keeping them. The two found pleasant accommodation in a substantial house called St Ola in Dunblane, near Stirling, where they could enjoy the excellent railway connection with Glasgow and Coatbridge. John was a successful manager and was liked by the men. He even prevailed upon the local council to provide housing for them. He had the provost and the town clerk entertained 'with ulterior motives, namely, twenty new council houses for his staff'.[8] But his visits to Southwick to see Muriel continued to be difficult. The Odhams parents – he mildly epileptic, and both deeply English and traditional – remained unimpressed by this odd Scot. John got the message; Muriel was cold and reserved, not wanting him to think she cared for him.

Nevertheless, in 1920, it suited John to press on and look for another house where he and Muriel would start their married life. It was, again, to be in Dunblane, where Charlie might also continue to live. Muriel did not care for the house of John's choice, finding it austere after the cosy embrace of her childhood home. But Dunardoch was large enough to accommodate John's mother whenever, according to him, she wanted to stay. She would have the best upstairs room, furnished with her things. The pattern which was to prevail throughout their married life had started: what he said went; no other view figured.

As I grew up, it was a little while before I recognised that a fierce current of responsive acquiescence flowed through our family: when John had decided, that was it. I had, gropingly, to learn to resist the impulse; capitulation on such a scale would have been death.

When Dr Reith died in 1919, his declining weeks were dragged out to the accompaniment of sibling fights as Archie, the oldest son, and Jean slugged it out across the landing in the manse in Lynedoch Street – and Robert, the second son, and his wife turned up, in John's view in order to scrounge. But, when John took out his discontent on Jean, he got back what he gave with interest. He and Jean both tried to take on the responsibility for managing their mother's will for her. John lost, and to his discomfort was added the inconvenience of having to share his mother with so many clamouring others.

But even while, as ever, he made waves in his new managerial job in Coatbridge, he felt threatened on a very different front. Young Charlie was starting to discover that he was an independent person: for him, it was becoming important to begin to cut loose from the relationship with John. But, whenever danger like this threatened, John set about dealing with the pain with an explosion of plotting, scheming and devising, all apparently on behalf of the other. That other, whoever it was, was rarely consulted, however, and so it was not difficult to see that this problem-solving exercise was to help John rather than anyone else. He was already too closely acquainted with the pain of rejection to be able to act rationally. Now, he decided, it would be prudent to get Charlie married off. Unrealistically, he thought that, if he managed Charlie into marriage, this would consolidate things between the two of them. Charlie, too, would set up house in Dunblane, and all four would live in regular and harmonious touch. Accordingly, John made contact with Maisie Henderson, who lived very substantially with her wealthy mother in a mansion called Argaty on the edge of Dunblane, a delirious mixture of the sixteenth century and Edwardiana. Like Muriel and her sad tendency to fall in with John's plans for her, Charlie too, good fellow that he was, went along with the idea as soon as he knew what it was. Or perhaps he liked the idea anyway.

Things went merrily with Charlie and Maisie. But John began to grow uneasy, finding to his dismay that he himself was becoming more and more excluded from their doings. His own scheme had turned nasty and bitten him: Maisie was a more robust character than he had noticed; and, as he entered on a new and strident dislike for her, she, no longer Miss Henderson, or even Maisie, became Jezebel – an unpleasant woman in the Bible, married to King Ahab, on both of whose heads descended the spectacular wrath of the prophet Elijah, to great effect.

And so John and Muriel were married, she with a tear or two, in the Doomsday Church of Kingston Buci in Southwick near Brighton in the summer of 1921. He got away from the reception as soon as he could and went upstairs with his brother Douglas and Charlie to pray. Of all the older brothers, Douglas stayed a friend to John, steering a hard path between concurring in the depth of the relationship between John and the younger man and issuing gentle warnings.

John took Muriel to the Isle of Skye, off the west coast of Scotland, for their honeymoon. This was an alien landscape for her in which, on a bad day, the Cuillin Hills could look like a Gustav Doré illustration from Dante's *Inferno*, and John a character from it. Things were not going too well for them both – and so, getting desperate, he said that they would walk from Sligachan to Loch Coruisk. He strode on ahead in gloomy self-absorption, she battling through some way behind, keeping going as best she could. They covered nine miles of rocks, bogs and high slopes with plunging burns until they reached a black lagoon lying deep below those 'bare black Heads, evermore doing deeds of darkness, weather plots and storm conspiracies in the clouds',[9] as Coleridge said. How unlike the warm Downs of the south which Muriel knew, her Sussex home with oak-shaded lanes, meadows and 'so many butterflies ... purposefully running up the stairs of the air' – Coleridge again. When they got back that night and she threw out the mangled remains of her shoes, he did manage an appreciative note of her stamina; and, with a tiny and temporary access of self-questioning, he wondered if he had been a little harsh, perhaps?

But, back in Coatbridge, things were not looking good. Beardmore's were losing orders, and John had to make many redundancies. He was no longer enjoying the work. On the one hand, he had greatly increased productive efficiency through a new card system regulating the shop floor; on the other, he had possibly overestimated the market for the oil engines and pumps.[10] He had reorganised internally, something which he relished and carried out at great speed and to great effect; but the next part, in which he would study the market and see if it was in a position to absorb the new rate of production – this was less to his taste. He had little appetite for putting himself in a position where he had to be open to the influences of others and decide in the light of them, and clearly felt that his lofty disregard for others and conviction as to his judgements were more than enough. Such care for one end of the production process and cavalier disregard for the other worked prejudicially against the good of the firm and his own future within it. The scene closed unhappily with his departure.

But it was when Charlie, who was busy making a go of things with Maisie, informed John that he had little feeling left for him that he nearly came apart. In his desperation, John sought out the Psychological Clinic in Glasgow – even though he was one of those sceptical patients who imagined that, having read his Freud, his Jung and his Pfister (a pastor in Zurich and follower of Freud), he could show those doctors how much he knew. In those early days in the history of psychotherapy, it may have been the Clinic for Psychological Medicine founded by Dr Oswald in 1910 in the Western Infirmary in Glasgow which John attended. By then, in

1921, it was being run by Dr David Henderson. Muriel, in John's view, could not or would not understand his torment, adding to it by remarking that she could be happy when she managed to forget about Charlie – a remembering that they had in common. What an irony it was that Charlie, through no fault or actions of his own, interposed himself between John and Muriel in their marriage by continuing as the focus of both their loves – not in the happy, far-off way of fairytales in which John had seen the three in gentle harmony, but like some effluent discharged into the current of their lives.

Charlie was engaged to Maisie – and, six months into John and Muriel's marriage, Muriel was in touch every day with her family and also sending for the doctor, so worried was she about John's mental health. Charlie tried to do his bit too. He and John would make a return visit to Comrie while Muriel was away visiting her family. As they explored old haunts in Comrie, climbing again up Monument Hill, it snowed heavily. John was thrilled, never more at home with the elements than when he could do battle with them. It almost seemed to John as though he and Charlie could rediscover their old relationship, and things could again be as rich as they had been before. But Charlie said he had to find a telephone; he needed to ring Maisie. While he spoke away in the telephone box at the post office, John leaned over the parapet of the old bridge and considered the River Earn below, as swift and black as the feelings which now engulfed him.

Charlie was married in Dunblane Cathedral, John and Muriel both facing up to the wedding, he firing criticisms like missiles at everyone and everything, especially the bride's mother.

Then John started to flirt with the girl in the large house opposite Dunardoch – the acute sense which he claimed for himself of the distinction between right and wrong demonstrably a matter of expediency only to be exploited or discarded on a whim. All his days, he clung tenaciously to what he regarded as his sole right to deviate. But these, and related matters, were never talked about. In Dunblane, Muriel saw, gossip whirled round the little township, and John cared not – except that, like one possessed, he was standing at midnight on the eve of his thirty-third birthday at Charlie's front gates at Argaty. He took the opportunity of an invitation to his old boarding school, Gresham's in Norfolk, to speak about himself as a 'borderline case'. This stretched the good manners of the public-school system almost to breaking point: a melancholy prophet in confessional mood was as remote from their experience as that of a deep-sea diver from an astronaut. John told them: 'I would recommend one real friend rather than a dozen lesser ones. It may be the divinest thing in your life. Few attain it. Take care, however, that the loss of it, for whatever reason, will not destroy your mental equilibrium. I speak from experience.'[11]

Meanwhile, relations between Argaty and Dunardoch deteriorated even more as uncomplimentary missives travelled to and fro. With John's mother temporarily ensconced, Dunardoch became the house

> Where sits our sulky sullen dame,
> Gathering her brows like gathering storm,
> Nursing her wrath to keep it warm.[12]

Feeling it her duty to intervene on behalf of her son, Mrs Reith set off purposefully to cover the goodly step between Dunardoch and Argaty, an angry bonnet on top. When she got there, she possibly was told to mind her own business – and this would have been a fair response. At last, John pulled himself together sufficiently to go to London to look for work, filling in time by helping the coalition Conservatives with their election arrangements. Muriel stayed in Dunblane, trying to manage the servants, whom she feared, and the accounts, which she did not understand.

It was by now October 1922. As was his wont, John attended church in London, returning after the morning service in Regent Square Church of Scotland to the evening one. He hoped for a word from on high that he might hear and interpret. He never forgot the words at the service one night from Ezekiel 22:30: 'And I sought for a man among them, that they should make up the hedge, and stand in the gap before me for the land, that I should not destroy it: but I found none'. John, with unfailing self-dramatisation, saw himself as Ezekiel's man. Not very long after hearing these words, on 14 October 1922, an advertisement for general manager of the British Broadcasting Company appeared in the *Morning Post*. John had put to sea at last. His preoccupation with Charlie fell away a little as that landscape dropped astern; he drove himself at the new job with all the application and drive of one escaping an army on the march. In an incredibly short time, the BBC was itself making news.

NOTES

1. Carlos Fuentes, 'How I Started to Write', in Phillip Lopate (ed.), *The Art of the Personal Essay* (Anchor Books, 1994).
2. Ian McIntyre, *The Expense of Glory* (HarperCollins, 1993), p. 71: quote from the Diary of John Charles Walsham Reith (hereafter '*JCWR Diary*'), 29.12.16.
3. McIntyre, *The Expense of Glory*, p. 71: quote from John Reith, *Into the Wind* (Hodder & Stoughton, 1949), p. 68.
4. McIntyre, *The Expense of Glory*, p. 72, from Reith's letter to his father, 25.2.17.
5. H. L. Mencken, 'On Being an American', in Lopate (ed.), *The Art of the Personal Essay*.
6. McIntyre, *The Expense of Glory*, p. 98.
7. Reith, *Into the Wind*, p. 6.
8. From summarised Reith diary as quoted by McIntyre, p. 99.
9. Richard Holmes, *Coleridge Early Visions* (Pantheon, 1989), p. 329.
10. John Hume and Michael Moss, *Beardmore: The History of a Scottish Industrial Giant* (Heinemann, 1979).
11. McIntyre, *The Expense of Glory*, p. 112, from *John O'London's Weekly* magazine, 1926.
12. Robert Burns, *Tam o' Shanter*, lines 10–12.

3

Out of a Broom Cupboard

WITH HIS appointment as general manager of the new British Broadcasting Company, John was in touch with those powers of his which were to fashion the new enterprise and make him a national figure. He turned the stern inheritance of his youth to his advantage. The Almighty, he claimed, was ever at his side, supporting the objectives of broadcasting: to educate, inform and entertain.

The British Broadcasting Company was formed on 18 October 1922; its shareholders were all manufacturers of wireless apparatus. A benign control of broadcasting was at that time already in place, since all transmitters had to be licensed. Broadcasting apparatus was vested in the Post Office and in the person of the Postmaster General. 'The policeman of the ether' was John's name for this important person, who was to figure large in the BBC's plans, negotiations and achievements for many years to come – and, depending on who occupied the position, the said 'policeman' was spoken of either tolerantly or disparagingly.

The wireless manufacturers were forming a single company from a committee of the 'big six', their income deriving equally from the licence fee and a royalty of manufacturers' sales. The BBC was 'simply to provide broadcast programmes', and the manufacturers had a licence now agreed with the Postmaster General for the 'creation, establishment and operation of stations as a public utility service to the public by means of wireless telephony and/or wireless telegraphy. The stations were to provide news, information, concerts, lectures, education material, speeches, weather reports, theatrical entertainment ...'.[1] Apparently, no-one noticed that the instrument – that is, the *wire-less* – at the heart of all this planning activity was designated by a negative.

A few days ahead of that meeting in October 1922, at the Institute of Electrical Engineers, the *Morning Post* had carried an advertisement inviting applications for the posts of general manager, director of programmes, chief engineer and secretary. John Reith, innocent of the work that was already going on around broadcasting, and not even knowing what was meant by it, applied for the first position, writing to Sir William Noble, chairman of the Broadcasting Committee and one of the first directors of the BBC. He told him about his engineering and commercial experience and about what he had achieved in organisational and administrative appointments of considerable responsibility, ending with the resounding statement that 'the appointment is of the nature and degree which I came to town hoping to obtain, and I should not apply if I did not feel capable of discharging its responsibility to your satisfaction'.[2]

He wrote his letter in the Cavendish Club and despatched it into the Club's letterbox. Then, having consulted the *Who's Who* entry for Sir William Noble, he set about retrieving the letter from the postbox, working on the club staff with ingenuity and insistence to bend the rules and open up the box for him. That done, he rewrote the letter with an additional paragraph: 'I am an Aberdonian and it is probable that you may know my people', he said.

No doubt the story that he would make of this incident was already forming in his mind, a story that he would tell down the years recalling the start of a great new institution in British life. He was not to know that a leading journalist had been offered the BBC job but had turned it down because it was not, in his view, large enough. John was interviewed on 13 December 1922; Sir William Noble was especially friendly towards him, and there were three other interviewers present. Among other questions, John was asked about dealing with letters of complaint – to which, no doubt, he gave a very adequate reply – after which he was 'informed that the general manager would, in a short time, know everybody worth knowing in the country'.[3] He had, wrote John, sounding undeniably smug about his continuing ignorance, 'no idea what the letters of complaint were about nor what would cause such notoriety'. After Noble had telephoned the next day to offer him the job, he renewed his efforts to find out what he was to manage, and he met Arthur Burrows and C. A. Lewis, already appointed director and deputy director of programmes respectively. Together, they went to look at office premises in Savoy Hill. Over a drink with Burrows afterwards, John continued to try, without disclosing his ignorance, to discover what broadcasting was. When Burrows remarked that he was lucky enough to have a voice that seemed to carry well, John was even more perplexed. It was not until he was able to speak with his school fellow Jack Loudon – having without success tried to turn around every casual conversation to broadcasting – that he knew at last what it was. But he never felt harassed by his ignorance or in too great a hurry to dispel it, since it provided a singular demonstration, to himself at least, of the sterling quality of his self-reliance.

Then he rushed back up to Dunblane, where his poor wife waited patiently all on her own except for one or two servants in this – to her – unknown country and where, as a shy person, she must have had few friends. But John's arrival was not exactly soothing, as, turning up without warning, something he so loved to do that he never lost the habit all his life, he bypassed the front door and its bell and went stealthily to the back door. Locked. Muriel was thrown into great alarm in the dark of a December evening, hearing someone trying the door She must have been hard put to it, when eventually the front doorbell rang, to open it a

41

crack. But John had not thought of these things, so excited was he by the news he had to give. He wrote to his mother from Dunblane, pressing her to stay at Dunardoch. This gave satisfaction to him, but less to Muriel. Since his mother did not take up his invitation, he called on her in Glasgow on his journey south after Christmas, telling her that she must go on living in order to see him gain a knighthood. This would not, he said, be too far in the future. He was distressed at leaving her. He was also extraordinarily accurate in his forecast.

Even though I scarcely knew my grandmother, I had little doubt, later on, that she was the most important woman in John's life.

The conditions under which he first started work for the BBC, at 9am on Saturday 30 December 1922, were meagre – contrasted, he felt, with his own tremendous capacities. But, captain of his own ship at last, he was blissfully happy. 'I worked', he wrote amiably enough, 'out of a sort of a broom cupboard.'[4] That morning, he had walked into the offices of the General Electric Company in Magnet House, in Kingsway, London, where a notice told him that here indeed was a company for him to be general manager of. The doorman wanted to know his business.

'The broadcasting company', said John.

'Nobody there yet, Sir; we're expecting them on Monday.'

'Who's the "them"?'

'The new company.'

John said that he was the 'them'.[5] And so they both rose up in the lift to the second floor, stepping out onto cheerless tiles in the half-light of yellowed stained glass and dark wood. The doorman clattered shut the metal concertina of the lift, and a chilly echo travelled down the building.

As the doorman unlocked a nearby door, he looked curiously at the young giant he had let in, but, leaving him to make his own explorations, shut the door behind him. The new general manager was on his own with the sound of retreating footsteps and the clanging of the lift door.

John was in a room about thirty feet long and half as wide. There were some tables and chairs and a door at the very far end, as he said, 'inviting examination'. Behind it was a very small room with a table, a chair and a telephone. 'Ah,' he said to himself, 'the general manager's office', and sat down in a practising sort of way. The door swung shut for some reason, and so he wedged it open again and surveyed the bleak space he had come through. He tried the telephone – the outside world suddenly had an allure of some kind – although he felt that the explanation he had given to the answering voice could have been foolish: were they prepared, he enquired, for calls for the BBC? – because the BBC was on the job. Soon, there came a knock at the door, and a man entered wearing a silk hat and carrying two attaché cases and some legal books. Like Livingstone and Stanley, they presumed. The secretary and the general manager shook hands gravely, and John made his first managerial decision: he would need at once to replace the secretary with a new appointment. Already, a furious current was gathering speed to start to drive what was to become the smooth turbine of the BBC.

On the questions as to who did what and who reported to whom in the new company, Sir William Noble had been quite clear. 'We're leaving it all up to you', he said easily. 'You'll be reporting at our monthly meetings, and we'll see how you're getting on.' Clearly, John had succeeded in projecting a wholly encouraging picture of himself. He found this entirely satisfactory, a picture already growing in his mind's eye of himself at one side of the boardroom table, Sir William opposite, and the directors around, he giving them an able and concise report on progress, programmes projected for transmission, the growth of the categories of education, information and entertainment (now in that order), new posts filled and to be advertised, and finances.

Though rooted in commerce, the BBC was already beginning its long climb upwards to the assumption of the ideals and lofty purposes of a public broadcasting service – John Reith their tireless inventor and protagonist. Already, an agreeable concept was forming in his mind that broadcasting should give the people not what they want but what they do not yet know that they need. He warmed more and more to that idea – not only of a public service but also of one that would carry indelibly the Reithian impress.

Finally, and deftly, he would share with the Board some of the problems that he and his staff faced, thereby steering them unawares past some of the issues on which he would prefer that they did not fasten. In so doing, he would hand them back their role to advise and guide, now enhanced in their own eyes with this confirmation of their great wisdom and experience. John had already developed a fine line in high-flying deviousness. To him, it provided such a natural path to progress that he would, equally without shame, later explain to me some of his methods. He would become all amused at himself and his exploits.

BBC broadcasting had officially started on 14 November 1922, the day of a general election. From the staff in the Birmingham Station came this account of the first announcement: 'Tonight, and until further notice, we will give ... copyright news bulletins specially prepared for the British Broadcasting Company by the several English news agencies. It is my intention tonight to read these bulletins twice, first of all rapidly and then slowly, repeating on the second occasion, wherever necessary, details on which listeners may wish to take notes.'[6] Matters went less smoothly in Manchester, where, in an excess of enthusiasm, they had engaged the band of the Grenadier Guards to play without having calculated whether the bandsmen and their huge instruments could all fit into the limited space available. Several sat on the piano; but, when it came to the tenor solo, the vocalist, being a small man, stepped up onto a podium made of heaped-up books, from which to come level with the microphone. Unfortunately, in reaching for his high note, the climax of an emotional build-up, he took a step back, and the microphone faithfully picked up the succession of crashes which ensued as he slid under the piano.[7]

The pre-Reith picture of the BBC in the late autumn of 1922 was one in which any kind of coherence or strategy was conspicuously missing. The three stations in London, Birmingham and Manchester were each made up of small groups producing programmes in the evenings, no-one knowing what the others were doing or where they should be heading. In Magnet House itself, as Arthur Burrows described it, the six telephones rang continuously. But, because the studio was in Marconi House in the Strand, people were bound to keep sprinting between one and the other. One jaded staff member remarked that he functioned on a diet of beer and meringues, these being the most easily assimilable 'in the extremity of haste'.[8] Those early days, before the effects of the new general manager's administrative zeal were fully felt, were written up a year later by a pioneer in the new *Radio Times* of 28 September 1923:

> Those were hectic but happy times. A whole crowd of us were herded together in one small room; all but the General Manager, who had a cupboard to himself, so small that he had to sit like an Oriental at a bazaar. 'Uncle Arthur' and 'Uncle Caractacus' would be 'broadcasting' at different 'phones a yard apart. Captain Eckersley would be dictating a highly technical letter and an intensely humorous burlesque at the same time. That is probably the origin of simultaneous broadcasting. Then the 'phones would be ringing all over the place with all sorts of queries ...[9]

As for John, he simply remarked that there was so little space that it became necessary 'to place one's hat on top of one's walking stick against a wall in order to find room for it'. One of his small team found himself near to breaking point: he, like everyone else, was working twelve hours a day because, as he saw it, 'We had been appointed guardians and attendants of the most voracious creature ever created by man – a microphone'.[10] So much did he feel the strain that he told his general manager that he would break down if things went on like this much longer. To which John replied: 'You might let me know when you are going to do it, then we can arrange to take it in turns'.

But these were the circumstances under which John was less likely than any other to collapse – as well he probably knew. He found the experience of sailing in uncharted waters exhilarating. After all, 'very few knew what broadcasting meant; none knew what it might become' – and now his ambition for it was fuelled by a certainty of a providential kind that he was predestined for a role of immeasurable significance. What he envisaged was something on a scale that no-one else was yet contemplating. Achievement looked him in the eye; and, loyal to the talents he knew he had, he responded with vigour and emotion. The enterprise of which he was now general manager would be made to coincide with the mighty image that he, John, had of himself. He would be the master builder, the visionary, the leader of men, the warrior in whose command lay even the ether itself. In the drama that unfolded before him, he was the lead player on the world's stage. In that role, he never slackened on performance. Of all this, he was entirely assured through his God, who was ever compliant and at his side, and through whose intervention this opportunity had opened out before him. The words of Ezekiel 22:30 were seldom out of his mind: 'And I sought for a man among them, that they should make up the hedge, and stand in the gap before me for the land'. Nothing stood in the way of John and this realisation of his dreams.

Now, in 1922, BBC programmes were on air, and the broom cupboard was dense with activity. Most of the issues with which John had to deal were new to him. To make up, he supplied masterly speed and confidence in assimilating new information on questions of copyright, performing rights, Marconi patents, associations of concert artists, authors, playwrights, composers, music publishers and theatre managers and, of course, wireless manufacturers.

Thirty-five years on, giving a public lecture, as he was wont to do, on the place of the public corporation, John was faced by a questioner with an elaborate enquiry. The lecturer regarded him silently until the questioner, unable to bear the suspense any longer, needed to know if he had been confusing. Another ghastly silence. Eventually he got his deserts. 'Oh no,' said Lord Reith, 'I'm not confused. I'm very intelligent, you know.'

Peter Eckersley, the BBC's first chief engineer, recruited by John, and as gifted an entertainer as he was a technician, took a whimsical view of the general manager. He said this of his first morning with the company:

> On the morning I joined, I was summoned to see Mr Reith. He outlined my immediate problems ... 2LO, the London transmitter, installed on the roof of Marconi House, was interfering with the Air Ministry receivers over the way and must be moved to a new position. I had better be satisfied that the new stations, to be erected in Glasgow, Cardiff, Bournemouth and Belfast, were being properly installed ... Several of the new technical publications were asking for articles on our future plans: publicity was essential. He suggested I should go and see the new press man, Smith, who was coming down from Glasgow. Was it necessary for me to live in Essex? Hadn't I better get a house in London at once? And perhaps a better suit of clothes might help.[11]

Peter Eckersley, very much his own man, was already displaying an unusual attitude: not only was he not in awe of John, but also he regarded him with rare objectivity. It was not long before he earned that unusual commodity: John's respect.

A few years on, I had no difficulty in picking up on how John seemed rather to encourage people to adopt a cringeing attitude towards him – and then he would think the less of them for cringeing. He never, I noticed, seemed able to talk to and with people around his dining-room table in a simple way – but rather, everything had to be a performance, he making platform statements. The people sat nervously around, wanting to join in and working hard to try to do so and thereby to win the favour of his attention. One man, deciding to be bold and address the circle of people instead of speaking directly to John, gave himself away by glancing at John to see the effect. I realised that, for me, too, things were to be no different: I could expect to be distanced and to have to be deferential and to make, as it were in my own way, prepared statements if I was to be heard at all. But, as a very small person, you do not have that capability.

Now that John had secured his appointment to manage the BBC, he set about investing in it his wild religious improving drives.

Robert Bridges, the Poet Laureate, a relative of John's wife Muriel, pronounced that Providence had raised John up to run the BBC and save the country. That the Almighty took this personal interest in his destiny remained John's conviction, which followed him with disturbing insistence throughout those long years of an engineering apprenticeship – but of whose steadfastness, when eventually he came unhappily to leave the BBC, he became less sure. Now, when at last broadcasting opened up to him, and when at last he knew what it was, he turned it into a mission – not because he longed for an enlightened population, but because he felt compelled to impose his reforming zeal upon a dull proletariat. Not that anyone put it like that. As Prospero said: 'This isle is full of noises, sounds and sweet airs that give delight and hurt not'.[12] And, he might have added, that inform, educate and entertain.

On Christmas Eve 1922, the first religious address ever to be broadcast had already been given by the Rector of Whitechapel, the Rev. J. A. Mayo. Not surprisingly, it was still early days when John made possible for himself a visit to the Archbishop of Canterbury, Dr Randall Davidson. Winning the recognition and approval of the most eminent personages in the land meant a lot to John, regardless of whether it was entirely for the standing of the organisation and the tide of influence and goodwill which would thus be engendered, as he always argued it was – or whether, as I felt to be nearer the mark, it was as a favour to himself.

In regard to the Archbishop, who was both vague about broadcasting and usefully curious, things went well. The Archbishop asked where he could hear it. Seizing the moment's inspiration, although unsure if he had not over-reached himself at last, John asked the Archbishop if he and Mrs Davidson would care to dine with him and his wife at their home.[13] This was accepted and arranged; and, soon afterwards, the Primate and his wife were received in the flat that John and Muriel had recently acquired in Queen Anne's Mansions. John was at pains – in more senses than one – to mask the acute back spasms which had caught up with him as well as some alarm caused by the occasion. Muriel, too, was struggling to manage her fright. Nevertheless, when John, unseen, turned the knob on the wireless set, and music filled the room, their guests were, as John remarked in his diary, most surprised. The Archbishop, who was particularly fond of piano music, asked if such a thing would be possible. John immediately rang the BBC and was put through to Stanton Jeffries, BBC director of music, who, in response to the request, obliged with his own rendering of Schubert's *Marche Militaire*. Mrs Davidson flew to the window to check whether it was open. John luxuriated in his own personal power; and so great was the impact on the Archbishop that, the next day, he called a meeting of church leaders in his room in the House of Lords – and a religious advisory committee had begun. Dr Garbett, Bishop of Southwark, was to be in the chair; and, with representatives from the Free Churches, the Roman Catholic Church and the Church of England, it was quaintly called the Sunday Committee.

If the religious leaders were keen to follow up the possibilities of broadcasting, the Newspaper Proprietors' Association, and the Newspaper Society, speaking for the provincial newspapers, were less so. When John had taken up his post, a restrictive arrangement was already in place with the news agencies in which the BBC had 'Temporary and provisional permission'[14] to transmit news summaries, lasting no more than half an hour, every evening. Then the NPA told the BBC that if, as was likely, it wished to advertise its programmes through them, it had to pay at the going rate. But John was in touch with Gordon Selfridge, the wealthy entrepreneur who advertised his store daily in the *Pall Mall Gazette*. Of his own free will, he offered the BBC the use of his space in that newspaper. The circulation of the *Gazette* rose, and the NPA backed off, saying, in an embarrassed sort of way, that its members had to make their own decisions. But, in John's mind, another idea was already forming, which was seven months later to become the *Radio Times*.

Meanwhile, Viscount Burnham, a press baron and member of the Sykes Committee on broadcasting and the Post Office, said publicly that the newspapers had nothing to fear from the broadcasting of news. 'On the contrary, insofar as it increased public curiosity and stimulated public interest, it rendered splendid service to the community.'[15] John himself had already observed that the BBC's half-hour evening news slot bore no relation to the sales of evening newspapers, other than possibly to enhance them.

It was not long before the new BBC ran into more trouble and 'an unenviable amount of public attention before we were quite ready for it',[16] according to John's understatement. Like some other people with outsized egos, he loved a crisis. The opportunity to demonstrate how emergencies could be handled with a show of effortlessness was irresistible. The BBC and the Post Office had trouble with the issuing of licences for broadcasting, largely on account of the low number of bona-fide applicants for BBC licences. The BBC only received five shillings of the ten-shilling licence from the BBC licensees – or from those in possession of BBC-marked sets. The wireless manufacturers who then comprised the BBC were disappointed with their income, and the company itself was seriously underfunded for some months.

Moreover, foreign suppliers were selling wireless parts which could be assembled together by amateurs with relative ease, with the result that the rising number of these experimenters was interfering with BBC transmissions. The Post Office could not – or would not – investigate; but Peter Eckersley, the BBC's brilliant engineer, argued that any moves to chase up offenders would rob the BBC of public support, which was already being eroded by some warm criticism in the press. Eckersley must have argued ably. Even on his sunniest days, John would assume a person guilty unless proved innocent – a paranoia which, while useful, did little to sweeten the atmosphere in later days for those in his vicinity.

John became a member of the Sykes Committee, which was constituted primarily with a view to supporting the interests of the Post Office. The committee met a great many times before the BBC was even one year old, resolution finally emerging with the help of off-the-record conversations between John and the new Postmaster General, the amazingly named Sir Lamington Worthington-Evans. The BBC was to be protected from foreign competition until the end of 1924, during which time its share of the licence fee would rise from five shillings to seven shillings and sixpence. Those constructing their own sets would pay for a fifteen-shilling licence, as would those who had already assembled theirs. During a ten-day span, the number of licences increased from 180,000 to 414,000; the Company was now out of crisis.

Godfrey Isaacs, managing director of Marconi, overflowed with congratulations to the BBC's general manager, and minuted his message which spoke of Reith's 'consummate ability and tact'.[17] The directors promoted John to managing director and voted him ten guineas with which to take a holiday – neither of which, in all probability, he accepted. Work – masses of it – was his life.

Anyway, there were a thousand things to attend to, as well as his great new idea of the BBC's own magazine promoting its own programmes on a weekly basis. In 1923, he wrote: 'Everything is now in shape for a BBC magazine, and from various alternatives I chose *Radio Times* for the title'.[18] He wrote a weekly editorial; Newnes were the publishers, with editorial control. The 285,000 copies of the first issue could have been doubled, with the BBC hardly into its second year. Gladstone Murray, a man able to build substantial connections for the BBC in numerous directions, was appointed director of publicity – and well he filled his role.

John's response to his Board's idea that he should receive a percentage of the profits was in one sense sagacious. It would have quadrupled his salary, but he recognised a conflict of interest: 'the trade had put me in office; expected me to look out for them; there was a moral responsibility to them. I would have thought it hardly proper to accept the money.'[19] He was also, however, inhibited about receiving *ex gratia* payments of any kind. Indeed, the whole business of earning was unexpectedly confusing for John, who would make no attempt to argue for remuneration for some extended piece of voluntary labour in which might lurk a moral dimension. If, inadvertently, he were to transgress such a boundary, his father would appear at his side with a holy reprimand.

In later years, he toiled without suitable renumeration for the North British Locomotive Company, where he had served his apprenticeship and which was now, in the 1950s, set for liquidation. Another ten years on, himself more than ever heavily in debt, he accepted the chairmanship of the State Building Society following the discovery of fraudulent dealings at the most senior level. Later, the shareholders got their money back plus one shilling in the pound, and the success was published abroad. But John felt that it was taboo to profit from another's misdeeds. Had some of the clarity that he had been able to bring to the State Building Society been available to him in his personal finances, his last bank statement might have stood a little more healthily than at £76.

By the end of 1924, with BBC staff in the head office alone numbering over 100, John still knew them all personally. It was not just the senior appointments who received the Reith treatment: the office boys and assistants learned about broadcasting as a vocation; and, despite the grand people with whom he had to do, John was seldom out of touch with his own down-to-earth origins. In those days, he apparently had none of the difficulty, which he claimed for himself in later years, of 'not recognising' someone. But, since he regarded this incapacity as a distinction rather than a difficulty, it never caused him a real problem.

In his third year at the BBC, John was asked to write a book about the experience so far, and so he went for a short time up to Rothiemurchus to write *Broadcast over Britain*.[20] In a chapter called 'Beyond the Horizon', he wrote about the standards to which the BBC worked, in all its activities. The association with religion was, he said, 'definite though restrained'. Although it might have been possible to work only with the material which the great faiths have in common, the case for Christianity was, in his view, undoubtedly made by its being 'the official religion of this country'. Even though this line was much criticised, the complaint – if complaint there were – was to be directed not against Christianity as such 'but against the patent limitations and deficiencies of its presentation and practice.... The Christianity which is broadcast', he went on, 'is unassociated with any creed or denomination. It is such that all except the hypercritical or the extreme may hear not only without offence, but with approval and profit.' Writing the book in the shortest possible time, and in this section more than usually given to rodomontade, John continued: 'it is a thoroughgoing, optimistic, and manly religion ... while the secularising of [the Sabbath] is one of the most significant and unfortunate trends of modern life'. But John's views on comparative religion were neither particularly deft nor probing.

When, in April 1928, the BBC moved from Magnet House to Savoy Hill, a far-reaching change had taken place. For the first time, administration, performance and equipment were all accommodated under the same roof, on an airy site with a broad prospect of the River Thames. The Savoy Hill era, which was to last until 1931, had begun, in which you could be almost sure to meet the great figures of the day – H. G. Wells, Bernard Shaw, G. K. Chesterton, Hilaire Belloc – enjoying a club atmosphere with whisky and soda before an open fire.[21] A certain radiance attached to innovation and to the BBC's growth, which, despite critical moments and emergencies, continued steadily. Though criticised, the BBC was rising luminously from out of its own aura of romance.

It was also, with dismaying speed, outgrowing even the new premises, converting and absorbing neighbouring offices into its orbit, with makeshift arrangements consuming the time of hard-pressed staff. Everyone made the best of the studios, even though they often hindered performances, heavily draped as they were with layers of thick material and deep carpet. This need to control reverberation also muffled voice output in a most dismaying way: singers were hard put to it to project any sound at all as they viewed the layers of dust deep on every fold. There was no ventilation – and, after a brass band had been playing, it was clear that something had to be done. The largest studio, which could take the chorus and orchestra, could only be used following negotiations with the Institute of Electrical Engineers, above whose council chamber it lay.

When one member of staff remarked that they all worked in a certain pandemonium, he was making a comment that John would not have relished. Stuart Hibberd, who joined as an announcer, told how, as a newcomer to Savoy Hill, he had been made to feel at home; one of the family, in fact. There was an 'all-pervading pioneering spirit, which seemed to proclaim from the housetops. Here's a wonderfully worthwhile job. Nothing matters but broadcasting – unless it's better and more extensive broadcasting.'[22]

There was plenty of evidence that this was happening, as more and more wireless aerials rose above the rooflines, with eight main broadcasting stations hard at work, and then several relay stations in heavily populated areas. These were evidence of Eckersley's aim that 'everyone should be able to hear one programme clearly on a cheap set'[23] – even though, in many places, reception was nigh on hopeless. The reception in Sheffield resembled 'an insurrection in hell',[24] as E. H. Shaughnessy, engineer to the Post Office, described it. The solution was simultaneous broadcasting. Rather than many local transmitters requiring many local programmes, a new system was introduced whereby different stations were connected by telephone wires, so that 'the output from one microphone would operate many stations simultaneously'.[25] The first simultaneous broadcast was the news bulletin of 29 August 1923. What was talked of now was 'the new wireless era'. Even though John's engineering experience was in a different field, he took pride in continually adding to his understanding of Peter Eckersley's expertise and giving him as much support as possible.

But there were still areas in need of extra powered servicing: the reception in the countryside was very poor. One high-powered long-wave station was needed; and, in the summer of 1925, the new Daventry station, built on Northamptonshire's Borough Hill, was opened by the Postmaster General. The prime minister, Stanley Baldwin, unable to be present, wrote to John about how aware he was of the way in which broadcasting could contribute to the happiness and knowledge of society. Daventry he saw as another milestone along the road to improving general wellbeing.[26]

John, meantime, was clear on the constitutional arrangements needed for broadcasting of this nature: 'broadcasting should be conducted as a public service and under public corporation constitution'. This formative statement, the basis on which the BBC was to move into the future, was not in fact the product of unalloyed Reithian vision. It came from David Sarnoff, who at the age of 15 had been the office boy to Guglielmo Marconi, and who by 1922 was already laying down the groundwork for broadcasting in America. He said: 'Broadcasting represents a job of entertaining, informing and educating the nation, and should therefore be distinctly recognised as a public service'. His recommendation was for 'A Public Service Broadcasting Company or National Broadcasting Company' to be set up in the USA.[27]

John's approach was characteristic: he not only embraced the Sarnoffian idea of the purpose of broadcasting – which, in the sequence which he favoured, was to educate, inform and entertain – but also went on to impose upon it his own unavoidable and audacious objectives, deciding himself how the interests of the public should be met. Although no-one would do things that way today, part of his contribution to what was to become the concept of 'Reithian standards' was to notice that here indeed was a task: that of recognising the public mood of the day, interpreting it, adapting the response and acting. His instinctive – rather than considered – prescription, which survived then in all its arrogance, but would not today, was, in short, that what he said went.

Down the years, it has been John Reith who has been credited with the original inspiration of public-service broadcasting, and with a public corporation set up for its delivery. But, even though it was not, after all, through his personal road to Damascus that this came about, but rather through his shrewd observation of the tides and currents of his own times to which another's vision was ready to be fitted, he made those early BBC years the determining moments in the history of a great institution. To be the vehicle for the formative idea is no less prophetic than to be its originator. John Reith was perhaps the only man who, anticipating the latent power of wireless, could work with a bunch of wireless manufacturers with commercial objectives and then, with incredible speed, go on to build an institution in which – as its output progressed from crystal sets and earphones to loudspeakers and mounting listener numbers – he might invest far-reaching benefits and ideas. This was a grand concept on an international scale. A unique

55

opportunity had been met by a man uniquely endowed; a leader, a crusader and an originator of ferocious energy, a man of such contradictions that we can hardly be thinking of the same man, however great his failings. One newspaper commentator noted, on the subjects of entertaining biography: 'their lives were so odd you could not possibly have made them up'. This applies aptly to John Reith.

NOTES

1. Asa Briggs, *The History of Broadcasting in the United Kingdom*, vol. 1: *The Birth of Broadcasting* (Oxford University Press, 1961), with the permission of the BBC, p. 127, from the BBC's early Objects of the Company, ch. 3.
2. Ibid., p. 137, from letter, Reith to Noble, 13.10.22, with the permission of the BBC.
3. Reith, *Into the Wind*, p. 82.
4. Ibid., p. 87.
5. Ibid., p. 87.
6. Asa Briggs, *The Birth of Broadcasting*, p. 140.
7. Briggs, p. 140, from Leslie Baily, Scrapbook for 1922.
8. Briggs, p. 141. A. Burrows.
9. Briggs, p. 13, from *Radio Times*, 28.9.23.
10. Briggs, p. 138. C. A. Lewis.
11. P. P. Eckersley, *The Power behind the Microphone* (Jonathan Cape, 1941), by kind permission of The Random House Group.
12. Shakespeare, *The Tempest*, Act III, Scene 2, line 147.
13. Ian McIntyre, *The Expense of Glory*, p. 124: *JCWR Diary*, 16.8.23.
14. Ibid., p. 122: *JCWR Diary*, 9.4.23.
15. Briggs, *The Birth of Broadcasting*, p. 210, from *Bournemouth Daily Echo*, with their permission.
16. From J. C. W. Reith, *Broadcast over Britain* (Hodder & Stoughton, 1924), p. 67, with their permission.
17. McIntyre, p. 130, quoting *JCWR Diary*, 9.10.23.
18. McIntyre, p. 127, from *JCWR Diary*, 10.9.23.
19. McIntyre, p. 128, from Reith, *Into the Wind*, p. 90.
20. Reith, *Broadcast over Britain*, pp. 193–4. Reproduced by permission of Hodder & Stoughton Ltd.
21. Briggs, *The Birth of Broadcasting*, pp. 211ff. Gale Pedrick BBC programme: 'These Radio Times', 18.12.53.
22. Stuart Hibberd, *This – is London* (1950), p. 3.

23. Eckersley, *The Power behind the Microphone*, p. 63, quoted in Briggs, p. 214.
24. Evidence by E. H. Shaughnessy, Chief Engineer to the Post Office, given to the Sykes Committee on Broadcasting. Quoted in Briggs, p. 216.
25. Briggs, p. 216.
26. Ibid., p. 224: letter, Baldwin to Reith, in Diaries enclosure volumes, 21.7.25.
27. Quotations in this paragraph are from Briggs, p. 59: letter, David Sarnoff to E. W. Rice, 17.6.22, quoted by G. L. Archer, *Big Business and Radio* (New York, 1939), p. 31.

4
Making Waves

OHN'S relish for crises was realised in the General Strike of
1926. He saw to it that Winston Churchill did not dismantle
the BBC's independence from government; rather that it played
a pivotal role. The prime minister was guided by John to the
airwaves; a little later, His Majesty himself. But, when these highlights
died away, depression readily overtook the new Director General.

'I do not say that I welcome crises, but I welcome the opportunities
which they bring.' So wrote John Reith as the General Strike of
1926 plunged the nation into emergency and the BBC into its
greatest challenge so far. The BBC's fragile independence was at
risk, while at the same time, because few – if any – newspapers
were being printed, the country looked to the BBC for its news.
John launched the BBC into its key role in style: following the
arrival of a messenger from Downing Street to his home in
Westminster late one April night, he ordered all transmitters to
be connected to his private line. He himself made the midnight
announcement that the first industrial stoppage had begun with

the complete shutdown of the mining industry. Never one to miss out on the essentials of such moments, John judged his own to have been 'an impressive performance'; instantly, he saw the dramatic possibilities of the nation in crisis and the part that he would play. The General Strike was to last nine days; the BBC's news service was crucial.

John was in his element. Not only was he now experiencing power of the kind of which he had always dreamed; but here, even more significantly, was a source of new ways in which he might emphatically assert his autonomy from his own disparaging family – those figures who carried on with their detestable assertions in his innermost being, but who could now lend wings to his words and to his decisions.

An emergency such as this made inevitable calls on John's unusual powers to fight battles and secure territory. Quick to exploit them, he secured the independence of the BBC for the next eighty years – and, too, the nation's esteem for public-service broadcasting and for the body of men and women raised up to reach such inspirational heights of integrity and authenticity.

What he laid down then was to be reflected in the storm of 2004 when the crisis arising out of the death of Dr David Kelly and the Hutton Enquiry led to the resignations of the BBC's two most senior figures. Comments then on the BBC mostly reflected the high regard in which it was held, along the lines of 'The BBC is the envy of the world'. Baroness Williams said: 'It is the finest broadcasting system there is', while others remarked that it is the public funding of the BBC which underpins its impartiality and the quality of its public-service remit.

Back in 1926, John Reith obtained approval from the government's officer on its Emergency Committee, J. C. C. Davidson, to broadcast several daily bulletins to replace the single evening slot, Reuter's supplying the material. The BBC's news service was never again to revert to its earlier limited provision. As the BBC stepped into this key role, it again ran the risk of being commandeered through the government's emergency regulations as a reward: many in government were jealous of its pivotal position. Some things, one might say, do not change.

In his diary, John described how, attending a lunch at the Traveller's Club, the prime minister, Stanley Baldwin, detached himself from the group he was with to come over and speak to him. 'He said we had the key situation now and everyone depended on us. He asked if we were properly protected, and I said we were everywhere. Savoy Hill is hotching with policemen and special constables. He said the Government had no alternative but to break off negotiations on Sunday night, and he seemed ready to talk to me much longer. I said he ought to broadcast soon.'[1]

John's penchant for cultivating the top people was developing fast. Sometimes, in later years, I would feel that he was painting himself in relation to them in too rosy colours: there seemed to be so many and such very eminent people, all of whom apparently approved of him. One day, I overheard my mother voice her similar doubt: a little tentatively, she said to him that she wondered that he knew quite so many important people. 'You don't think that I've been making it up?' he said, snappishly. 'Oh, dear, no', she said, abashed. 'Oh no!' 'Well, I can tell you,' he went on rapidly, 'the new American Ambassador, Joe Kennedy, made it known that he wanted to meet me, and so, newly arrived in this country, had me to lunch yesterday. A mutual friend, he said, had advised him to get me along because I was politically detached and knew most people in the country.[2] Over an hour and a half's questioning, I was able to tell him all he wanted to know. Most grateful, he was. He appreciated my advice, he said.' He broke off. 'Is there anything wrong in that?' He turned round in his chair to confront her. 'Oh no – oh dear me, no', she said again. 'Of course not.' Nothing more was said; but, for me, at this time not yet having gathered some sense of personal autonomy by learning to survive boarding school, I felt again cast down as to how one was ever to make one's way in the world, as I both wanted and was expected to do, in the face of such dazzling accomplishment. Was he really as brilliant as these people seemed to find him, or were they just taken in?

John's diary entry went on: 'Stanley Baldwin was walking up and down the Cabinet Room while Davidson and I leaned against the mantelpiece and explained our views – at least, I said what I thought and Davidson joined in. Every time I made a point, the PM stopped in his perambulations and faced us. He said he entirely agreed with us that it would be far better to leave the BBC with a considerable measure of autonomy and independence. He was most pleasant.'[3] Mr Reith should attend the Steering Committee of the Cabinet, said Mr Baldwin, where, lined up for him, were, among others, Churchill and Lord Birkenhead. At that meeting, Davidson endorsed the prime minister's clear preference for the BBC's independence; but, due to weak chairing, the matter was left unresolved. This provoked from John a powerfully written document for the prime minister's attention: his fight for the BBC's independence was continuing to match his personal fight for his own. 'The BBC has secured and holds the goodwill and affection of the people. It has been trusted to do the right thing at all times. Its influence is widespread. It is a national institution and a national asset. If it be commandeered or unduly hampered or manipulated now, the immediate purpose of such action is not only unserved but also prejudiced.'[4]

Baldwin, in his dealings with the BBC's managing director, was almost compliant: better to leave well alone than to open out the way to a battle between the Cabinet and Reith. But it must have irritated his Chancellor no end. Despite this, after a delay, the Cabinet decided to leave the BBC to operate on its own.

Now the prime minister did want to broadcast. John decided that he should do this from John's own house rather than Savoy Hill. Was this because he wanted to impress his mother, who was staying with him and Muriel? John went to collect Mr Baldwin on a Saturday evening early in May, returning to Barton Street with the prime minister and a phalanx of police outriders. Baldwin seemed unfazed by either the national emergency or his first experience of broadcasting. 'See what you think of this',[5] he said, and tossed his manuscript to John. 'It's tripe', he went on, and sat down easily at John's desk, where the hefty microphone was already in place. John suggested something personal with which to end, and produced a purple passage off the cuff, to which Baldwin said: 'Excellent. Write it down if you have a legible hand.' At 9:30pm, John, leaning over the prime minister's shoulder in the direction of the microphone, announced: 'London and all stations calling – the prime minister'. But the prime minister was taking the opportunity to light his pipe, striking his match beside the microphone to do so. Then, as he started, John went and sat in a large armchair in the corner of the room; but, since the leather was squeaky, he got up again quickly. Then he remembered having noticed that the final paragraph of the speech could be improved. The prime minister still had two more pages to go, and so John quietly removed the sheet below the top one, made his changes and then replaced it, slipping it under the top one as before. Undeterred, Baldwin read on, scarcely pausing even at the alterations.

When the broadcast was over, John's mother, listening through the door, tried to vanish as it opened suddenly and exposed her with her ear to where the keyhole had been. Her son did the only thing possible in the circumstances and brought her in to be introduced. After that, prime minister and managing director together rode back to Downing Street, leaving John's mother, as intended, greatly impressed.

Quite often, John read the news bulletins himself – again an opportunity for performance. He did this, he said, because listeners were finding some announcers sounding anxious. But, on 12 May, as he was reading, someone put a note down in front of him. The TUC, said the scribble, had sent a deputation to Downing Street: the strike was called off. John made the announcement and, as soon as he was off the air, set up preparations for the evening bulletin. By the time he was on air again, he had messages from the King and from the prime minister to read out and his own encomium prepared.[6] It was couched in heavily brocaded language and attributed the nation's happy escape with reverence to Almighty God, with diplomacy to the prime minister, and with modesty to the BBC. By now, launched deeply into melodrama, he called upon the energies and sensibilities of fellow craftsmen to join with him in the repairing of the gaps and the building of the walls of a more enduring city. He was making his allusion to the Old Testament passage which had so stirred him as he heard it shortly before replying to the BBC's advertisement for a general manager. Now John's words flowed in inexorable sequence into the lines of Blake's *Jerusalem*. Not content with recital alone, John had had an orchestra quickly assembled to play softly behind the lines – and then, as his voice died away, the music surged forward, swelling to a choral entry for the final verse.

He was overcome with excitement: he had made pure theatre of this historic moment, and the response was enormous. The '*Jerusalem* business' filled switchboards and postbags for days to come. Baldwin wrote congratulating John and his staff – and, for most people, the BBC's impartiality was a matter for praise. Not so for the Labour Party, however, who were understandably miffed at not having had their time on air as had the Tories and the Liberals. The Labour MP Ellen Wilkinson addressed meetings up and down the country excoriating the BBC; and Peter Eckersley, the chief engineer, was not entirely happy either. He wrote:

> My job was to sort out the news as it came in higgledy-piggledy and arrange items under headings. My tidy sheets were sent to the Admiralty where, so we gathered, government censors would pass it for broadcasting. I therefore shared with a few others the staggering experience of comparing all the news as it came in with that which was considered fit for public consumption. Many of those beside myself who had been proselytising the BBC as the impartial public servant were bitterly disappointed. It was not so much that the news was altered as given bias by elimination.[7]

Station directors were sent circulars to the effect that nothing calculated to extend the areas of the strike should be broadcast; but broadcast messages from the TUC's General Council were allowed, as well as Labour demonstrations, union leaders' speeches and those critical of government. In a memorandum to his senior staff when the strike was over, John conceded that the Labour Party had grounds for complaint, but maintained that the decision flowed inescapably from the declaration in the High Court that the strike was illegal: the BBC was unable to permit anything which was contrary to the spirit of that judgement or which might have prolonged or sought to justify the strike.

In response to the whole episode, John's staff wrote to him in memorable terms: 'It is your leadership that has made the BBC what it is and therefore in the emergency able to do what had to be done ... you never failed to keep a steady hand on the tiller and gave confidence to us all'. How well they knew that, for their man, there could be no metaphor more telling than a nautical one. But, outwardly, he affected a certain indifference to these loyal words.[8]

The story of the General Strike, another amazing episode in the life of the BBC was, like others, heard by me in mournful retrospective. I was never very clear what was meant by 'the General Strike', and mundane explanations were nowhere to be had. Teaching the children had no part in John's programme, since, as progeny of his, they were expected to absorb information and become competent by a process of silent osmosis. And so, here was yet one more cloudy triumph involving the highest in the land, the rightness of the BBC and further proof of John's unerring judgement and power. As for me, enabling of any kind was unlikely to be found at home.

But, as well as Peter Eckersley's voice of doubt on the BBC's role in the General Strike, there were almost certainly others questioning the sensationalist treatment of a political event that had caused suffering to many. Even my mother, behind whose comments wisdom might be found, had her view. 'I'm afraid Daddy does not have very good taste', she said.

Professor Harold Laski was a political scientist and socialist with Marxist leanings. There is no evidence that he ever met John; but he would have heard him on some public occasion. John would never have allowed anyone with communist leanings on radio. Laski wrote, with rare perception:

> His deep-set eyes look as though, at any moment, they may let loose a tempest. He is vehement, determined, aggressive,

masterful. He works easily with you while you agree with him. When you disagree, no one can quite tell, least of all he, what will be the outcome ... There is a fanatic in him. It is one of his gifts and one of his limitations. It explains his power of work, his energy and his drive. But it means also that he carries about with him a bundle of dogmas – social, religious, ethical, political – and he has a tendency to make them the measure of all things and all men. Sunday is what the lawyers call a *dies non* on the wireless, because Sir John will have it so. Controversy is always a little tepid and half-hearted, because Sir John believes we ought not to go too far.[9]

Or, as the psychoanalytically minded would argue, we should not upset father. Or, again, as we have noticed, his powers of reasoning and of lateral thinking, while well developed in some areas, were limited in others.

It was true that, by this time, four years into its life, the BBC had acquired extraordinary standing, even though those in government thought John Reith freakish, and others viewed him warily. Many still looked to him with admiration, among whom were most of his increasing staff. His gaunt, battle-scarred image peered over every shoulder. While allowing his staff much freedom, he also required that they work to their very best – all the time. His reputation was as widely travelled as that of his institution. Asa Briggs remarked that, in 1924 and 1925, he was managing the BBC as though it had already acquired the mantle of a public corporation, even though it was still a public company. Written and published in a hurry, John's *Broadcast over Britain*, although couched in corporate terms, amounted to his personal manifesto for 'the preservation of a high moral standard in broadcasting' and its remit as a public service.

The responsibility weighs heavily with us; let there be no misunderstanding on that score. It is realised to the full; it is apt to become an obsession. It is a burden such as few have been called upon to carry. Whether we are fit or not, is for reasoned judgement only, but at any rate it is relevant and advisable

65

that our recognition of the responsibility should be known. Pronouncement may be reserved till the proofs of the efforts are established.[10]

If this was, as John said, a burden, it was one that he carried without reluctance. The BBC was being made most aptly to fit his aspirations. The elements making up this particular responsibility were set out with care. Within the driving force of the BBC, there could be no room for the profit motive – even though its own origins had been in the commercialism of the manufacturing interest. Secondly, its 'parish' was the United Kingdom, with boundaries expanding to become the British Empire. This concept was the basis for planning, over which, in the third place, unified control was to be exerted: 'in a concern where expansion is so rapid and the problems so unique, unity of control is essential'.[11] (This statement, with its grammatical impropriety, bears witness to the speed of its construction and lack of the author's customary fastidious scrutiny.)

Ahead of John lay his claim that he was, with increasing frequency, to make on behalf of the BBC's dominion: that is, its monopoly. Used only circumspectly at the outset, the word had become enhanced by the time of his autobiography in 1949, when it had become 'the brute force of monopoly'. Now, however, he was imaginatively tuned into the dynamic of his audiences and his publics in just the way Ralph Waldo Emerson wrote about in his *Shakespeare*:

> The great man ... is he who finds himself in the river of thoughts and events, forced onward by the ideas and necessities of his contemporaries ... Great genial power, one would almost say, consists in not being original at all; in being altogether receptive; and in letting the world do all, and suffering the spirit of the hour to pass unobstructed through the mind.[12]

One could certainly argue that John's was not a very original mind. But he was particularly receptive to the movements and urgings of the day, then going on by drive and extrapolation to usher in a redesigned contemporary.

The range of the BBC's broadcast programmes was considerable. With great care, John had appointed J. C. Stobart to be director of education, with an Advisory Committee formed principally of representatives from adult education. Their task was to plant education firmly in the culture of broadcasting. Then came the Advisory Council on spoken English, set up in 1926. The BBC had its own brand. Instead of regional accents, there had to be a single style, BBC-speak: standard southern English, or Received Pronunciation. Here, the Advisory Council bore all the marks of having been leaned on in this less-than-happy example of 'unified control'. The BBC's official voice was through its announcers – all dressed up in dinner jackets, butterfly collar and starched front before a disregarding microphone. Behind them stood John Reith, the conformist, the Establishment Man: he with his own mixed utterance of London, Glasgow and the United States insisting on Received Pronunciation.

A committee chaired by George Bernard Shaw and including Robert Bridges, the Poet Laureate, and the writer Rudyard Kipling acted, as it were, 'as a special gardener employed to weed out impurities of vowel or diphthong and cultivate the lawns of phrasing and inflection', as Alvar Liddell, one of the early voices of the BBC, is credited with saying. John did not see that the BBC would have been better to have sustained dialect and to have valued locality; nor did he know how very middlebrow was his own culture. But pushing back frontiers, opening up new territories and stretching minds to new capabilities were things he thoroughly understood. At times a fair stylist himself, he understood the work of the Advisory Council even though their more creative obscurities eluded him.

In his managerial capacity, he had, despite some people's grumbles to the contrary, an enlightened approach to delegation – and, indeed, a rare creativity of his own. 'In the moment of creation,' said Arthur Miller, 'when his work pierces the truth, the artist cannot dissimulate, he cannot fake it.'[13] Intimidated by Bertrand Russell, H. G. Wells and George Orwell, having very little to say about the Eric Gill sculptures adorning his own Broadcasting House, and looking upon the composers Benjamin Britten, Aaron

Copland and Ralph Vaughan Williams as aliens, John did not, to his great credit, prevent what he did not understand. Instead, he delegated to those who did. When he did not understand something, as was to become so painfully obvious in relation to television, he simply backed off and covered over his ignorance.

The Musical Advisory Committee, under Sir Hugh Allen of the Royal College of Music, had first met in July 1925. Among its members were Professor Donald Tovey, Sir Walford Davies and Sir Landon Ronald. John always noticed the titled before the others. It was Sir Walford Davies who turned out to be a natural communicator on the air: a populariser for music without ever becoming a salesman for cheap goods. 'He used the piano with consummate skill', wrote Stuart Hibberd, 'and had that sense of intimacy – of having a little chat with one listener or one family alone – which broadly speaking is the pre-requisite of all successful broadcasting.' Broadcast music, on average three hours and twenty-five minutes a day, occupied more broadcast time than any other subject.[14]

On the concerns of the Religious Affairs Advisory Committee, John necessarily had strong views. He was hardly into the BBC before both the compulsions and the frustrations of his years of youthful indoctrination from the Glasgow manse were making themselves apparent. As Asa Briggs said, 'it was because Reith believed that the final truths of religion were beyond controversy that his own position was controversial'.[15] He took the line that the Christianity that was broadcast should be made up of the common denominations of all creeds, their differences obscured. This anodyne mixture would easily smooth over controversy of any kind, John felt. He, after all, was almost more uneasy with controversy than he was with the secularisation of the Sabbath, preferring to take an absolutist stand on matters which were more naturally subject for discussion, views and argument. In itself, religion offered him little comfort. He had had enough of it to make himself miserable but not enough to stabilise and secure him. In early College Church days, the singing of the metrical psalms and the Old Testament readings were as near as you could get to Father – either in heaven or in the manse.

The two were sometimes muddled. He was always striving for that faith once believed by his Christian forefathers and which he tried to recreate within himself, filled with the granite pieties of an earlier Presbyterian North-East Scotland.

And so, he did not like it when opinion prevailed – and differed from his. A dinner guest, more daring than most, wanted to know his views on democracy. John made his familiar statement: 'I believe in the democratic principle but not in democratic process'. As intended, the dinner guest retreated; there was no discussion to be had. But then another guest had to have a go, only to find himself decapitated on the subject of Christianity and personal belief: 'I believe profoundly in the Christian ethic,' came the magisterial reply, 'but am a poor practitioner'. John knew that he could not argue, and so made it an impossibility. As to his poor practice as a Christian, he was not greatly bothered.

The increasing secularisation of the Sabbath was, however, now to be countered by the benign influences of broadcasting. John's drive to invest in the BBC a high moral tone was much more to do with leaving with it the indelible imprint of John Reith than it was to do with zeal for the nation's health and wellbeing. He urged on the Religious Advisory Committee a weekly – and then a daily – religious service. The Sunday talk of the very early days was given by well-known preachers. John always went for the figures who were already well known in their field, such as the Rev. T. B. Clayton of Toc H, the Rev. G. Studdart Kennedy and Gipsy Smith. The Sunday talk developed into the Sunday service; and the first-ever outside broadcast was from St Martin-in-the-Fields, with the vicar – who had an adventurist spirit – the Rev. Dick Sheppard. The response to this was gratifying in the extreme.

After that came the weekday half-hour studio services, with organ accompaniment because piano was 'reminiscent of the village hall'. *The Week's Good Cause* of a Sunday evening started in 1926; the first *Epilogue* later that year. John would have argued that, at a time when religion was no longer retaining the centrality in people's lives that it had had, the BBC's stand was contributing significantly to the stemming of the flow.

His initiatives for righteousness were let loose on the country, to the gratification of the persuaded and the resentment of the heathen, as he would call them. It was all 'very worthy and dull', said Frank Gillard, esteemed war correspondent and veteran broadcaster (later director of sound broadcasting), thinking, too, of the diet of talks which bulked out the weekly programmes. But John could no more walk free of his indoctrinated past than he could prevent himself from using its pieties to outdistance his parents' certainties through his own comprehensive promulgation of the Christian message. Professor Harold Laski put it this way: 'A man as dominating as he could easily be a little more audacious. The big thing for wireless to do is to provoke people into thought. ... That is the really big thing to do.'[16] But that was not within John's power.

Out of his own limited cultural grasp, now exposed to a whirlwind of administrative dynamism and political wheeler-dealing, John introduced a new wing to the establishment and reinforced the existing structure.

A memorable outside broadcast had already been made in 1924. King George V opened the British Empire Exhibition in Wembley on 23 April and was estimated to have been heard by 10 million people. It was relayed to Manchester, Leeds and Glasgow, the *Daily Mail* having given massive publicity to its arrangements for large crowds to assemble in selected centres to hear it. The newspaper commented in its leader afterwards that 'of all the wonders of yesterday ... the most wonderful was the broadcasting of the King's speech and of the whole audible pageant at Wembley'.[17] It had, indeed, been a triumph in the mastery of the technical complexities of outside broadcasting.

Such a high as John had experienced after the General Strike could only, for a man of his temperament, be followed by a great gloom. After his mother's long stay in Barton Street, she returned to Scotland and was followed by sorrowful letters of his that told her how much he missed her. My mother, not surprisingly, seldom had a good word for Mrs Reith senior. Rumblings of a knighthood neither cheered John up nor prevented his restless thoughts about the possibilities of leaving the BBC for other openings, especially in America. Those in whom he confided – and they were few – found his attitude incomprehensible. But then, so too did he. Given that he felt so passionately for and about the BBC, could it have been that he feared becoming overwhelmed by these very feelings?

Throughout John's life, he seemed to be straining after yet another personal Everest – almost as though he was convinced that just one more summit would, at last, complete for him that demolition job still outstanding on all those internal figures of his childhood, who were still continuing, in his experience, to rubbish his creations. Even in his extreme old age, when he and Muriel had left London for Edinburgh, I learned to my astonishment that he still had hopes of being recalled to the BBC to rescue it – a sort of de Gaulle figure. Sir Hugh Carleton Greene had journeyed to Edinburgh to meet him; I found them, of equal height, staring uneasily at one another across the drawing room. But what John had sadly misinterpreted as a recall to London was simply Greene ensuring that, in the forthcoming controversy over a committee of enquiry into the BBC, he did not have John Reith as an enemy.

But, back in 1926, it had seemed that the mounting prospect of the BBC becoming a public corporation had in it, for John, the makings of a concealed threat.

The BBC's remit had now become incontrovertibly national, with international connections widening by the day. Nothing less than radical change was appropriate. In working for the stabilising of the BBC's autonomy, the very route by which John hoped to establish it – through the assumption of corporation status – threatened his own freedom and supremacy. With the structure set, there would come a Board of Governors and their chairperson who would be active and interventionist in a way that the old Board, with their *laisser-faire* approach, would never be, having left John, as Sir William Noble had said at the outset, to do the job and then 'to come and tell us how you're getting on'. Suddenly, he saw that he was going to have to negotiate for his high objectives, treat others as equals and accept compromise. Somewhere, he was sensing that some things were beyond him, as Mary Agnes Hamilton, with her acute perception, noticed:

> For his own convictions one can see him going to the stake, but like too many potential martyrs, he has little patience with the differing convictions of others. Others in fact represent his Achilles heel; he blocks his own vision and deflects it dangerously. Generous and unfailingly kind to those below him, warmly considerate of their welfare, ready to put himself to endless pains to serve them, he lacks, tragically for himself and for his fellows, capacity to collaborate on terms of equality.[18]

Because aspects of the corporation status that was on the way for the BBC upset John, he was in poor fettle as he and Muriel decided to attempt a holiday, something to which he did not incline naturally. For a cross-Channel trip, they seemed to need an inordinate amount of luggage, setting off for the coast in their Lanchester car – a more substantial equivalent of the memorable vehicle driven by Jacques Tati in *La vacance de M. Hulot.* John had loaded it with the mathematical precision of his strategic approach whereby large regular objects went in first, with smaller ones by degrees wedged around them. Irregular items – they had tennis rackets and a large circular hatbox – went in last. A curious skill of his was to be able to stow away more items than the capacity of the container apparently allowed, something which never failed to sweeten his outlook. And so, off they set to revisit the French centres of war that held significance for them both. They visited the scene near the Battle of Loos where John had been wounded, and the graves of Muriel's brother Valentine and former fiancé Gilbert Grune. But, on the second, as Ian McIntyre comments: 'Reith did not distinguish himself by his delicacy. He said that he supposed that "if he had appeared she would readily go with him and leave me". He became uncompanionably melancholic and while "idiotic people danced to the jazz all afternoon, including the revolting Charleston" he took himself off to the far end of the hotel and read Spengler's *Decline of the West.*'[19] He quite enjoyed being a misanthrope.

1. John Reith.

2. *George Reith 'of the Clyde' (1811–89). Born: Stonehaven. Died: Glasgow.*
General Manager of the Clyde Navigation Trust, 1864–88. John's grandfather.

3. Captain Reith, 5th Scottish Rifles c.*1917.*

4. Charlie Bowser and J.R. c.1919.

5. Engaged to Muriel Odhams, Southwick, 1919.

6. *Winston Churchill at BBC microphone at Savoy Hill.* © *BBC*

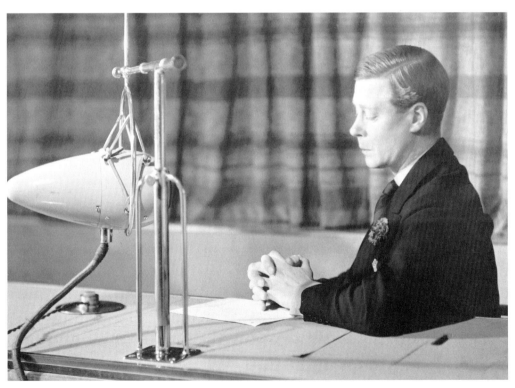

7. *The Duke of Windsor: 1935. HRH the Duke of Windsor broadcasting to the Empire from Broadcasting House.* © *BBC*

8. *John Reith at his desk in Broadcasting House, March 1934.* © *BBC*

9. *John and Marista (aged 2).*

10. Family portrait showing Christopher (aged 6) and Marista (aged 2).

11. Mary Agnes Hamilton. © BBC

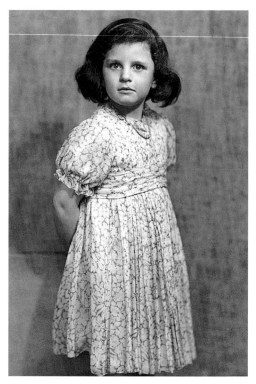

12. Marista (aged 5).

13. Marista and John, c.1950.

14. With Christopher and Marista.

Of this, as I grew up in his family, I had plenty of experience – more and more, it seemed, as frustration and gloom took hold in response to the falling-away of his public life. Something would trigger a rage – a failure to be recognised in a New Year Honours List; a poor school report for my brother Christopher at a time when I was too young to prompt any such damning documents; or, more rarely, his feeling unwell. His voice would rise and his fist crash onto the table. The telephone, perhaps because it had been the vehicle for some unwelcome message, would be hurled to the ground, where it would lie, the receiver separate and buzzing inconsequentially. This was like a storm when the lightnings and thunderclaps are directly overhead. Then, as the pyrotechnics move away a little, they leave behind them a heated disturbance onto which a loaded and uneasy quiet falls. So were the aftermaths of John's meteorological squalls, he in an enveloping black cloud of personal despondency, and those around not quite liking to speak – and everyone, especially John, wondering how, without losing face, one might break out of this impasse.

As I grew up, I began to notice what an awful lot of emotional space was taken up by my father's upheavals. My mother, a not unsympathetic person, when her husband's sombre state swept her into one of her own, could not take on teenage glooms and inconsistencies as well, and simply became impatient. But what parent has not done that with adolescence? For my part, I accepted that, while his commotions commanded attention, mine were not sufficiently important – so I would get on with the job of managing on my own.

My opinion was not asked when it was decided that I would go away to boarding school. Aged 14, I was both appalled and certain that it was for the best. At St George's School, Ascot, there were teachers who could listen to you. I began to do reasonably well.

John and Muriel came home early from their holiday in 1926 because Muriel's father was gravely ill. He died shortly afterwards, and John took it upon himself to criticise severely his mother-in-law's arrangements for the funeral, which he considered shoddy: the single horse drawing the hearse had frequently to be rested on the steep hills involved. Later that year, John was to find his brother Douglas, normally not lacking in avuncular advice to John, and never entirely disapproved of by him, very ill and looking terrible. He had contracted a tropical disease as a missionary in what is now Ghana, and he died a year later. 'He tried to help me when I was young', wrote John, as usual exercising a fearful economy in regard to any possible emotional excesses. Although, for the rest of his life, he referred to 'my deceased brother Douglas', it lacked the contumely with which he spoke of the others.

Only the image of Beta, the second oldest in the family, remained unsullied. A trained hospital nurse, she had nursed him in his infancy but had died of a form of meningitis. Of 'my poor brother Ernest', he spoke seldom and then only with reluctance. Brilliant, popular, dux of the Academy and a competent violinist, he became mentally ill, and, after some years at home, saw out his time in the Crichton Lunatic Asylum in Dumfries. This was a place where mental illness, despite the obloquy of its Victorian name, was treated with new and enlightened understanding.

John himself was seldom free of threats in many forms. In 1926, it was a committee set up the previous year by the Postmaster General to look at the future of broadcasting and the emergence of a British Broadcasting Corporation established by Royal Charter. The 27th Earl of Crawford and Balcarres, who had served in the Cabinet and was a connoisseur of the arts, was to chair it. John submitted his memorandum to the committee without consulting anyone. His response to a government-appointed committee and its authority was a rebellious one: looking ahead to the coming of a new chairman and Board for the BBC, he saw his freedom of action curtailed, and did not like what he saw. Before the committee, he hedged on questions of constitutional detail. 'I may have my own views', he said; 'my own colleagues on the Board, my own Chairman, will have theirs. I do not think it would be quite right for me to give my opinion.' 'We will make up your mind for you', said Lord Crawford pleasantly. 'I do not imply that it is not already made up', retorted John – singularly with neither grace nor diplomacy.[20]

But, despite these and other discouraging signs, the committee – in working towards the fundamental change in the BBC's authority – recommended that that freedom which it had to air controversial opinions and arguments should continue, provided that the quality was high and that opinions were distributed with scrupulous fairness. When the Postmaster General reported to the House of Commons on the Committee's recommendations, it was to give the government's agreement to the BBC's service passing over 'as a going concern' to the new authority that was to be established by Royal Charter as the British Broadcasting Corporation. Restrictions were to be retained on the broadcasting of controversial material, while those restrictions remaining to do with the frequency of news bulletins were lifted.

John was still not happy, even though the Crawford Committee – which was, broadly speaking, liberal – moved with the climate of the BBC as it had been carefully nurtured towards its flowering as a public corporation. He must have seen that Crawford was realising the very ideals towards which he had been working. The committee followed the ways in which he had been 'growing' the old company in the direction of something more expansive and more considerable, and exerting more influence over the British scheme of things. The Charter, setting up the British Broadcasting Corporation for the next ten years, was presented to the Commons in the autumn of 1925.

His next meeting with the Earl of Crawford was very many years later and was again a source of some embarrassment to him. Nearly thirty years on, he and the Earl found themselves as rival candidates for the students' Rector of St Andrews University. Neither knew at the outset that the other was standing – and John, perhaps aware that his behaviour in 1925 had left the Crawford Committee justifiably irritated with him, was now quite disconcerted. I was a student at St Andrews at the time, although it was certainly not on my initiative that he became a candidate; I merely became the subject of large and gratifying student pranks. John lost to the Earl, and was both mortified and relieved — and a friendly lunch ensued amid the art treasures at Balcarres House, with the Earl and Countess the most urbane of hosts.

NOTES

1. This quotation, and those in the opening paragraph, are from McIntyre, *The Expense of Glory*, p. 141, from *JCWR Diary*, 4.5.26.
2. Reith, *Into the Wind*, p. 306.
3. McIntyre, p. 142, from *Diary*, 6.5.26.
4. Ibid.
5. Ibid., p. 143, from *Diary*, 8.5.26.
6. Reith, *Into the Wind*, p. 113.
7. Eckersley, *The Power behind the Microphone*, quoted in McIntyre, p. 146.
8. McIntyre, p. 147, from memorandum to Reith, 17.5.26.
9. McIntyre, p. 187, from *Daily Herald*, 31.3.31.
10. Reith, *Broadcast over Britain*, p. 34.
11. Briggs, p. 237, from Reith, *Broadcast over Britain*, p. 64.
12. Ralph Waldo Emerson, *Shakespeare*, by permission of Oxford University Press.
13. Arthur Miller, *The Final Act of Politics*, *Guardian* Saturday Review, p. 1, 21.7.01. Reprinted by permission of International Creative Management Inc. © 2000.
14. Briggs, p. 284, quoting Stuart Hibberd, *This — is London*.
15. Briggs, p. 272.
16. Harold Laski, *Daily Herald*, 31.3.31, as quoted by McIntyre, *The Expense of Glory*, p. 187.
17. Briggs, p. 291, from *Daily Mail*, 2.4.24, with their permission.
18. Mary Agnes Hamilton, *Remembering my Good Friends* (Jonathan Cape, 1944), p. 285.
19. McIntyre, p. 150, from *JCWR Diary*, 17.8.26.
20. Briggs, p. 335. Oral evidence of Reith before the Crawford Committee, 23.2.26, by permission of the BBC.

5

A Board of Governors

*T*HE BBC's transition from company to corporation was celebrated in style, with prime-ministerial support. The Christian message had been promulgated, as had the Empire Service itself, reliably on the airwaves. But John was falling into a strained relationship with his Board of Governors; the arrival of his first child disconcerted him, and his talented chief engineer found himself fired.

Two and a quarter million licences had been sold, and 500 telegrams and 12,000 letters of congratulation had been received by the BBC. In 1926, the British Broadcasting Company was going out in a blaze of glory. A valedictory dinner in December 1926, attended by the prime minister, Stanley Baldwin, marked the passing of the company into governance through a Royal Charter for broadcasting, a system outside government control. Press coverage was massive. In the speech that John Reith made that evening, underlining the new Corporation's dedication to public service, he laid claim to further substantial territory: 'We have broadcast the Christian religion and tried to reflect the spirit of common-sense Christian ethics which we believe to be a necessary component of citizenship and culture'.[1] John tended to carry his religion like a banner – in those days, at least.

In addition, the BBC was building up a programme service for what, in a short time, was developing into a mass demand. Neither popularist nor propagandist, the BBC was to keep up a never-ending campaign for continuing independence: Winston Churchill, then Chancellor of the Exchequer, had not, so far, succeeded in taking it over and making it speak for government. But it was already a prized institution, run to great effect. Frank Gillard wrote that never before had a public service gained such status and repute in so short a time. John Reith was famous throughout the land.

On the technical side, the BBC could reliably find the best engineers to work under the gifted Peter Eckersley, with the prospect of international broadcasting moving towards realisation. John Reith envisaged an Empire Service; but, because other countries were taking steps to open up their transmitting stations, he made sure that there should be 'no chaos of the waves'[2] either in Britain or in Europe. 'Our colonial cousins are now looking to us to suggest some things from which they will benefit', he wrote. The Post Office's high-powered long-wave transmitting station in Daventry was at work, and British programmes were being transmitted to the then dominions and colonies. By 1926, the BBC was in touch with what was happening in pretty well every corner of the world, and senior people from many countries reached John's office, international praise pouring in. Despite the awful struggles which he had with himself, John's achievements through the BBC mounted up; there seemed to be no barriers to the creative openings available within it.

Most happy when he could, without restraint, think big and bring about large results, he had in a relatively short time become conspicuous on the world stage. If occasionally, in the later years when I knew him, he could experience – even briefly – power and success, in them he could sometimes find contentment. The capacity to think big – this was his gift to broadcasting. When Malcolm Muggeridge called him 'a great man' (even though he went on to qualify it by noticing that he was also hung about with littlenesses), he was principally in touch with John's largeness of vision, to which he coupled a relentless energy. He had no difficulty in doing without sleep if the need to implement what he saw called for it. Throughout my young childhood, I was usefully distanced from him; nevertheless, there was also the experience of the large-scale conditions in which I grew up, the powerhouse behind them, and the stimulus of them both.

But now, in the early BBC, John was going to have to work with a Chairman and a Board of Governors involved with the BBC's affairs in such a way as he had not previously experienced. He viewed the curtailment of his power with alarm. He certainly believed in government by authority – provided that he was the authority. But the Chairman of the new Board, Lord Clarendon, and the four Governors had been appointed, and now he found it 'very irritating to have Clarendon and other people nosing about'. The noble Lord – George Herbert Hyde Villiers, 6th Earl of Clarendon – had a long lineage and titles but, in John's view, a most abbreviated grasp; and 'silly Bertie's' habit of running for cover at the sight of trouble kept him well exercised and John in a constant state of high alert. Already, the Chairman had persuaded the Postmaster General of the value of his view on one contentious issue as opposed to John's.

And then there was Mrs Snowden. Well known in the Labour Party as bossy, ambitious and a troublemaker, with a conspicuous ability to make a drama wherever she could, she trumpeted her dislike for John. She thought him a frightful egoist and not at all what he was cracked up to be.[3] John looked around for the most pungent sobriquet, making do in the meantime with 'a poisonous creature'. But, as the insults flew, so he concentrated his efforts, emerging from the Book of Revelation with the 'whore of Babylon'. The points of contention between them were as trivial as together they made them inflammatory. These two Governors figured too large in John's cosmology, and his injured and tumescent ego propelled him variously to an archbishop or a prime minister in search of justice.

Of little use to him with Lord Clarendon and Mrs Snowden were the devices of his well-practised stagecraft, through which, by disclosing only a measured amount of himself, he excited fascination in those around him. But, in the vicinity of these two, he found himself to some extent dismantled, exposed like a snail without its shell and left only with a burning antipathy towards them in place of his legendary power.

Some years later, he would draw up his hate list — a subject he liked to raise so that people would become curious and enquire, and he could then enjoy their incredulity. 'Usually,' he would explain elaborately, 'it has seven names; occasionally one name drops off at the foot while a new name appears to head the list.' The unspoken question next was not hard to detect. Instead of answering it at once, he would carry on repetitiously: 'The principal hate heads the list, while those who no longer merit a place are removed. Usually it is headed by Churchill. Then there are Montgomery, Mountbatten, Dalton ... my future son-in-law now joins the list.' This was Murray, whom I married in 1960. At this, only the boldest could mutter: 'But *surely* ...' 'Surely *what?*' he would come back with some force, disallowing any offence lodged within his statement other than that which he, the innocent sufferer, must experience through his daughter's fall from grace. Although Murray and I only came to learn through hearsay of the distinguished company he now kept, the news reached us reliably enough through one or two creepy people who felt that they might enhance personal prestige by appointing themselves go-betweens. At the time, however, well used as I was to his funny little ways, the greater hurt was always going to be his.

And so, in 1926, when the BBC staff got together to celebrate the new status, John was not in party mood. But his faithful deputy, Vice-Admiral Charles Carpendale, took him by the hand and towed him into the big committee room where, to his astonishment, all 100 of his staff were gathered in cheerful congestion. The admiral made funny speeches and handed over a pair of antique candlesticks. Then came a letter from the prime minister's office offering John a knighthood. The prophecy that he had made to his mother four years earlier, along with the injunction to her to live long enough to experience it with him – this was now true. Unfortunately, his enthusiasm had unaccountably waned in the interval, and the delay in his reply lasted so long that the prime minister's private secretary had to do what he almost certainly had never done before: he had to chase up a potential recipient for their reply. At last, John got down to a letter, which he showed to Carpendale; but he said it was 'too snotty' and that John had to rewrite it. Carpendale had a great way with him; and, as well as brushing up on John's nautical language as a vehicle for everyday business exchanges, this time he talked him into a reasonable reply in which he accepted 'the wretched knighthood', as he would call it – that is, until he got more used to the idea and found that he did not mind quite so much after all. Having gone through an apparently unnecessary performance and a reluctance to receive the knighthood, John, I noticed, found it entirely to his taste and spoke his titled name quite pompously.

But, for him, short temper and restless gloom followed achievement. His personal emotional see-saw was seldom in equilibrium. Christmas time in particular had become, for him, a sad memorial to his lost friendship with Charlie Bowser, whose birthday fell within the festivities. The season was marked by great throwings-out and burnings of his letters. He had 400 left from earlier clearances; now, in 1927, he kept twenty only. But, having been reminded by them of Charlie's great love for Muriel at that time, and the way in which 'Jezebel' had come in and spoiled everything for all three of them, he burned the last letters too. I used to wonder who Charlie was, about whom my mother stayed tight-lipped and who seemed to be the same person as 'Bowser' – his name discharged by my father as though by a gun.

On such occasions, this was just the moment for another explosion over Mrs Snowden, who, having agreed with the other Governors that no press interviews should be given, nevertheless sparked off several column inches of press criticism of the BBC by doing so. Lord Clarendon said that he would speak to the Postmaster General and have her removed – but lost his nerve and failed to do so. John's contempt for him knew no bounds; and, not for the first time, John felt that he would have to walk out of the BBC and find other work. He continued to be burdened by his own slender tolerance of difficult circumstances, especially when they came attached to particular personalities. In 1928, with the BBC only into its sixth year and with an enviably steadfast image, John shared his disquiet with Montague Rendall, a Governor with whom he was on good terms and who tried to reason with him against doing anything precipitate. He spoke with Lord Stamfordham, the King's private secretary, who, no doubt feeling himself to be out of his depth, reached for the safeguard of Buckingham Palace notepaper for his reply. Rather stiffly, he gave John the benefit of his advice that, if there was no longer scope for his powers, he should look elsewhere. This was unenlightening.

Stanley Baldwin, when his help was called upon, wondered what effect John's departure would have on the BBC, and John replied easily that it would not suffer. They talked about openings, discussing nothing lower than the Canadian High Commission, the American Embassy and India's viceroy, posts which John coveted. Nothing came of these, perhaps because, unknown to either participant, leaving the BBC and finding another prestigious post was not, after all, the issue. John was more likely to be looking for an escape route from another anguish which, kindled by the unhappy relations with two of his Governors, stirred up the old pains associated with his unaccepting family and of his displacement from among them. Unconsciously, he felt that if he left the BBC he would escape these persecuting figures. Whatever the faults of his hates – and they were no doubt many – it was more significantly true of John that, for all his rugged exterior, actor's devices and feigned indifference to criticism, he was unable to function in the vicinity of people who did not value him, accept his lead or confirm for him his own uncertain self-image. The search for employment, were that possible, of even greater eminence than what he now had was a search for a position in life from whose elevation he could cut loose from all those harsh family figures within and the denigration and disapproval which went with them. Or so, simplistically, in an unthought-out way he felt. But the problems on which he sought advice were more the concern of a psychotherapist than of a prime minister. John had taken himself off for consultation in earlier years, and was to do so again much later on; moreover, he studied Freud and Pfister, saying that he was doing so to enhance his power over people, when more probably he was trying to help himself.

I suppose that, for a child, adult changes of mood and unpredictability are especially disconcerting – and it was in these in particular that his instability showed itself. Often, the feeling that things were volatile, haphazard and dangerous surged through the household, and there was no knowing what would act as the trigger. Once it was a puppy, newly introduced to the household. John, no lover of animals, decided in his terms to tolerate Muriel's enjoyment of having dogs inhabit her large house and garden. Muriel, thinking to introduce Larry, a red setter puppy, in due course to replace the ageing Rufus and in the meantime to learn from him some of his gentlemanly manners, found that she had imported a problem child. As well as having fits, Larry tended to bark at night. This, on anyone's terms, stretches tolerance to the limits; but when, in the early hours, I heard the animal's barking turn to screaming, I crept to the balcony to see my father in his red dressing-gown bending over to thrash Larry with his leather belt. A few days later, Larry disappeared. But that scene never quite left my mind.

The possibility of John's leaving the BBC became a source of fevered press speculation, which was then countered unconvincingly by a release from Savoy Hill bearing unmistakable signs of authorship: 'as far as is known, there is no foundation in the report that Sir John Reith intends to resign in order to take up a post in the City'.

Expressions of regret had been moving about the Corporation variously and with vigour. John had created the desired effect without the associated action, and had done himself some good in the process. Sir Henry Wood, the power – with John – behind the Promenade Concerts, worried that what had been the happy relationship between them would now find him having to work with someone else. One can only speculate how far one narcissist could be heard and understood by another. Not very far, probably. Sir John never liked Sir Henry.

Of all the people in the BBC or outside it who had some understanding of John and the ways in which his zones of torment could so quickly ignite, Charles Carpendale, his deputy, was one. Peter Eckersley had remarked of the admiral, when he came on board, that 'he was a martinet on the quarter deck and a good fellow in the ward room'. He cajoled, encouraged, soothed and even challenged his boss through the worst of his personal weathers, easing the prolific yield of his broadcasting outreach into the public domain.

In this uncertain state, John went into his first experience of fatherhood. Christopher John was born at home, in Barton Street, Westminster, on 27 May 1928; and John found that a newborn baby was unappealing. He was further disconcerted when, a few days later, feeling it his paternal duty to return home early from the office and take tea with Muriel and the nurse, the latter, meaning well (which, as we know, is the high road to misfortune), thought she saw her moment and unexpectedly put the bundle in his lap to hold. His way of recovering from a derailment such as this was to set about securing places for his son at preparatory school and at Eton and arranging for his baptism in Lambeth Palace by the Archbishop of Canterbury. Water from both the River Dee in Aberdeenshire and the River Jordan was used; the child must have been drenched. Then there was the embarrassment to be straightened out of his not having called on the services of Dr Archibald Fleming of St Columba's Church of Scotland in London.

Winston Churchill heard of John's possible departure from the BBC, and now, as Chancellor of the Exchequer, drew out the throttle on the engines of a new charm offensive towards John. Churchill assured him that the recent news that he was not going from the BBC came to him as a great personal relief. Churchill was angling for a live broadcast of his budget statement, knowing that the prime minister was not in favour of broadcasting from the Chamber. He piled on the flattery, telling John that the prime minister had such a high opinion of him and how much he was influenced by him. But John had his own line on these things and, unmoved by the blandishments, arranged for Churchill to have fifteen minutes the evening after the budget. Their associations were always to be made up of point-scoring, the one against the other, and throughout my young life I was to hear Churchill's name pronounced with more obloquy than that of most others.

The political parties, now alive to the powerful effects of broadcasting, were all working on the Director General for air time, and had to be treated with scrupulous fairness. John escorted Stanley Baldwin to the studio for his, and threw in some editorial work on the way there. The prime minister's speech was delivered to great effect. Then it was Ramsay MacDonald's turn, this time in Newcastle, whither John went and where he found him in poor shape. MacDonald was very appreciative of the coaching in techniques of broadcasting that he received on the spot. John did not take to Lloyd George, even though not unnoticing of a certain magic which attached to him. When it came to his turn, Lloyd George was extremely nervous, and this affected his performance. Once more acting as producer and coach, John put a note in front of him: 'TOO SAD', it said in large letters. Apparently, this device, which would have seriously put off others, had the desired effect, and Lloyd George's delivery suddenly improved. Nevertheless, he still had to be appeased for not having been awarded a slot in the same week as the others. 'The parties', says Ian McIntyre, 'were left in no doubt that although the Director General of the BBC was at their service, he was not their servant.'[4]

But it was not always a flawless leadership that John offered his staff. After the general election of 1929, when results were broadcast as they came in, listeners were claiming that announcers were showing bias in the way that they read the results. Without pausing to check whether there was any accuracy in this, John took to reading the results himself, displacing those staff who had rehearsed for the purpose. The microphone, as ever, acted as a safety valve for John. And then there had been a scene, claimed the press, between Sir John and Eric Dunstan, the BBC's senior and well-respected announcer, who had then left. Dunstan, a former diplomat, was a person of some consequence, and was in the process of marching out of the BBC when he encountered distress at the switchboard. Now the callers were saying that the present announcer was too fast and too indistinct, and so Dunstan's last task before resuming his outward march was to convey the latest dissatisfaction to John and ask him to adjust. 'I will not read any slower and I am going on announcing', snapped the Director General, and turned his back on Dunstan, who was by now almost out of the room anyway.

Professor Harold Laski had his views on some imperfections inside Savoy Hill:

> At a conference, he seems to talk as though he is in charge of the national well-being. He speaks with the urgency of a pontiff. You too rarely hear from the admirable and efficient staff he has gathered about him. He gives the impression that the BBC pivots too exclusively upon his private sense of right and wrong ... There is still not a sufficiently comfortable atmosphere at Savoy Hill. He has gathered about him brains in plenty. But he has cramped their usefulness and their creative quality by being too dominating in his governance.[5]

But it was with some anguish that John found that he would have to fire his chief engineer. Peter Eckersley had been with him from the very start, having accepted the offer of the most exceptional engineering job in the country at the time. He was an ebullient character who, before the BBC discovered him, had already been carrying out his own investigations into the transmitting of messages by wireless. Working out of a disused army hut, he had spent many happy hours improvising broadcast entertainment and contributing dotty songs of his own. He and some others had completed their programme planning in a nearby pub, half an hour before going on air. Then, seized by the idea of more live music, they hired Lauritz Melchior, the tenor then at the top of the performing tree. At his command was a considerable volume of sound; and, not having quite understood the physics of the airwaves, Melchior was anxious for his voice to reach across the North Sea to his native Denmark. He gave everything he had to his opening note, and it was tremendous. But it never reached Denmark. He had shattered the mike and shut down the generator.[6]

Seven years on from then, Peter Eckersley became the guilty party in an action for divorce arising out of a relationship within Broadcasting House. John, with great reluctance and some self-righteousness, dismissed him. He would see himself as standing for that body of belief and the execution of those standards that belonged to the Free Church of Scotland. In such a situation, he was scarcely himself a free agent. Nevertheless, on some other deviant in the BBC, a little later, a lighter sentence was imposed. This man was no longer allowed to read the *Epilogue*. And so, when John's mother came for her annual visit and he took her to tea at the House of Commons, he introduced her to Ramsay MacDonald. Lady Astor, the first female MP, came up next, and with typical directness asked Mrs Reith whether it was from her that her son got his Mussolini traits. We have no record of her reply. Perhaps Lady Astor, as well as living up to her reputation for blunt speaking, was also perceptive. Perhaps she scented scandal.

Not so many years later, John was to cause my mother, most un-characteristically and with fearful effort, suddenly to say to me: 'Do you think there is anything going on between Daddy and Joyce Wilson?' (Joyce was at the time his secretary, a post which was to be renewed from time to time.) Out of shock and an overprotected childhood, I could only make a feeble reply that I was sure I did not know. Just like the public, with their myth of Reith, I, enclosed in his family, lived with some misperceptions and was only able to recognise the cultivated image. My mother's lonely anxiety brought the scales tumbling from my eyes and, with them, a wonder: where does one go to find dependability? Until that moment, I had thought that I lived under the same roof as its monument: a man I scarcely knew but about whose well-defined image I had been sure: a man of bad-tempered incorruptibility.

John had made a many-faceted invention of himself, and it was there to protect him from the confusion that he daily faced within. On the practical level, everything in his vicinity demonstrated an impeccable orderliness and method: even the trivia of life figured large so that every length of string, deposited in the string box, had to be coiled and secured ready for further use. In the tin boxes containing his voluminous diaries, each was placed with mathematical precision. To be untidy – and how often we, his family, were found to be grievously wanting – was a sin against heaven. Whenever he found something to tidy, he was, he said, doing 'the Lord's work' – he was a Christian soldier, marching as to war against the enemy within that he so feared. He was replacing the bewilderment inside with an outward precision.

And so it was another, larger and very public part of his personal construct that made him a famous figure. This one was festooned with morality and stabilised, apparently, by integrity. Its incorruptibility was rooted in religion. It was utterly admirable, and the public, on the whole, admired it. There is a fascination in watching a reputation making itself. But very few people could know how true of John Reith was the remark by Marcel Proust, the nearly contemporary French novelist, that 'One becomes moral as soon as one is unhappy'.[7]

And so, John had to part with his brilliant engineer. Scarcely admitting it, even to himself, he was hit by doubts. And then he went silent on the subject of Peter Eckersley. But, of Eckersley's work, Professor Asa Briggs, author of the three-volume definitive *History of Broadcasting in the United Kingdom*, wrote with admiration. In 1923, 'Engineering ... had three aspects ... the maintenance of a high technical standard of broadcasting by the existing stations; the spreading of the broadcasting service into new areas of the country hitherto uncovered; and third

... research'.[8] It was Eckersley's ambition – although he was a technical expert – to use his unique skill to 'enable the listener to forget about the technique of the service'. But he was unable 'to sit back and watch the wheels go round' as he had supposed he might. 'Our enthusiasm', Eckersley had written, 'was maintained by a competition with ourselves; we were on trial against the measure of our ambitions and so we never became complacent.'[9] His going was a sad loss to the BBC.

Luck, or the allure of an unusual job, brought Adrian Boult to the BBC as musical director in 1930. He was given his head to do what he loved to do: to support contemporary composers and performers and to promote their work with radio talks and *Radio Times* articles as well as performances. People enjoyed working with him because he laid claim to no artist's licence to withdraw into some kind of creative subjectivity but went in for clear thinking and crisp communications, virtues not always to be found among distinguished conductors, as he himself was to become. No wonder John's eye fell on him. At their first meeting, Boult was given to understand that he was to *direct* the BBC's music. 'If conducting could, now and then, be added to directing without impairing it, well and good.' Sir John added, however, 'that he did not like sending for his Director of Music in the afternoon only to be told that he had gone home to rest as he was conducting that evening'.[10]

It was in 1930 also that moves had been made towards the formation of the BBC Symphony Orchestra for 110 players. But other London orchestras became concerned, nervous of the resources at the BBC's command and of the competition. They wished the BBC's orchestra to be reserved for studio work only, and so John called a meeting of eminent musicians, Thomas Beecham and Landon Ronald among them. He was persuaded by their argument that an orchestra, confined to a studio and always lacking audience stimulus, would deteriorate fast. But Boult himself liked studio work, finding the red light a stimulus in itself and enjoying not pouring himself yet again into what he called his 'penguins'. The Symphony Orchestra came together for its first rehearsals over a week in the Central Hall, Westminster, and was given, as Boult said, a most fitting welcome to the Corporation by its Director General. After their first session in the Queen's Hall, Boult was sent for by John. 'I do not pretend to know', he said, fiercely eyeing his almost equally tall director of music, 'about these things, but everyone tells me that the orchestra plays better for you than anyone else. Would you like that post?' Boult took the job of conductor as well as that of musical director, welcoming the flamboyant conductor Toscanini to the podium and the day's great piano soloists to the platform: Rubinstein, Moiseiwitsch, Myra Hess and many more. Already the orchestra was world-class.

John recognised, and then tended to become sentimental about, only a limited number of musical extracts. He would refer often to Wagner's *March of the Valkyrie* from *Lohengrin* in such a way as to suggest that he had selected that at random from his range of many esteemed favourites. One day, I asked him about Bach's Brandenburg Concertos, and he looked into the middle distance and pronounced them 'very fine' in such a way as to leave me in no doubt that he had not the faintest idea and that the subject was now to be discontinued. And so, it was with accuracy and honesty that he said to Boult that he 'did not know about these [musical] things' — but at the same time did no damage at all to his directorial powers.

For a little while, John thought seriously about a job offer he had received. It was on the railways. Both through his grandfather and through his own engineering apprenticeship, he was drawn to the railways. Since things were so bad with Lord Clarendon and with Mrs Snowden (later to become Lady Snowden when her husband became Chancellor under Ramsay MacDonald), he considered the job offer very carefully. He would be technical vice-president in charge of 100,000 men in the London Midland and Scottish Railway. But a £7,000 salary he thought insufficient; and he did not relish the idea of being a junior vice-president. Much upset, he took his troubles to the Archbishop of Canterbury. Dr Davidson was sympathetic to John, although it was perhaps of dubious comfort to be told that he had more influence than any man, past or present. (Others might say: what about Leonardo da Vinci, or Jefferson, or Aristotle? This was an exaggerated claim made on behalf of a man with an excessive ego.) But, being of a melancholic disposition, John no doubt dwelt on the insuperable problems that he had with the Red Woman and the Noble Lord. 'A thorn in the spirit is worse than a thorn in the flesh', said John to Stanley Baldwin, who chose instead to be hugely amused.

It was surprising that, in the circumstances, he did not accept the opening with the LMS. He could have negotiated for a salary increase and looked towards an easier prospect for himself in which he would not remain a junior vice-president. Having turned down the job, he continued instead, as was his wont, to exchange greetings with the engine-drivers on the line out of Marylebone to Beaconsfield in Buckinghamshire (he and my mother had moved to a rented house there after Christopher's birth). Greetings to the drivers were made easy by the fact that he always chose the foremost compartment in the front carriage in the forlorn hope that fewer of his fellow human beings would follow him this far up the platform.

Aged 17, I was occasionally on the same train with him. On one occasion, as we walked along the platform, the driver came forward to ask if I would like to ride on the footplate. Greatly excited, and my father wafting approval, I climbed aboard. The guard blew the whistle, and we eased forward gently. But a gasping reality followed as we entered the first of many tunnels. Apart from the furnace, which was being constantly stoked, the light was quite extinguished and the air to breathe reduced to a choking soup of soot. We emerged only to plunge into another tenebrous gullet waiting open-mouthed to receive us.

Now, the last tunnel astern, the driver was asking if I would like to drive. He showed me how, and explained the signalling ahead. I gripped the levers by which we would, as he said, collect more speed. 'Just draw her out gently', he said. Expecting resistance, I hauled away – from which followed a fearful juddering and plunge. Finally, the driver took control while I envisaged crowded carriages in which, with the passengers seated facing each other, knees banged together, briefcases leapt from overhead racks, and, according to temperament, alarm or fury followed. I looked back to find my father peering out of his compartment window, his homburg askew. He shouted to know if I had done that; but he was not annoyed. At Sudbury and Harrow, I thought I should return to more conventional travel, even though – much blackened and inevitably associated in the minds of the other passengers with the recent happening – I found myself regarded with unwelcoming looks.

More cheerfully, by December 1932 an up-to-date news service, although still without money or mandate, had been made available across the continents. It presaged one of the most splendid of the BBC's initiatives: its World Service. Despite his troubles, John still retained a zest for existence out of which he could forge ahead most creatively. At last, when it looked as though the Italians were going to get there first after all, John got the ear of his government. Invited to appear before a cabinet meeting, he argued at his most impressive and came away having secured agreement for a fully mandated World Service parallel to the domestic service. The moment was good: war was already in the air.

Years later, in 1991, when Marmaduke Hussey, the BBC's then chairman, was invited to Prague to meet President Vacláv Havel, he visited their parliament, the Chamber of Deputies. Unexpectedly called upon by the presiding officer, Hussey was given a resonant greeting, recalling how that great institution which was the BBC had remained true and steadfast throughout many long years. This tribute crystallised the ultimate motive and purpose of the BBC and its World Service, drawing, as it does, 53 million listeners, with the number still growing. In 1991, even the most critical press were remarking that the World Service was not only a great success story but also one of Britain's finest contributions to international understanding.

In the long-drawn-out aftermath of 11 September 2001, when a new government was installed in Afghanistan, one single reporter was among those invited to attend the inauguration. Although within the new Kabul administration many factions continued to disagree with one another, there was one thing on which, for the occasion, they achieved consensus: the BBC World Service, and no other, was to be represented as the new government was sworn in. From the BBC in London, reliably impartial, the word 'terrorism' would never disturb the airwaves. The BBC's service is still the most trusted in the world, with its robust commitment to impartiality and the liberal values of democracy and fairness. John had invented what the UN Secretary General, Kofi Annan, was to describe as 'Britain's greatest gift to the world in the twentieth century'.

On Christmas Day 1932, King George V spoke globally from his home at Sandringham. *The Times*, in its leader the next day, commented that one day, perhaps, we should know, from somebody's memoirs, just how this could have happened.[11] John Reith's memoirs obliged. Negotiations had started in 1927 with a suggestion from him to the King's private secretary. A message from the King to his people on Christmas Day would be very impressive. Next, ahead of a visit by the King and Queen to Broadcasting House in June 1932, John had spoken further with Lord Wigram, the King's private secretary, who cautioned against taking the matter any further until after the royal visit. When that had gone smoothly, the private secretary advised that the invitation should come from Downing Street; and, at last, on 24 November an announcement could be made. John wrote up the story of the broadcast in his diary:

> An anxious afternoon for all concerned in the BBC. So many things that might go wrong. The complications and the delicacies of timing and switching and relaying from one part of the world to another. Nothing went wrong; all excelled. The King's message impressive and moving beyond expectation. It was a triumph for him and for BBC engineers and programme planners. Reports

were received with extraordinary rapidity from all over the world and two thousand leading articles were counted in Broadcasting House. A selection of letters, received from all over the world, were bound into a volume and sent to the King, who was said to be much moved.[12]

With an image such as this, it was no wonder that John could impress the highest in the land, the public both internationally and at home, and himself. The prime minister, Ramsay MacDonald, said very publicly that the country, if not the world, owed the BBC a debt of gratitude for its courage in maintaining the highest standards.

That same year, with the departure of Lady Snowden from the Board, Mrs Mary Agnes Hamilton came to take her place. A woman of great acuity, she admired John very much but was also highly critical. In her memoirs, she noted: 'While I was at the BBC we talked and thought too much about the Director General and too little about broadcasting'. The talk tended, she said, towards a 'fascinated mixture of affection and repulsion'.[13] Both domineering and morbidly sensitive, with everything either a personal triumph or a personal insult, he was to her one of those people who never grow up out of the illusion that Carlyle denounced so passionately: the illusion that the universe is made for them. His inability to voyage into the minds of others was at times a catastrophic flaw for broadcasting. She found him to be an Ibsen character: an autocrat, intimidating but feeble at the core; one of those strong men who look stronger than they are.

NOTES

1. Reith, *Into the Wind*, p. 116.
2. Briggs, *The Birth of Broadcasting*, p. 322.
3. McIntyre, p. 155, Mrs Snowden to Lord Gainford, Chairman, 1.5.27: the Gainford Papers MS100.
4. McIntyre, p. 174, from *JCWR Diary*, 10 and 16.4.29.
5. Harold Laski, as quoted by McIntyre, p. 187.
6. McIntyre, p. 121.
7. Marcel Proust, *Within a Budding Grove*.

8. Briggs, p. 202.
9. Eckersley, *The Power behind the Microphone*, pp. 64 and 80.
10. Sir Adrian Boult, *My Own Trumpet*, chapter 9, para. 1, V. 17.
11. Reith, *Into the Wind*, p. 168.
12. McIntyre, p. 168.
13. M. A. Hamilton, *Remembering my Good Friends.*

6

Broadcasting House

*T*HE DIRECTOR GENERAL did not feel at home in the new Broadcasting House, despite the originality of the building. But he made of it a pulpit more illustrious than his father's, and set himself passionately to establish order all around. His 700 staff gathered to hear him and found his actor's skills captivating; but, on the development of television, he saw little other than threat.

In 1932, aged 42, ten years on from his appointment as Director General of the BBC, John Reith occupies his fine new office in Broadcasting House. His room reflects the bow-shaped prow of the building surging forwards into the heart of London and its affairs, and embellished with the controversial statue of Prospero and Ariel. On the subject of Eric Gill's sculptures, and this one in particular, the Director General is silent; the naked Ariel, the sprite of Shakespeare's *Tempest*, was, after all, rather well endowed. Outwardly, the building imitates nothing but the very best of 1930s architecture, its pale Portland stone, devoid of any decorative excesses, exuding personality and confidence, and calmly containing the energies and contentions within.

Like the eighteenth-century Romantic poet Thomas Gray, who would not be so well known were it not for his *Elegy in a Country Churchyard*, so the architect, Lt-Col. Val Myer, would be less well known if he had not conceived Broadcasting House. He, with the BBC's consulting engineer Marmaduke Tudsbury – the only BBC associate who could call his boss 'Walsham' – designed the building with a core, or central donjon, to contain the soundproofed studios. They were proofed, that is, against all except the Bakerloo underground railway line below, whose periodic thunder they never could exclude. Around the central donjon, they arranged the service and administrative areas. Here, we have a functional modernism without the mannerisms of the time.

The entrance hall is strong, simple and coherent. It has no dust-gathering filigrees, no softening curves other than those that have to imitate the exterior of the hall as it inclines towards the front doors. The vista is one of lines, angles and resolute rectangles; the motifs of the mosaic floor continue upwards through the square pillars to the angled lighting and take in, on their way, stylised fluting, framed within more rectangles forming the cornice. The architect has, as required, absorbed and reflected the no-nonsense style of his client, to whom a sonorous Latin tribute has been compiled and spread across the hefty horizontal of the entry. It announces: RECTORE JOHANNI REITH PRIMI, and has been included against the (not so very strong) will of the said Rector, or Director General. Meanwhile, in the midst, there is the sower: Eric Gill's strong and silent figure, hard at work broadcasting in his own style. The sculptures cause surprise, not only to the Director General but also to those who, wishing to appear contemporary, keep their views to themselves.

But, for John Reith, the building holds little excitement. He is as unmoved by how it appears as by what, for him, it signifies. 'I was not happy about the new Broadcasting House,' he wrote peevishly, 'but had not urged my own view against that of others. It was really too early to contemplate a comprehensive headquarters for British Broadcasting.'[1]

Why did he not urge his views? Surely a move by the BBC to its own purpose-built Broadcasting House signalled a new triumph? It was scarcely his style to keep his opinions to himself, sidelined in deference to those of others. He gloried in his powers of persuasion and argument, and regarded the insistence of his point of view as being that most conducive to the wellbeing of this great and growing institution. His reluctance to underwrite the new building, most carefully thought out to reflect and house operations and organisation, was not to do with the initiative itself. He would have intervened if he had thought that the move away from Savoy Hill, with its overcrowding and piecemeal arrangements, would damage the BBC's reputation or interfere with its delivery.

The doubts and difficulties about the building which were suddenly now almost overwhelming him were closer to home and bit into those insecurities of his which he had worked so hard to cover over. Probably he neither recognised nor understood the central and perplexing question: where would authority be in the new building? *His* authority, that is. Might it perhaps be dispersed throughout and thus diminished? The relationship between him and his staff would, from now on, be different. In Savoy Hill, *he* had been the integrative principle, whereas now the building intervened with its own arrangements for devolved power. John's position and his ownership of power, in his black mood, he saw as compromised. His mind was filled with the picture of an increasing array of deputies and departmental carriers of responsibility, operating at a distance from him, sheltered in contained bureaux of effort throughout the building. It had not happened before, but, this time, delegation stood for disintegration. He was uncomfortable with the building's most contemporary statement because it challenged his more pompous attitudes. It was not only Eric Gill with whom he felt out of tune; it was lonely at the top and, he found, most unsatisfactory. Moreover, this new Broadcasting House, with its authority and purpose without and its firm system within, was already signalling a new epoch in another form. The BBC was no longer an idiosyncratic invention insisting on a foothold for itself in the 1920s whirl of the political, commercial and social life of the country, but was, instead, now an institution arrived. It was an essential construct with its place in Britain's national consciousness and its establishment system; a figurehead in the eyes of the world and the opinions of the nations. The Corporation did not simply speak to the nation – it belonged to it. But, as John saw controllers who were no longer directly under his watchful eye, he was in the meantime isolated, with the Governors, at the top of a pyramid of power. Not for the first time, the crisis with which he had to struggle on his own was large and personal.

I was to witness many such incomprehensible mood-swings as I was growing up – especially in relation to the question of adolescence. The growing child has become wayward and inconsistent and, at times, utterly perplexing to those around it. The parents find it hard to believe in their offspring. Perhaps institutions, coming of age and finding themselves less and less indebted to the lone inspiration from which they have come, set up similar cross-currents of aspiration and operation.

For the uneasy parent that was John Reith, whose own growing up had been hard and confusing, the only thing to do was to make warning sounds about a forthcoming severance between him and his children: from the BBC, and then later on, when my tiresome teens struck, from me. But since, as a parent, one is acting out of confused feelings, a decision, and the release that would attach to it, is elusive. John had another six years ahead of him in which he would love and hate his BBC, until, like a diver who has hesitated too long on the bank, he plunged in clumsily and distressfully and then announced to a bewildered world that he had had enough.

And so now, in 1932, he is not enjoying what he sees, and he starts to plant in the BBC more and more of his youth's influences, in particular the old orthodoxies of the College Church in Glasgow. He stakes a claim to exclusive territory. At the heart of Broadcasting House is the religious broadcasting studio designed by Edward Mauffe, architect of Guildford's twentieth-century cathedral. In the hallway in Broadcasting House, its entrance arch also carries the unmissable dedication in clear gold letters: DEO OMNIPOTENTI – to Almighty God.[2] And on the broad curved front of the western elevation of the new building is the spectacular BBC coat of arms sculpted out of the stone, along with its devout motto: 'Nation Shall Speak Peace Unto Nation'. This is the inspiration of Dr Montague Rendall, a former headmaster and now a Governor of the BBC. His eirenic injunction, however, is displayed in disconcerting proximity to the personal premises in which storm the most bellicose Director General of all time.

Nevertheless, a new church with its own liturgy and its own dogma is being fashioned by John Reith. It is to be for him a pulpit with a greater range than his father's; its congregation that of the British Empire. Its elders, or ruling body, are the early BBC Governors, who, in calm acceptance and prayerful mood, subscribe to the tenor of the gold-lettered invocation to Almighty God: 'TEMPLUM HOC ARTIUM ET MUSAREM ...' – 'This temple of the Arts and Muses ...'. Still in the words of Dr Rendall, the Governors have gone on to pray that 'that good seed sown may bring forth a good harvest, that all things hostile to peace or purity may be banished from this house, and that the people, inclining their ear to whatsoever things are beautiful and honest and of good report, may tread the path of wisdom and uprightness'. Truly, Mount Zion is come to Portland Place; Dr Thomas Chalmers speaks again, John Reith the mouthpiece for his crusading evangel. It is all up there, classical Latin construed by Dr Rendall.

When broadcasting opened up to John Reith, he turned it into a mission. One cannot help noticing the way in which John arranged for himself the platform of the ether from and through which to persuade an increasing number of the nation's population under his direction to look to better things. In the same way, his father, the Very Rev. Dr George Reith, had climbed into his pulpit every Sunday and, with evangelical fervour, commanded the attention of a swelling congregation. The BBC was formed, as it were, as a projection of the father's Christian moral message and with what R. L. Stevenson called 'the freezing immunities of the pulpit'.[3]

These were then moulded by John, with some enhancement, into a staged performance. But, unlike his father, John did not so much aspire to heavenly things as invest religiosity into the BBC. He did not have the consolation of the faith in which he was brought up, as much as his personal experience of the Almighty endorsing his worldly aspirations in a most worldly way. Public worship appealed insofar as the sermon might measure up to his histrionic ideals of preaching, as learned from his father's eloquence. But there were few clerics who could do that; and, when asked by Malcolm Muggeridge in 1961, during a televised interview, to read from his father's last sermon, he began – but, as his voice cracked, he gave up – and then stopped altogether. The idea of sharing his God with a gathered congregation was unappealing. John's line to fatherhood was a direct one: his father and the biblical Father. They were not discrete figures but intertwined. Either or both in his experience were to be found beside him at his desk offering a quiet injunction, or on the summit of Cairn Gorm in the Scottish Highlands, when they might appear in the manner of the prophets of the Old Testament.

'Without me ye can do nothing.' When his father was dying in 1919, he had spoken thus from the Bible to John. To whom did the first-person pronoun refer? To John, it was usefully ambiguous. In one of his televised interviews with Malcolm Muggeridge in 1967, he explained, not for the first time, how the Almighty was there in his appointment to the BBC. 'I felt I could – mark you, with the help of the Almighty, and I say that seriously – I could do whatever was required. I would say that the Almighty was there in my receiving that job and was there in the execution of it. I am a little frightened of what I am going to say – I felt as if it had been laid on.' As the journalist and novelist Auberon Waugh remarked, he needed to be admired, but he despised sycophants – that is, when he recognised them as such. Thus, from the BBC's early beginnings, Sunday programmes were serious and solemn, worked out of a non-denominational Sabbatarianism, their educational and intellectual standards such as only he, John, felt were appropriate. There were services, talks, 'bottled' music. There were no satirical shows; there was no unscripted material, argument or political discussion. George Bernard Shaw was unimpressed, describing the BBC's output as 'atheism tempered by hymns'.

Religiosity in the BBC also took another form. Anyone looking for a job in John Reith's day, and up for interview with the Director General, would have done well to adjust to the signs of the devotional life within. 'Do you believe in the teachings of our Lord Jesus Christ?' was not, even in those days, the stuff of the normal interview – and, unless warned, the candidate would have to feel himself an infidel among the congregation of the God-fearing. John was, however, unbothered by the inconsistencies in his position, in that he found a lot of the matter of the said teachings unappealing – such as reference to the meek inheriting the earth and the poor in spirit being blessed – and so, without difficulty, he edited all that out of his life. But, whenever there was someone to listen and hear, such as on the television, he excused himself by explaining that, as we have already noted, while he believed profoundly in the Christian doctrine, he was a poor practitioner – something he clearly saw as a mark of distinction, because he said it so often.

He certainly was not concerned about his poor standards and was never going to do anything about them. In the sense that John saw himself above the law, he himself was one of the elect. His view reflected a form of the earlier Antinomianism, as it was called. This attracted a strong but discreet following in Scotland in the eighteenth century among people who saw themselves justified by their faith – even as justified sinners, as they expressed it. A form of debased Calvinism, *Confessions of a Justified Sinner* by James Hogg ('the Ettrick Shepherd') of the Scottish Borders, was published in the early 1800s and was pivotal in exposing this mid-Enlightenment phase in Scottish history. It lingered on in condoning a ferocious egotism in a one-to-one assumed relationship with the Almighty. Perhaps John Reith would not have thought of himself as Antinomian – but what is interesting about him, as someone has remarked, is not Reith, an ordinary limited person, but the effect that he had on people. I am reminded of Mesmer, a man whose hypnotic effect was so great that he gave his name to the science he uncovered, using his extraordinary powers of magnetism for healing purposes. John's powers, at their best, were for releasing new capabilities in people and enlarging the spectrum of human accomplishment.

If John Reith was considered a genius, it was not so much because of the brilliance of his intellect – which more closely resembled a street made up of indifferent buildings with gap sites, and some very fine buildings in among them – but because, as a misanthropic soloist, he was paradoxically also in among the press of the people and the thick of events; an anomaly, both outside his time and in tune with it and with his country. I quote again this passage from Ralph Waldo Emerson: 'The great man ... is he who finds himself in the river of thoughts and events, *forced onward by the ideas and necessities of his contemporaries* ... Great genial power, one would almost say, consists in not being original at all; in being altogether receptive; and in letting the world do all, and suffering the spirit of the hour to pass unobstructed through the mind.'[4] Emerson's description was right for John Reith – provided, that is, that he was free to pursue his own way as a soloist, free of political constraint, the restrictions of democracy and the agendas of consensus systems.

'At last one man can sit at a microphone and address the entire world, now that that man has nothing to say', said G. K. Chesterton rather unkindly. His remark may not have been personally directed, however. Far from reflecting the crises of the 1930s, the BBC's output of talks, drama and religion relied on academic addresses delivered with an after-dinner technique, totally scripted and on the whole anaesthetised against rumours of war from the continent and other unedifying matters.

In his own office, John sat at his desk opposite the door so that every entrant was drilled with his look. The room, with its fine pale panelling, was bright with natural light; a line of blue hydrangeas stretched like a small hedge across the balcony outside his window. Everything in the room was arranged with geometrical precision and reflected his inner child's delight in order and arrangement: he was pathologically afraid of confusion in any form, and quaintly believed that, to get to heaven, your affairs had to be in perfect order, your accounts up to date, your shirts neatly stacked and the picture on the wall centred to within a centimetre. A large part of the Lord's work, he said, consisted in getting rid of rubbish. Order and method were, for him, forms of high art, the Lord endorsing them.

For his secretaries, however, whose absolute loyalty was his, he was the man who, when the pressure was on and the meeting impending, did little to familiarise himself with the forthcoming issues and arguments, preferring to award himself the gratification of a public display of fast thinking and incisiveness. And so he would set about rearranging the furniture in his office; and, instead of typing up preparatory papers, his secretaries found themselves heaving away two apiece at one end of a desk, a table or a bookcase, while he sweated at the other end, straining to impose a new order on things. He liked the feeling of energy and purpose in this way displaced, and it was worth the onset of lumbago that would follow.

Preparations over, a meeting would be held in the Director General's office. As the first visitor arrived, John would wave him to a seat, an impression of gold accompanying the gesture. John wore his father's wedding ring and a signet ring, and across his waistcoat there were not one but two watch-chains. To one was attached a large gold pocket watch. He would often consult it and replace it carefully, even though a second dial, with the numbering and hands like tendrils, was strapped to his wrist. The two were checked daily to make sure that they agreed. On the end of the second chain – his father's watch-chain – a seal was attached. Mounted in gold, it carried his crest with the spread eagle. Scattering thanks, the visitor would usually sit taut in his chair like something on sale from a surplus store. Others would arrive; and, when they were seated, John would stride quickly to and fro, which would mean that the meeting with the DG had begun. The group would uneasily follow his movements back and forth and feel vaguely disadvantaged, knowing that he could dispense kindness, vision, misery, humour and small-mindedness in equal measure. Then, shatteringly, he would shoot them a smile and a chuckle of disarming warmth and friendliness. The views of Mr Smith were not only sought but apparently also stored for further consideration – accurately stored in John's elephant memory, without the need for pen and paper. Emboldened, Mr Brown would contribute his qualifying clause – only to experience it rubbished as being of no account, unworthy of acknowledgement. 'The mystery of the leader as performer is as ancient as civilisation',[5] wrote Arthur Miller. John Reith would not have thought in that way, but he thoroughly understood and practised 'leadership which required the artifices of theatrical illusion'. 'We are moved', said Miller, 'more by our glandular reactions to a leader's personality, his acting, than by his proposals or his moral character.' Under John Reith, some people rose above themselves and excelled, while others sank and were never seen again.

On 4 May 1932, at a general staff meeting in the new concert hall of Broadcasting House, every seat is occupied. All 700 of the BBC staff are gathered, and expectation rises through the quiet buzzing of exchange. With a curiously quick and light step, John Reith walks onto the platform and stands before his staff as they offer a brief precursory applause. It dies away fast, but still he stands, so that suspended expectancy verges on tension; they wait, as it were, under the shadow of his eyebrows. He has not forgotten the dignified performance of his minister father's entry before the massed congregation of the College Church and the dense hush that surrounded it. On the full wave of this now useful anxiety, he rides in, exploiting their riveted attention and challenging them with his vision of the truths which surround them and which soon, through them, are to become the power of broadcasting. 'The Corporation should be more an organism than an organisation',[6] he tells them. No division, branch, department or section should work to itself, since none can do good or ill without affecting the whole. 'We are a new and vitally important experiment in the management of a public utility service ... we can show others the way.' Finally, he tells them, a man (he has forgotten the women, of whom there are a fair number) cannot be happy in a job unless he can work with heart as well as with head or hands. They can count on him to help them. All 700 rise to his presence and his utterance as though to a magnet.

The more distanced he is by his accomplished stagecraft, the more fascinating he becomes, and the more it seems to each person present that he or she is the focus of John Reith's words, spoken with undeniable immediacy. 'Acting', said Stanislawski, the nineteenth-century Russian actor and theatre director, 'is the art of public solitude.'

However aloof, inaccessible and mysterious was this lofty Scot, a Prospero with power to enchant, his invisible Ariel touching each with his spell, he was also the man who, for many of them, in the cramped conditions of Magnet House and Savoy Hill, sat in their midst exerting leadership and drive to a vexatious extent. This earlier experience of proximity contrasted tellingly with remoteness, adding, if anything, to enthralling performance. And how they all, each and every one, loved a performer.

'The actor lies', said Arthur Miller, 'with all the spontaneity that careful calculation can lend him; he may nevertheless fabricate a vision of some important truth about the human condition that opens us to a new understanding of ourselves.'[7] With his actor's sense, John Reith could gather up his staff to be the vehicle for his messianic aspirations and ideals. It was not so much *what* he persuaded them of but that he *was* persuasive, each person now provoked into his or her energised dedication to the task. 'Art', went on Miller – and John's approach emerges as an art – 'has always been the revenge of the human spirit upon the short-sighted';[8] and the BBC, or Reith's Revenge, was his assault on 'the self-congratulatory ignorant prosperity of society's new success people', as George Eliot said. It was also an attack on those who liked to stay in the rut rather than get out of it – if only to leave room for others to climb in, as John liked to remind youthful audiences whenever he had a chance.

For neither the first nor the last time, the power that John had to command and compel his audience was almost unequalled – except, perhaps, by Winston Churchill. He had, for the time being anyway, disposed of the chill that he experienced when first confronted by this noble building and its arranged spaces and designated areas. For the BBC's early days of make-do and improvisation, he had drawn on his army experience of inadequate accommodation. But now, adjusted, his reforming zeal percolated into every department and initiative: rather than an end in itself, broadcasting was to be a means to social betterment. He was a management fanatic who, while preferring controllers to producers, did not, on the whole, inhibit what he did not understand, but allowed others to open doors to the contemporary.

Janet Adam Smith, a young Oxford graduate, as assistant editor of *The Listener*, was peculiarly able to open doors to the literary contemporary. *The Listener* was a weekly journal providing serious reviews of broadcast music and talks, including some transcripts also. As was true for others carrying responsibility, John invested a huge and powerful trust in them to work boldly in the field of their expertise. Much of this included looking to the future and working with the brightest minds of the day, whether in poetry, drama, music, philosophy, engineering or the natural sciences, and so on. He himself neither enjoyed nor understood the ways in which they would voyage into the distance. But it is clear that, as long as these people were distinguished in their field and were prepared to come on board and work for him, he was not particularly bothered if their language was foreign to him. Janet Adam Smith's father, the Very Rev. Sir George Adam Smith, formerly Principal of Aberdeen University, had been a friend of John's father. *The Listener* had not, in 1929, taken its place among the weighty regular publications of the day without experiencing difficulty. The Newspaper Proprietors' Association again became alarmed about the BBC's publishing ventures, convinced that it would not confine itself to the scripting of broadcast talks but would expand into review articles, commentary and opinions – and, most dangerous of all – would be illustrated. The NPA set off to make its declaration of war to the Postmaster General; but he stayed tight in his bunker, feeling secure in clause 3(d) of the BBC's Charter, in which it was given considerable liberty in the range and purpose of its published material. The NPA's next move, a meeting with the prime minister, was quickly followed by John Reith's own visit; but to neither blandishment would the prime minister rise. His response to John's, however, was the flattering assertion that he would know best how to handle the dispute; the prime minister was sure of that – which was true. But John needed to let him know that he was again about to distinguish himself.

And so John, as ever, prepared stage and setting for himself as sole actor. Rather than receive a delegation on BBC territory, he took himself, alone, to the NPA headquarters. 'I was alone,' he wrote, 'deliberately so. The greater the number that sit on one side of the table, the greater the advantage to him that sits alone on the other.'[9] The NPA's chairman, Lord Riddell, had twelve of his office-bearers on either side of him, while John, for the greater part of an hour, sat regarding them, stonily editing his face and saying nothing, taking notes occasionally. Then he let fly: he 'wasn't having it', he said, and he did so in several different ways. The policy of the BBC, he said, was designed amply to fulfil the aspirations of both print and sound, and to their mutual advantage. The NPA climbed down. Having managed the opposition to his satisfaction, John emerged happily. His secretaries, well practised in the art of reading his moods, heard with relief the cheerful rattling of starched cuffs – he liked to express moments of cheer by shaking his large hands against the sides of his head and creating a benign commotion. Chuckles on the telephone and something approaching merriment in his dealings with colleagues and visitors were heard. The secretaries also knew, however, that change could sweep in from nowhere like a blizzard in the hills, fast and total in its effect.

John's interpretation of events remained lofty. The way in which the Lord endorsed his worldly aspirations was a privilege not apparently granted in later years to Haley, Jacob, Greene or Curran, all Director Generals between 1944 and 1971, his ferocious egotism propelling him nearly to the top of the tree before abandoning him to inevitable downfall. With Milton, he could have said:

> ... And in my choice
> To reign is worth ambition though in hell:
> Better to reign in hell than serve in heaven.[10]

Despite John's pleasure in having single-handedly achieved a great victory, his Board made no reference to it. John went on to note in his diary how burdened he was with a sense of his own ability – something which was not conceit. Two days later, *The Listener* was on sale. But more and more contemporary poets appeared on its pages, and complaints both from inside the Corporation and from outside grew. Cecil Day-Lewis, Irish-born poet, and Herbert Read, art critic, appeared in a 1933 *Listener* poetry supplement, with pride of place being given to W. H. Auden's *The Witness*. Miss Adam Smith was summoned to the presence.

> The D.G. wanted to know why there was so much that seemed odd, uncouth, 'modernist', about our poems. He was not choleric, like the outraged pundits who wrote to us from the Athenaeum, but puzzled. He made it plain that he was not objecting to modern poetry as such any more than to the modern music broadcast by the BBC, but I think he was anxious that poems which appeared in *The Listener* ... should be recognised as having merit by responsible and informed persons beyond the paper.[11]

Miss Adam Smith suggested that T. S. Eliot be invited to act as arbiter. Eventually, the latter, for a ten-guinea fee, looked into *The Listener* and pronounced on the merits of a weekly publication including poetry. While ambivalent, he was not destructive: '*The Listener* was one of very few weeklies in which he would not dissuade any promising young poet from seeking to appear' was his economical response. Janet Adam Smith continued:

> For the rest of the time that I was at *The Listener* there was still abuse from the Athenaeum, still muttering within the Corporation, and I had to be ready with a glib paraphrase of every poem in case it were challenged by someone in the hierarchy. (I remember trying to explain Dylan Thomas's *Light breaks where no sun shines* to the retired soldier who was a Controller of Programmes.) But from Jove there was no more thunder.

But, despite the achievements, when rumours reached him of posts of national and international importance needing to be filled, John's old dissatisfactions and restlessness assailed him. One night at the Athenaeum, he dined with John Buchan, a Conservative

MP already well known for his novels. Buchan remarked that both Baldwin and MacDonald had been pondering on the shortage of able men for the important jobs, and enquired whether John Reith would think of a Governor Generalship – or Ambassador to Washington? This was deeply unsettling for John, even though he was at the height of his powers in the BBC and was never, apparently, working better than under the benign chairmanship of John Whitley. Indecision, that scourge of his, again visited him. (Even worse: shortly afterwards, Geoffrey Dawson, editor of *The Times*, made similar remarks to him over lunch about significant vacancies.)

This time, John had his answer ready: 'The difficulty of being Governor General of Bombay, from my point of view, is that there is a Viceroy over the Governor'. And so he spoke to Sir Maurice Hankey, Secretary to the Cabinet, who agreed that he was talked of in connection with various positions, but that his lack of parliamentary experience was thought a drawback by many. But, Sir Maurice enquired, would he be interested in railway nationalisation? John that said he would be interested in the permanent position of Postmaster General. Already, like a child with his sandcastle on the beach, he was starting to harbour destructive urges towards his own creation of the BBC, a portent of what was to follow in six years' time in 1938.

The arrival of television, as inevitable as it was distasteful to John, was something from which he had to back off. Never at home with what he might consider 'the pleasure principle', he felt that television, in an unexamined way, suggested levity without demand. He found himself unable to enter the fray sufficiently to have imposed on it anything like the rigour accorded to wireless. He might have felt that he could not stem the tide of populism – that, anyhow, was one theory. Nor had he fallen out with his fellow countryman, John Logie Baird, in spite of a less-than-happy encounter at Glasgow Technical College, where they were fellow students. Of his experience, Baird had written:

When I left school I went immediately to the Royal Technical College, Glasgow, travelling up and down from Helensburgh. The

Technical College was an extremely efficient national institute. The students were, for the most part, poor young men desperately anxious to get on. They worked with an almost unbelievable tenacity and zeal. There were, however, a few exceptions, gentlemen's sons, well off and with no real anxieties as to their future. Among these was a tall well-built youth, the son of the Moderator of the Presbyterian Church, by name John Reith. I met him for the first time in rather unfavourable circumstances. I was, and still am, very short-sighted and, at the beginning of one of the classes, the professor asked if those who were short-sighted and wanted front seats would hand in their names. When I went up to the platform to give him my name, three large impressive young students were talking to him. They talked on terms of equality; in fact there was a distinct aroma of patronage.

The young gentlemen were of the type we would today call 'heavies', and they boomed with heavy joviality at the poor little Professor who was distinctly embarrassed and ill at ease. I interrupted timidly and handed him a piece of paper with my name on it. As I did so, the heaviest and most overpowering of the three 'heavies' turned round and boomed at me: 'Ha! What is the matter with you? Are you deaf or blind?' I simpered something in inaudible embarrassment and he turned his back on me, and the three 'heavies' walked out of the classroom booming portentously to each other.

This was the first time I saw Reith. I did not see him again for twenty years. Reith did not distinguish himself in his examinations, he was worse than I was.[12]

But, in the BBC, it seemed that John wanted to help Baird.

At every growth point in the BBC, John delegated. There was, for instance, the graceful handing-on of all things musical to Adrian Boult, including the formation and conductorship of the BBC Symphony Orchestra. J. C. Stobart opened out the BBC's broad educational umbrella, and under Peter Eckersley the engineers stormed technical mountains. But, with television, rather than empower his staff with large responsibility, John himself withdrew from the scene. If he could not see the implications of television, they certainly did not, and they proceeded instead to fall out among themselves.

It was not a good start for television. In part, the issue disabled John; he was, it seemed, up against some internal embargo, a personal one particularly his own. Anthony Kamm, working on a biography of Baird, wrote to me:

> He (your father) never attended any demonstration of television, and he usually managed to be on holiday when significant events in television took place. Though it was at his instigation that the original Television Committee was set up, he disagreed with its enthusiasm for the medium. Indeed, he could not bear any encomium on its future possibilities ...
>
> These were certainly enormous difficulties between the Baird company and the BBC, and I was beginning to feel that the problems were magnified because your father did not want to have more to do with them than he had to, and left it to his staff to sort them out.[13]

After John had left the BBC, the Corporation presented him with one of the first television sets ever made, working by way of a lid and a mirror to right the upside-down image; but he would never look at it. There was Sylvia Peters, one of the first announcers on BBC Television, and the mast at Alexandra Palace with simulated power circles jerkily emanating from it. But, in our household, one seldom got to watch the television.

To try to understand why John's effective self was not available for this new service to come, or able to apply to it his customary prescience, one might look to his background in the Free Church of Scotland, built into which was a most restricted view of life. In the Free Church, the hearing of the Word was all. The preaching of the Gospel, the church believed, was carried out to greatest effect without the distraction of any images. And so, its new churches were no more than boxes for the hearing of the Word. Colour, decoration and adornment in any form scarcely appeared in its buildings as they sprang up across the country after the 1843 Disruption. Austere and featureless as many of these churches were, the only thing for their congregations was to attend to the Word and submit to the preacher's eloquence and conviction.

Emotionally swayed in this way, John seems not to have considered that seriousness of content and purpose might not, after all, be the exclusive property of the spoken word and of music – that television, as well as radio, might be enlightening, educating, enjoyable and entertaining. John Reith, it seemed, looked out at television from the scarcely opened door of an unadorned Free Church building, the glass of its windows frosted and crinkled as a barrier between the worshippers within viewing the distractions of worldly matters without, whether rural or urban. And so it might be that John Reith's rejection, in a sort of grim totality of what he took to be the levity of the visual arts and all the signals of gathering interest in television, went back to the influences of his youth.

In the same way, but without such comprehensive effect, he looked at the new Broadcasting House building, and was unmoved. Today's journalistic simplifications based on an assumed hatred of John Logie Baird are convenient but inaccurate.

NOTES

1. Reith, *Into the Wind*, p. 158.
2. Ibid.
3. Robert Louis Stevenson, 'Talk and Talkers'.
4. Ralph Waldo Emerson, *Shakespeare*, by permission of Oxford University Press.
5. Arthur Miller, quoted in 'The Final Act of Politics', *The Guardian* Saturday Review, p. 1, 27.7.01. Reprinted by permission of the International Creative Review.
6. Reith, *Into the Wind*, p. 159.
7. Miller, ibid.
8. Ibid.
9. McIntyre, p. 170, from Reith, *Diary*, 11.1.29.
10. John Milton, *Paradise Lost*, line 261.
11. McIntyre, p. 191, from J. Adam Smith, 'T. S. Eliot and *The Listener*', *The Listener*, 21.1.65, by permission of Professor Andrew Roberts. Quotations in the following paragraph are from this same source.
12. Antony Kamm and Malcolm Baird, *John Logie Baird: A Life* (NMS, 2002); 'T.V. and Me', *The Memoirs of John Logie Baird* (Mercat Press, 2004).
13. Antony Kamm, letter to the author 7.10.2000, by permission of NMS Publishing Ltd and Antony Kamm.

7

Mrs Hamilton

*A*S A SMALL child in the garden at Harrias House, Beaconsfield, I was captivated by this fierce lady's willingness to listen to me. Then I noticed her attention drawn to something else: my father was approaching. I was disappointed, and she was not pleased. I went to look for my mother – before, I hoped, I was found by the nanny and again interrupted. My mother was arranging flowers for another dinner party that night; she enjoyed the flowers but not the company.

A photograph shows my father seated in a garden chair, a shaft of sunlight landing on a small bundle in his lap. It looks as though the shawl and what it holds have been placed there; the parasol, which he grasps, has been handed to him to shade this infant, perched on his high and bony knees. But John Reith's face, ever so slightly turned away, suggests that he finds the infant entirely resistible. From the picture, it is clear that my mother has worked hard to persuade him into a pose; already you can see that he is telling himself that this ordeal will soon be over and he can get back to the important things at his desk. Ah! Here comes the nurse, all in her white starched rig, a galleon with sails unfurled to a following wind. He does not, however, as she expects, hand her the baby, but, pressing against the chair-back, moves his arms away and the sunshade too, for her to lift up his daughter. He cheerfully hates the nurse but recognises her uses: the infant is starting to wriggle, squeezing up her already closed eyes into a look of pained affront, winding up for the kind of noise which is absolutely for somebody else to deal with.

There were plenty of those 'somebody elses' in my very young life – all those people who came in from elsewhere and were not my mother. Nannies, they were called – and I could not think why they were there and not my mother. Because there seemed to have been several of them – maybe they did not stay very long – none figures particularly. There was one exception, however. She was called Nannie Foxley, and I remember her because she found my older brother more appealing than me. If I thought about life, which I didn't, I accepted this as one of life's facts: my brother was preferable to me. He had wavy hair and looked charming in a kilt.

Once, when I was two, my mother was away for three months. I did not know that she had gone with my father to South Africa. There they were in the hall, all dressed up to go, and the maids and the chauffeur moving the mountain of bags out to the car for loading. I looked down at them from the gallery above, and called out to my mother not to go away – did she have to go? Please not to – because I really thought that, with my pleading, she would take off her coat and decide not to go. But, instead, she looked dreadfully sad – and then the nanny came and took me away, and I thought my mother had gone forever.

I had an unusual name. It came about through somebody's bad handwriting, and so it had – at the time anyway – an assured uniqueness. When I grew older, I was to hear the story many times, told by my father to admiring listeners. Ever mindful of his Kincardineshire antecedents, and wishing to incorporate his mother's name, Mary, in mine (I had been born on her birthday, on 10 April 1932), my father sought the help of the editor of the local Kincardineshire newspaper, who helpfully sent him some ideas, among which was 'Mariota'. This my parents misread as 'Marista' — and I am glad that they stuck with their mistake.

It did, at the time, however, provoke this poem:

45 Doughty St.
W.C.1
2.9.32

My dear MaRista MuRiel Reith
The R which ripples through your name
Shows that, though born on England's heath
You really stand for Scotland's claim,
Blessed by the waters of the Dee —
The best of streams for you and me.

Perhaps you may not have to dwell
Among the mountains and the glens
Which once your Kinsmen knew so well
In all of thackit butts and bens.
And yet your heart will surely beat
When North you turn your little feet.

When you can scale old Cairn mon Earn's
Dark fir-clad slopes you'll stand as Queen
Above the gently sloping Mearns
And catch a glimpse of Aberdeen.
You'll notice how the Slug road steals
Past your ancestral Clachanshiels.

Although it's hard, as you may find,
To learn the names of capes and bays,
You'll have a map within your mind
Of where your fathers spent their days
Before the days of railway trucks.
It is not like your native Bucks.

When you are ready for the road,
I shan't be fit, I fear, to climb,

116

Or help you with your hiker's load.
And so, instead, I send this rhyme:
Which is my sort of BBC —
My dear Marista —

J.M.B.

I believe that 'JMB' was J. M. Bulloch, who I can only surmise worked in the BBC and was well acquainted with Kincardineshire.

Later on, when I was six, my mother and father, when they were not out to dinner, tended to make formal visits to the nursery. This was in the evenings for singing hymns, and they sat on either side of the fire, my brother and I attached to my mother's chair. It must have been a thin and straggly sound.

As a child, I viewed my father from a distance. That he was afraid of small people was something which dawned on me later; all I knew at the time was that I was uncomfortable when he was around, and that he was uncomfortable with me. I certainly could not know that, in claiming the small child's inalienable right to be the centre of attention, I had usurped what he took for granted was his. You cannot have two claims for power, especially when one of you, by the laws of nature, will always win. These things did not make for an easy relationship.

At the time, of course, I knew nothing, either, of the BBC, other than that somewhere, a long way from the nursery and the garden, my father had a large and important life — a place where he was king of the castle. Few would have known that, at the time, he was making repetitious statements to his diary doubting whether he should be much longer with the BBC. 'What a curse it is to have outstanding comprehensive ability, combined with a desire to use it to maximum purpose', he was announcing to the surrounding vacuum, without a shred of conviction. But, perhaps because at the time he was both powerful and unsettled in the BBC, he quite liked the idea of showing off his family by having them visit him in his room in Broadcasting House. We were ushered in, and there he was — hard at work, striding back and forth, talking to some people already there. Instantly, they rose and then evaporated, bowing. We were offered chairs, but still he continued to move about, my

117

mother watching anxiously from her place. There was little on the top of his huge desk apart from a shiny gold pen and ink-holders. Secretaries, especially Jo Stanley, came and went noiselessly, giving us friendly smiles. The balcony outside his windows supported a phalanx of red tulips. I whispered to my mother about all those brilliant blooms nodding in the sunny breeze, and she liked them too; but she was a little cowed at the business of broadcasting which, irrespective of our presence, went on in and through and out of that room with its pale wood panels, matching furniture and tulips looking in.

Then I found myself being regarded by a fierce old man with a lot of whiskers looking down out of a drawing in a frame. He was quite frightening, and I looked away. (Later on, he turned up in my father's dressing room at home.) My father seemed to admire him – for this was his grandfather. I sat on the floor, where I could take it all in and from where everything seemed to run as smoothly and easily as the great big car in which we rode. Eventually we left, with many polite people bowing us on our way. Our car, with Burness the chauffeur, was waiting at the door; but, before we got in, we waved to my father, who appeared on his balcony behind the tulips, waving too, for all the world like the captain on the bridge of his ship, enjoying himself. Although, while we were there, he hardly stopped working, he seemed quite to like it, and we did not mind. Afterwards, I asked my mother what my father did all day. A little vaguely, she said that he signed letters. Well, I thought, I could do that too – when I had learned to write, that is.

But it was from my father that I learned that there was a very different, very important place that was nothing to do with Broadcasting House or Harrias House. It was called Scotland. Instead of meadows, green and flat and with cows and white painted wooden gates, it had hills, wide open and covered in heather. Instead of the very occasional ambling stream, it had burns in plenty that were boisterous with rocks and waterfalls, tumbling down from great high mountains. Its people spoke with 'a Scots accent' – and, all in all, to my young groping mind, this had to be the real place to be. And so I felt at home when, set down for the first time on a Scottish heather hillside and with legs too short to make any sort of headway, I could happily flop about among the heather in flower. The pollen rose in sneeze-worthy clouds – and, as I examined the tiny flowerets which made up each spike, I smelled the honey smell which was for always.

Near at hand was our hotel. An abrupt presence, the Tyndrum Hotel rose unceremoniously from out of its heather surrounds, an alien planted temporarily among all those hills which, unlike the hotel, had neither beginnings nor endings. From our bedroom window high up, we heard the sound of bagpipes – wild and weird, sounding sometimes near at hand and then far away, carried up the mountainside on the breeze. There he was – a piper below, pacing to and fro across the courtyard as he played. He wore a kilt, a larger version of the one that Christopher so hated to wear that he lay on the floor and screamed. Now my father was saying to him that he must throw these pennies down to the piper. Being the older, and the boy, it generally fell to him to do the expected thing, and I did not have to. Christopher did not want to throw any pennies to anyone, but found now that he had to.

Outside again, I was busy making a new friend. A burn ran swiftly beside the old village street, on the other side of which was a row of old, old cottages with a door and two windows each, and smoke that drifted vaguely from out of each stubby chimney. Apart from the sound of the burn, all was quiet: no cars drove along this stony unmade road, because the road for the cars was a new one, smoothly surfaced and crossing right over the old one. When it came to that spot, my burn plunged underneath the new road and rushed out cheerfully on the other side. Meanwhile, any passing car just drove over the top of the burn without noticing this living thing below as it muttered, chuckled and sang in the sunlight and hurried on in case it should be late.

Back at Harrias House, there was Mrs Hamilton. She wore a skirt with very large black-and-white checks. Her skirt seemed to me to be a bit fierce. In the garden on a wonderfully sunny summer's day, she was standing beside the lavender hedge, listening to me. The lavender was a sea of mauve, and above it the rambler rose clusters were tossing their summer weight. The bees had set up an industrious hum around about, most intent on their task. Mrs Hamilton generally kept one eyebrow very much higher than the other, as though it was hooked onto the rim of her spectacles. She was attending to me very carefully, certainly not thinking about anything else. I was still trying to ride my bicycle, and I did not like to see new scratches appear on its cream-and-red paint because of all the times when, riding along the brick path, I had fallen off into the roses and lavender. And anyway, it had been Christopher's before becoming mine. But this time, while Mrs Hamilton listened, I got on much better and enjoyed not falling off. I stopped cycling; that was better for us both.

She had no children, I think, and nor did she talk in the way most grown-ups think they need to talk to children, in a bouncy sort of way with everything so awfully jolly. Perhaps it was because she did not know about things like bathtime, walks and changing wet socks that she could listen so hard now, while, all of a sudden, I found I had many things that I wanted to talk about. I had an idea that she might have had something to do with the wireless set which suddenly arrived in the nursery. It was a funny-looking thing with a large domed top and wooden rays like imitation sunbeams on its face. I liked watching the little window with a green light, which, like a fan, opened and closed with the on/off switch and produced a little plopping noise inside as the wireless came to life. I listened to the *Zoo Man* and *Uncle Mac*. But the wireless was not switched on much, except when the nanny insisted on turning on a Sunday-morning noise called a cinema organ. It followed its loud and tuneless way by straddling first one squelchy chord and then another, the sound bouncing uncomfortably around the nursery. I hated the cinema organ so much that I could scarcely eat my cornflakes. Could I ask her to turn it off, I thought to myself? But she will probably not mind about my minding – and then, as the noise goes on, I will feel even worse about it. I would try and bear it, I thought. Then I felt annoyed that I should.

But it was not about any cinema organ that I wanted to tell Mrs Hamilton but about a new piece which I was learning on the piano by a man called Handel. He must be a very great man to be able to write such a good tune, I thought. Mrs Hamilton nodded and asked more about the piece: what did I like about it? Had I heard Handel's *Water Music*? She hummed a bit and said she was sure that I would enjoy it. Meantime, the bees were minding their own business as they went on busily touching blossoms and moving on. Far away in the high tops of the old oak trees, the warm breeze shuffled the dense and twisted branches, making the dapples on the ground rush around a bit.

Mrs Hamilton had a walking stick. She did not seem to need it for walking; but it had suddenly become important to prod the earth under the lavender hedge quite fiercely and to go on to excavate a sort of hole. I wondered what it was that had annoyed her so that she needed to poke the ground so hard. Was it something I had said? Looking past her, I saw my father step out from the house. He moved quickly over to where we were; it was as if he would be coming to tell me that Mrs Hamilton was a very important person in the BBC – that she was a Governor, and did I know what a Governor was? – and then I would feel that I had been wrong to take up her time. And, no, I had no idea what a Governor of the BBC was. All the things which I had wanted to talk about now seemed silly. I fidgeted with the bike and wished I was not there. Now Mrs Hamilton was looking at me, saying nothing, but her eyebrow seemed higher up than ever, and the black-and-white checks even busier. My father came up and, instead of making an announcement to me about Mrs Hamilton, said to her that I was very intelligent, which I did not enjoy very much. I felt that it was not much to do with me anyway – but something to do with him.

Anyway, when Mrs Hamilton was around, I had noticed that my father seemed to have to work very hard, striding up and down the lawn as though lots of people were looking and hearing him make famous statements. They must both have important things to say about the BBC, I thought; but Mrs Hamilton was glaring into the distance, and I started away on my bicycle.

I saw Mansbridge, the parlour maid, coming up the garden path, and I cycled over to meet her. She was very nice. She wore a dark green uniform with a brown apron, and a brown twirl on her head. She was carrying a round brass tray, her hand spread out underneath it and a small envelope on top. It was a telegram for Sir John, she said to me; and no, there was not one for Miss Marista today. Mansbridge waited until the perambulations brought the two closer, and then stepped forward. 'Yes, Mansbridge?' said my father. He looked at her in a very kindly way. Everyone liked Mansbridge. 'There is a telegram for you, Sir', she said. He took the envelope, and Mansbridge stepped back. He opened it with his enormous first finger, read it quickly and handed it to Mrs Hamilton. Still Mansbridge waited; and then she said: 'The telegraph boy is waiting, Sir, if you wish to send a reply'. But his expression had changed.

'There is no answer', he said, as though to a public meeting. His voice sounded dangerous. 'Thank you, Sir', said Mansbridge, and turned to go, carrying her tray beside her. My father and Mrs Hamilton started to talk. I heard something about Lady Snowden, and then something to do with Babylon, which seemed to be about the same person. It was only years later that I understood what that was about. Slowly and deliberately, he started tearing up the telegram. He called out to Mansbridge, who turned around at once. He smiled at her. 'Have you got your tray?' he said. She held it out, and he put the by now tiny scraps of telegram onto it. 'That's what we do with people like that', he said. 'Sir', said Mansbridge, skilfully managing neither to agree nor disagree.

It was years after this that I sensed a stir in the house, and I ran along to the gallery to see what was happening. Down below, I saw Mansbridge lying on a sort of bed and being carried out through the front door. She looked terrible and different. When I was able to see my mother, I asked where Mansbridge was going and when she would be coming back. My mother said she was going to hospital, where they would look after her. Would they make her better so she would come back? They would look after her, said my mother again. I knew then that Mansbridge would never be back; and, although nobody said anything about dying, I knew then that people died. But how could they be there one day, so happy and important, and then suddenly nowhere? Once, there had been a granny in the house for a while; she was in the big blue bedroom. There were nurses coming and going, and my mother was always upset and somewhere else in and out and round about her. This granny never talked with me

– and when, suddenly, she was not there, the nurses had left and the blinds were drawn up and the windows opened, all I knew was that she had gone, and there was a lot to be said for that. But Mansbridge, who was my friend, had died, and I had not said goodbye to her.

Now, on the day of the telegram, my father and Mrs Hamilton resumed walking up and down, he pausing to sweep his hand across his bald head with a short impatient gesture and to make an announcement with raised voice. Mrs Hamilton waited, listened, made a comment and listened again. They paid no attention to the old red setter as they passed and repassed him. Stretched out on the lawn, Rufus picked himself up, and, with hanging head and tongue flopped out, he plodded a few paces before dropping down into a new shade. But, for me, everything had gone soggy and boring. Mrs Hamilton was no longer around to listen to me, and I was better out of the way. I wandered into the house and found my mother arranging lupins in a tall white vase. A luscious heap of blooms lay beside her on the garden-room table – blues, mauves and pink, and one that was special and different in among them. Each of its blossoms was both blue and white; it was a Russell lupin, she said. Already, the flowers were flopping a little in the heat; but their sweet and salty smell was all around. I picked out a particularly fat one which rose to a luscious spike in pink, with edible globules, and she put it in with the others in her display. But now she was saying that there was not much to choose from in the garden; some things were dying off. The soil was so stony that they could not grow, and there was all that ground elder: she had found it creeping into the roots of plants. I had thought that that was what the gardeners were for; but it was so bad, apparently, that they could make nothing of it. In fact, nobody could do anything to solve all the problems, which lay around like litter on the grass. My mother lifted up her vase and set off with it and its nodding blooms down the back passage. I raced ahead to open the swing door beside the pantry, and we were in the hall. There was plenty of space and light here and rich dark antiques, on each of which stood gleaming brass. The maids regularly collected up the brass and carried it into the pantry to polish it with Brasso. It smelled strongly. On other days, it was the silver – candlesticks, inkstands, ashtrays, a model of Broadcasting House and hundreds of spoons and forks — that was stacked up all around them, and tins of Goddards silver polish. The maids did not seem to enjoy these jobs very much. The gallery ran around three sides of the hall, and a stairway of broad steps made its way up the fourth side. 'These are very good stairs, shallow and wide,' said my mother, 'not steep and horrid.' I learned to notice bad stairs and feel smug about the good ones that I had at home with their blue stair-carpet and Greek key-pattern border. An antique refectory table stood below the stairs with benches on either side and Windsor armchairs, which my mother said were very special, at either end.

Now my mother put down her vase on the old oak blanket-chest, pausing while I found the raffia mat that was supposed to prevent any more of those ineradicable white circles from appearing through the old polish. Her lupins looked wonderful, I thought, beside the open door into the garden. Around the edge, she had put a few leaf whorls; and, for a little while anyway, the spikes would stay straight and pointed before starting to twist and loop about.

But, for my mother, it was not quite right: I knew that she delighted in her flowers and even shared it a little with me. But there was always something else about which only she knew and about which she had to worry on her own. It was as though the flowers were all very well, 'but ...'. There was a 'supposing if ...' — and then whatever it was would be very bad indeed. But she kept her reservations to herself, and you never knew what could take the worry away because you could not think what it was. My mother preferred flowers and animals to people. When other people were around and staying, and my father was making a brave show, she withdrew behind a put-on smile. But now the maids were drawing down the blinds to prevent the carpets and furniture from fading. The breeze made the lowered blinds bulge in and out, each one dragging its little wooden acorn on the end of its drawstring back and forth across the sills, making a hot little summer noise. My mother saw the nanny set off into the garden to find me; I heard her calling as she went. My mother said: 'You'd better go', and I think she was a bit sorry. I went out as slowly as possible. There was the nanny, fat with instructions and prohibitions. Whatever I was doing, it was her job, apparently, to stop it. 'Don't do that', she would say over and over again. Or, it was time to do this – and then that. Nannies had to rubbish everything they did not understand in favour of the world of Putting Away Your Toys and Getting Ready for a Walk; to the keyboard they awarded incomprehension and obligation, calling it Time To Do Your Practice Now.

Ever the conformist, my father had got himself this large house in the country. He made sure that the servants' wing was fully occupied and that his two young children had an entourage of nannies and under-maids, all well distanced from the purposeful part of the house. For my father and mother, for whom the 'old aims' were seldom particularly clear, even the end of removing friction was often lost as gales of criticism of my mother alternated with gusts of loud and guilty affection.

Grand people came as visitors to the house; but neither of my parents entertained with the fluency available to their neighbours, who had the benefit of heredity. My father liked to engage in his favourite game of outstaring his children, who were now (aged ten and six) permitted occasionally to visit the adult company. Before we could reach the haven of a chair, we had to stand about like chess pieces on a board, from time to time propelled by a hand on the shoulder onto another square. We stood silently minding our manners, hoping that no well-intentioned souls would feel that they should try to get us to talk. This, we had learned, is what you must never do; and so, not surprisingly, we were not very good at it. My mother offered frail conversational nothings at her end of the table and anxiously watched to see that there were no caterpillars in the garden peas.

But, on one typical occasion that I remember, she had a more pressing concern. Everybody had sat down at the table – except for the host. The maids delayed serving the meal as my mother considered the social hiatus opening up before her eyes. Agitating at her end of the table, she beckoned to the head parlour maid, who had to explain – with blushes – that Sir John was busy clearing the coal cellar. Then, in the midst of the maids fleeing in and out with hot dishes, he appeared, entirely black, for all the world as though he were Laurence Olivier playing Shakespeare's Othello, the whites of his eyes showing up grotesquely.

'Oh, John!' said my mother. And then, most unnecessarily: 'What *have* you been doing?' 'Goodness me, Sir John', said one of the ladies. 'You look as though you've been cleaning out the coal cellar!' 'That, Ma'am,' he said, with an elaborate courtesy that bizarrely contrasted with his appearance, 'is exactly what I have been doing.' But with this adjustment: 'I've been clearing, rather than cleaning, the coal cellar. I cannot', he went on, undeterred by his circumstances, 'tolerate a lack of a system. When I find it missing, I must install it and ensure that everything is done with the greatest possible efficiency.'

'Are you sure, Sir John, that what you've said applies to your coal cellar?' Scepticism lay heavily across this man's tones. 'Do you really think', he went on, 'that, to the servants whose job it is to carry in the coal and then to distribute it throughout the house, your system will at once be apparent?' An irritation with his host's lack of manners was showing. 'I have no doubt that it will be anything but apparent,' said the begrimed householder easily, a ghoulish grin beginning to struggle through the blackness, 'but I shall make sure that that is rectified.' Then, going on to explain that it was industrial inefficiency, springing from no proper sense of system, that was at present bedevilling the country, he left the room to go and clean up, his wife again becalmed amid the threat of a comprehensive silence.

On his return, he made announcements to the company about 'the Brute Force of Monopoly' — which I thought must be a very large dog on the end of a chain biting at a very small one called Monopoly. The bolder of the men leaned out over his raspberry bavarois to insert his serious and searching point. My father appeared to be engaging with the engine of his vast intelligence at full throttle, and his shrivelling stare was turned upon the man; but all he was doing was tuning into his capacity to surprise and, most likely, wrong-foot his audience.

My father's background had nothing in common with the lifestyle he had created for himself in both London and Beaconsfield. In the Scottish manse in which he had grown up, his parents were immersed in congregational responsibilities so that their large and turbulent family strove among themselves, their rampant tensions partly covered over by outward conformity. Now John, unawares, was inventing conformity – not this time through the church parade, but, with equal accuracy, to reflect the style of the landed and the titled of the day. He laid on his own spectacle of social orthodoxy and sustained it with a menu of servants operating out of a small mansion and gardens called Harrias House, near Beaconsfield. And then, without noticing, he was caught up in one of his old surges of rebellion against his early learning.

Suddenly, he had to rubbish the set-up he had created and in which, to some extent, he had confined himself. It was, after all, a self-imposed restriction. Different as this one was from the circumstances of his upbringing, it nevertheless amounted to a re-enactment in the form of many limitations on or dampeners of the original impulse and the pure spirit of drive and invention. The habit of reluctant conformity dies hard. Religious compliance and behaviour appropriate to the children of the manse was his childhood's qualifying experience; as a youth, he found his own forms of protest. Now social conformity, in his adulthood and in all his outward success, was the same pattern resurfacing, the restrictions as confining as ever, and the need to burst them apart the more insistent.

Responding to an inner need, one that seldom left him, he looked around for a new setting on which his meticulous sense of order and of system might be imposed. The coal cellar was an ideal candidate. Not only was it one of the few remaining areas in the house and grounds to have escaped his attentions, but also it had the great merit of being able to imprint its effects on anyone who went near. This bonus enabled John to put together yet another form of staged entry into the public domain, his actions conveying more clearly than might any words of his a general distaste for this contrived scene that he had now dramatically joined, doing so on his terms rather than anyone else's.

But, when he had left the dining-room, walking its length to exit by its main door into the hall, the head parlour maid had a further whispered exchange with my mother: would her ladyship like the footprints behind the guests' chairs swept up now, or left and done later?

8

The Sound of Music

I RESPONDED well to piano lessons, even though parental encouragement was rare. Unexpectedly summoned to play before guests, I froze – a fright from which I never quite recovered. To add to the discomfort, I apparently resembled my Aunt Jean, my father's elder sister, whom he resented. Though a talented pianist, she would never perform in front of anyone.

I was four when I started piano lessons. 'Buy a broom and sweep the room', I confidently played. Miss McLeary was my teacher; and I somehow felt that she had to be a good thing, because she escaped disapproval as she came and went from the house. Musically, this was a happy time: there seemed to be no difficulties, and as I made easy progress I seemed to be answering something that was already there, going on in my head. I sensed a general air of approval in the household, even if on the subject of Miss McLeary I felt cool. She and I went together to the baby grand Challen piano that was parked in the French window of the drawing room. This window was never to be opened, since it was felt that, if it were, it would make an easy entry point for burglars. If there was a good world inside — and it felt as though it was — there was almost certainly a bad one outside, which the piano, placed hard up against the window, was there in part to keep out, strengthening the defences against unwanted persons who might otherwise rush in and, with malicious intent, do a terrible damage of some sort. Thus, no guests of my mother's or father's, with languid ease and drink in hand, would flow through the opened windows and the homely porch and out to the lawn on a summer evening, to linger beneath stately oaks — now shorn of all but their topmost tuft — or to tread enchanted glades of roses and evergreen — now geometricised into the stunned regularity of a domino set. Like everything else, the garden and its growth had to be managed. Sometimes, even playing the piano felt far too abandoned to fit into such regulation — especially when I felt it become exciting.

The reality was that, as a nicely brought-up little girl, I had to learn to play. I was awarded an instrument, one that was already serving as a security device. This piano was part of a set ordered for BBC studios, I had heard. And so the teacher and I, she beside the keyboard and I at the centre, would position ourselves. With some dread of the next thirty minutes (my lessons were now extended from twenty minutes as I progressed), I fidgeted the piano stool into place, parking myself on its large tulip chintz in which the rest of the drawing-room furniture was dressed. With its shelves peopled with Copenhagen china figures, a Dresden tea service, Worcester cake plates and its miniature ivories, the drawing room breathed polite tea parties in which the ladies sipped daintily from wide open cups with floral design, holding on to their fluted saucer of most delicate bone china. As she drank, each kept her little finger pointing out prettily through jewelled rings. But the piano stool was broad and low and wrong for the piano; it could not be adjusted and was one more of the great unalterables of life where it was more important that something should look good — well-polished cabriole legs and laundered chintz — than actually do the job properly.

Before long, I was at work on the F Minor Prelude from Walter Carroll's *First Lessons in Bach*. Despite the teacher's close attention, I played well enough, and it seemed that just occasionally the music played itself as simultaneously I read the notes, heard and played them. Now the Mozart allegro vivace had become a runaway horse and the exuberant trills of the rondo a cat's cradle. I could not do it: I laboured under the blanket prohibition that one should never make a mistake; I gave myself a row that was bigger than anyone else's. I was trying to play under difficulties in what was becoming a rather unhelpful environment. My brother picked up the general message with the child's accuracy. 'What a ghastly noise', he said. And so, even at the age of four, I began to play behind shut doors, the piano nevertheless the centre of some magnetic field into which I was irresistibly drawn, so that, as I played, I felt neither solitary nor sorry. Hundreds of childhood hours were spent like that.

Parents then, as now, however dislocated their lifestyle, were still the products of their culture. In the ways of the English shires in the 1930s, praise or condemnation – or even anything enjoyed overmuch – were bad form. You did not show your feelings beyond the conventional expectations of society; and, in adversity, the stiff upper lip was the thing. There was little idea that children needed attention and approval as much as they needed food, and of such a kind that very few paid people – the nannies and so on – were able to provide.

'The English take their pleasures sadly after the fashion of their country.'[1] What mattered was the *done* thing. In the same way as you did not feed your dog at table so that it did not become bad-mannered and demanding, so you had little idea of spending time with your child, listening, taking part in the games and inventions, sharing the joys and upsets and generally being available. In the kind of household which my parents tried to imitate, *comme il faut* was buttressed by servants, structures and expectations, at the centre of which the children had to manage on meagre attention and little listening, staying in the nursery as expected. The things that mattered were the rest after lunch with the blinds drawn down, the duty walk, the punishment of the reluctant bowel and the administration of malt extract along with the children's own jug of full-cream Jersey milk. Nannies were paid to see to these things. In the meantime, intellectual stimulus, psychic health and personal development scarcely figured other than through all those lessons essential to a young girl's future social poise: music, dancing, painting and riding. For some, things had not changed since Jane Austen's day — at least, not in their parents' perception.

It seemed as though my mother, caught up in a lifestyle which she did not enjoy, felt as though she had somehow boarded the wrong train and kept trying to get off at stops along the way, while at the same time hoping to get it right in front of all these servants and all the visitors whom John said they had to have. Apart from her cousin Doris Naylor, Peter and their boys Robin, Hew and Richard, nobody seemed to come whom my parents *wanted* to see simply because they were old friends. Most visitors were received out of obligation and as a result of the BBC. Not that John would ever admit to *wanting* to see anyone — only to having to. The Naylors' visits were, for me, a matter for rejoicing. Unlike any other visitors, they seemed to feel entirely at home. As the boys rushed into the garden room, hauled out the garden carts, rode the bicycles and climbed unclimbable trees, I watched with feelings in which dismay at the sudden appropriation of my precious things mingled with a sort of cheering realisation that nobody apparently found anything here of which they should be afraid, and nobody was formal. As for Auntie Doris, there were so many things that were, to her, shriekingly funny that you began to notice that this was in fact so. My mother chuckled and began to enjoy herself; my father was finding that there was a whole lot here going on of which he could not quite disapprove — nor quite control either; and Uncle Peter's self-deprecatory humour surfaced readily from his comfortable shape and out of much buzzing and twinkling. But, since he was also Colonel Naylor, you respected Uncle Peter — as you did his ebullient wife.

I was quite unaccustomed to other children of my age, either coming to visit me or having me visit them. The very occasional children's party was something that happened within the intimidating interior of Hall Barn, near Beaconsfield, where dwelt Lord and Lady Burnham. Driven to its terrifying entrance, you stood, cold with fear, beneath a grimness which was its portico, set on huge severe pillars all of which together blackened out the sky. When the nurse tugged at the great metal bell-pull, the response was an unearthly silence. A distant, desperate hope visited: perhaps the inhabitants had fled? Been annihilated? But the scrunching gravel told of the arrival of more prettified children, all, in my perception, confident and happy, with nannies with silly faces and sillier hats. The door was opened by a grim-faced butler, and you were admitted to a great cavernous hall. There were more rooms to be crossed, ponderous doors opened and closed – and then the dense trebles of childish voices sounding nearer and nearer. The spectacle was as of some freak of nature that had occurred: reality could never account for such numbers of children running like automatons to and from the attendant nannies who now sat in a gossiping wall of starched bosoms around the room's edge. More than usually cocooned from my own kind, and therefore without experience of a world of people beyond the garden's high brick walls and cypress hedges, I was now isolated by the deluge of numbers, and no doubt clung to the nanny's knee as any port in a storm, longing for the sufficiency of my own inventions around my paints, the piano, my boats and my carts.

My mother did not quite get around to thinking that small children might have active minds, eager to absorb fresh experience, stimulated for more, and packed with enquiry. In fact, she clung to her own ideas about me, responding less to my being quite quick at my lessons with the governess and more eager that I become interested in things belonging to upper-class little girls. I would, therefore, enjoy dollies. There were plenty of opportunities: my father's fame and success attracted a regular flow of lavish gifts and bouquets to the house – that recognisable phenomenon where wealth and prominence draw largesse because people wish to be identified with it, and in a way that poverty and need can seldom match. And so, as yet again the postman pushed his bicycle up the drive and handed over another enormous parcel addressed to me, it was to be, I was almost sure, though loaded with promise, packed with disappointment. I remembered, as usual, to unknot rather than cut the string and to fold up the brown paper for further use. But, as I did so, and took off the lid, white clouds of tissue paper confirmed yet another no-hope package with a doll inside. Yet another cerulean gaze stared sightlessly up at me, flapping eyelids working out of inert china onto which apple cheeks were painted. My mother, quite unable to accept that, for me, this parcel had not only a charmless content but a rather repulsive one too, reached in for some of the attendant items with all the urgency of the Egyptian tomb-raiders seizing the gold that lay about the mummified body. 'Oh, look! Isn't that sweet!' she cried, holding up miniature vest and knickers with rosebud design for my conversion at last. 'Don't you think so? It's beautifully made!' In deep disagreement, I looked away but took back the clothes from my mother's hand between finger and thumb, dropped them back in the box and covered over everything with some finality, foaming paper and the lid secured in place. Another obligatory letter, painfully executed, to yet another faceless admirer of my father's lay ahead. 'You must', I learned, 'always tell the truth' — but with the understanding that *comme il faut*, such as offering warm thanks for something you hated, overrode the truth. And so, heavily impressing the paper with large irregular letters, I lied my way across lined and tinted sheets, leaving my mother disappointed and worried by my attitude to dollydom, and fearing that I was beginning to take after not even Aunt Jean but my father, and that she would have to pass on yet another dolly to the deserving poor.

Although she enjoyed Gilbert and Sullivan, my mother frowned at highbrow people like Bach and Scarlatti. She could never understand that music needed someone to listen as well as someone to perform: that the person playing, whatever their age and stage, must be heard. But she was not able to come and hear me because she was always being waylaid by flowers that needed to be watered, budgerigars' cages to be cleaned or raspberries to be picked, and having to push past all the servants who were there to do these things — except that they would not do them so well — and so she had no time to sit by the piano when I practised.

That left the nanny, in whose job description nothing of the sort featured or penetrated her limited comprehension; and the teacher, out of whose programme of instruction and correction a weak sun of commendation and recognition would occasionally and fitfully shine. But still I played — and often happily and well. Between governess lessons, I enjoyed sailing the fleet of boats that I had on the pond, where I would watch them put out to sea from out of the stalwart confines of the harbour walls, there to confront unknown hazards (usually a propeller fankled up in a leaf, or a clockwork motor fully unwound in mid-ocean). And then, suddenly, I would be caught by the magnetic pull of a tune sounding in my head, and I would run for the house and the piano. The boats I left becalmed in mid-pond, nodding in desultory and sub-nautical fashion in their drift towards the pond's hard edge.

In the house, some disagreeable imprints across the carpets produced shrieks from the nanny and others; but the ivory piano keys, though muddled, sang to me still. Then, one day, without warning, I was called upon to play before my parents' guests. They had begun to think that there was something going on here that they should notice and then possess. My mother, like Beatrix Potter's Mrs Tabitha Twitchet, had fine company to tea. She sent for me out in the garden. I experienced a shock of fear: I could not play in front of all those people. Poured into a frilly dress, I was nannied to the drawing-room door and then boosted into the room prettily to meet the guests. By now, the ladies were well ensconced in the tulip chintz armchairs. They leant beckoningly forward, each wanting to be so sweet with children. It seemed to me that these ladies wore their chairs like clothes, tight about the hips that season. The men were just resigned; one looked as though he had swallowed the east wind.

From the hearthrug, my father spoke as though to a boardroom meeting: 'This is Marista. They tell us she plays the piano well these days.' He looked meaningfully towards it – and, abandoning all hope, I swam to the keyboard and made some kind of strangulated response. My father stood behind the sofa like Ben Macdui in a thunderstorm, my mother sheltering behind the silver teapot as my fingers worked, each with the alacrity of a slug on a wet day. I fled from the keyboard and hid behind her chair. Everyone studied the carpet. Now my father would put on his act and I could keep hiding behind my mother's chair, away from the spotlight. He sent for a glass half-filled with water. This trick of his never worked, but he did it all the same. Staring up at a fixed point on the ceiling, he balanced the glass on his brow, trying to reach the floor and lie down with the glass still in place. The effort built up an agreeable tension in his audience, with giggles, gasps and chuckles alternating. This time, he reached the sitting position before becoming drenched and having to retire, leaving my mother and the guests trying to keep an already thin conversation from becoming irreversibly sparse, a maid mopping up in among them. Upstairs at last, I flung off the frills and ran to the garden to my den in the yew hedge to nurse my wounded pride. I sat there long enough to feel deliciously hidden when they started to look for me, and I heard the voice of the nanny calling, her starched bosom and stupid apron going satisfactorily in the wrong direction.

But when, at last, I began to make my way to the house, I met my father coming out. He was unsmiling. He was, he said, not for the first time, reminded by me of what he called 'That Dreadful Sister of Mine, Jean. She was a gold medallist at the piano', he said. 'She would never play in front of anyone. Quite weird.' He paused, and I pictured a lady with a cross face playing away superbly in a room in Glasgow, darkened by half-drawn blinds, a shut door, and grey buildings without. 'Never would play in front of anyone', he repeated. 'Utterly disobliging. Just kept it all to herself.' He was speaking in painful trajectories and giving me his fierce look, one eyebrow up and the other down, the unspoken question heavy in the air.

Already, it had been impressed upon me that, in all those many moments in a child's life which adults find especially unattractive, I could look like Aunt Jean. She was someone of whom it took not a lot, apparently, to remind my father. 'That dreadful sister of mine', 'my deceased brother Douglas', and many more: they all seemed to be as figures standing around him, crowding in on him at any time and under any circumstances. And then there was this someone called 'Bowser'. He never spoke the name other than as though he were hitting a nail on the head with a very large hammer.

But now, apparently, as well as looking like my aunt, I had picked up on a family pattern already in place where an accomplished performer refuses an audience. I must be very bad to be so like this very bad person, and had little or nothing with which to earn my parents' favour or kindness. On the other hand, there was a certain wayward distinction in all this which I did not mind. There was a strange alliance with my father born of negativity. I was clearly in line for attack, a form of attention which, oddly enough, produced in me an energised response of some kind. As to whether it was I or Aunt Jean who was in the firing line, I was not sure – or as to whether there was any difference between us. What was sure was that I was not going to be able to bring my father the personal satisfaction and gain for which he was looking through my being an outstanding keyboard performer. Had I shown signs of brilliance as an architect, a lion-tamer or a business entrepreneur, the same thing would have happened. My so public failure had told against him in a way that he could not tolerate. That I might have some views or feelings of my own on the matter clearly had not crossed his mind. But what I was starting to feel sure about was that this music of mine was being taken away. I could not have it any more. Could it conceivably be that it – or I – represented some kind of threat to him?

To be so clever at the piano as would satisfy him, one would have needed to be able to catch up with the wind or travel to the horizon and meet it. He was as far away as these in tuning in to me and what I might be able to do; or, more importantly, accepting what I could not yet do. Instead, he stayed with some bloodless ideal of his for me and in comparison with which I could do nothing but fall short. He and I had to coexist, while I would find as much as I could of selfhood from my mother, from my music, insofar as I could get a hold of what was left to me, and from the semi-rural environment in which we lived.

I had had a fright, that afternoon, when I had been called in from the garden, dressed up by my nanny and spooned into the drawing room. There, I had been suddenly so much the centre of attention for my mother and father and all those strangers in their tulip chintz chairs that all the talk suddenly stopped. When I had been told to go to the piano, the keyboard froze under my fingers.

And then, after that, and almost whenever I practised – without my noticing, or without my teacher noticing either – the inner music was starting to retreat behind some other activity, which was like a superimposed regulatory function that allowed for absolutely no mistakes whatsoever. To make a mistake was to launch a condemnation upon oneself, followed by self-criticism and an unworthiness which had no sooner settled than it was followed up by guilt. I had to go on trying harder and harder, even though, as wrists and hands stiffened with application, I was no nearer, but farther from my goal of effortless playing where the music itself could sing. That goal could not be available to me, since I was expected to go down a path of lonely excellence, and on another's behalf.

But still it mattered. Music, after all, is rooted in the innermost being of most of us and raises strong feelings, perhaps because its rhythm reflects the child's first-ever sensory experience of its mother's heartbeat while *in utero*. And so, because the world out there was a dangerous as well as an unregarding place, the music that I listened to or tried to perform became more and more an inner matter. In later years, I was to find the following extract from a paper by Sarah Nettleton arresting:

> When there is danger, disorder and constraint in the environment, the music that is within becomes a safe and uncritical resort; and while it stimulates both sadness and happiness simultaneously, it provides a relatedness to which it is possible safely to withdraw. For some children, music is a great deal less complicated than parents, in certain ways coming to take their place.[2]

That my father was complicated and unpredictable I had no doubt. But, I supposed, that was probably how fathers were. After all, I had no experience of any others.

NOTES

1. R. de Bethune, *Duc de Sully Memoirs.*
2. *The Inner World of the Musically Gifted Child*, unpublished paper by Sarah Nettleton, London-based pianist and psychotherapist, quoted with her permission.

9

Sea Lavender

Y FATHER had set up a lavish lifestyle, and I assumed that he had endless money. But he was heavily in debt. His anxieties increased as J. H. Whitley, the Chairman of the BBC, to whom he was greatly attached, became very ill. His death was shortly followed by John's mother's death. Incredibly, John took to celebrating Hitler and his policies. The family holiday in 1936 was not a success.

Back in 1930, when a new BBC chairman was to be appointed, John Reith privately decided that this was the role that he would like to have. In this way, he would be able to exert new leverage on Mrs Snowden and eventually get rid of her. The appointment of Chairman was in the prime minister's gift, and so John had been pleased when Ramsay MacDonald had invited him to meet to consider the candidates. After a little while, John had got around to saying what he really wanted to say: that he would very much like the job. He had followed up his arguments to the prime minister by letter. But his diary was to learn that he was disgusted with the prime minister: someone of whom John knew little, J. H. Whitley, formerly Speaker of the House of Commons, was to be Chairman. John had taken the opportunity to demonstrate his disgust when, attending the funeral in Westminster Abbey of Lord Davidson, Archbishop of Canterbury, he had 'directed a glare of malevolence' towards the prime minister, who, along with Stanley Baldwin, was one of the pallbearers. John, who inhabited a world of his own magic, always felt that he could cast a spell on anyone who had incurred his displeasure. He never doubted the efficacy of his vengeful looks, even though the supposedly injured party was unlikely, in this instance anyway, to have noticed.

Meanwhile, the Postmaster General had been explaining to the Chairman-designate that John Reith, on account of his instability, would not be at the BBC for very much longer. What the Postmaster General could not have understood was that it was through work, preferably without let-up, that John felt he could get a grip and at times be splendidly abled. But happiness, which for him could never be an overall state, he enjoyed occasionally only.

Many men who carry responsibilities, and who are leaders, nevertheless spend time with their family and take their share in fathering their children, who, bouncing with future potential, are eager learners, ready with play and inventiveness. But John's newly arrived family made him feel guilty; and, in turn, I felt uneasy with him. When he made up his mind to 'play' with us, it was never the kind of play in which you could easily lose yourself to fun and discovery. He had a rather painful ploy which was to place you on his high and bony knees to be jiggled about until suddenly a gap opened up and you fell to the floor. I giggled dutifully and without amusement – in the same way as I did in response to being tickled. Mercifully, these clumsy games were fairly quickly over, as he got bored. But they scarcely amounted to an understanding between us, and I was glad when it was all over and he would continue writing, which he seldom stopped doing, and I could go off on my own. The risks which gathered around him were fewer when he was safely at his desk in the big study, easily in control of his papers, his telephone and even himself, and almost content.

And then, in his London office, he had received a letter which he read with something like incredulity. It came from the new Chairman:

> May I say with what pleasure I look forward to being associated with you in the great work of which you are the creator. I hope our association will be mutually helpful in the service to which you have given such unstinted devotion and to which I will bring my very humble contribution in the spirit of an admirer and a learner.

As John wrote of this sea-change in *Into the Wind*, the note of astounded disbelief persisted. However much he might claim that it made no difference to him whatever Mrs Snowden – and, until recently, Lord Clarendon as well – might say and do, the reality was different: he did mind, dreadfully. And so now, after their first meeting, his diary was to learn what he felt about John Whitley:

> He was impressive in appearance; quiet and courteous; of a natural dignity; a man whom one could trust; who would be utterly sincere. Whatever he might have been told – and he would surely have been told a great deal – he would not allow himself to be prejudiced; would make up his own mind. At our first meeting we discussed broadcasting policy. At the end of it he said he had come prepared to approve what we had done and were trying to do; now he knew he did ... Was he actually saying all this, or was it a dream? There might, perhaps, have been a greater contrast between him and his predecessor; but one could not imagine it ... it seemed that a raging storm had been suddenly hushed to calm. In fact he brought, immediately, by his very coming, peace.[1]

John Whitley's background was in Yorkshire cotton. He had held a parliamentary seat for the Liberals and chaired the council whose task it was to find common ground between the civil service and the cotton industry. His gifts as a conciliator were recognised in the status accorded to the Whitley Councils and their achievements; he was an able Speaker of the House of Commons. His task of reconciling Reith to his Governors, and to one in particular, was probably as testing as any in his career. John found himself talking openly about his contumacious relationship with Mrs Snowden and about her efforts, as he saw them, to undermine him throughout the circles that she inhabited. Almost certainly, nobody, either before or after, had succeeded in asking John to forgive and forget: his was a paranoia which was apt to move in long before he had any evidence to support it. It was

> As if increase of appetite had grown
> By what it fed on.[2]

But John, now being asked, so to speak, to make a new start, was able to hear his chairman to the extent that he could state his terms: 'Do you really know', he enquired, 'how much you are asking of me?' Whitley was giving him the comfort and assurance that he craved but was usually too proud to accept. For sure, at no other time and in no other circumstances was John able to claim that he had succeeded in forgiving and forgetting; at no other time could he look out on the world in such peace. 'Free from internal strife, suspicion and distrust,' he wrote, 'one was able, undistracted, to get on with the job.' This was a cry of pain which was also the experience of relief from it, and from all the trials of his youth. 'I am now on quite agreeable terms with the Snowden woman', he wrote after a Board meeting later that year, not fully aware of the effect of the catalyst that was Whitley, even on his relationships. Only one other person succeeded in enabling John to change his views and regard them in a more peaceable way: this was Malcolm Muggeridge, when in later years they worked together on a television series.

John Whitley's arrival had been like the bursting into tender leafage of spring's young shoots following release from winter's relentless hold. It was, wrote John Reith, 'a period of light, understanding, and excellent wisdom'.

Why, I was to wonder later, were there not more John Whitleys who could break through into my father's harsh and lonely life so that he could look into other bright mornings?

Of course, as a small child, I made my own arrangements in response to what I perceived to be a hostile world outside the small one of nursery and garden that I inhabited. Visitors came regularly to formal lunches at Harrias House and represented for me threatened, if not actual, invasions from without. I delighted to spy on the enemy. And so, whenever the front doorbell rang and the maid's footsteps rattled along the downstairs corridor, I dashed for the upstairs store room – called the tank room – from whose small window, with little risk of being seen, I could look down on the group assembled outside the front door below, waiting to be let in. On one occasion that I remember, the women's dresses fluttered in the breeze, but their faces were hidden by strange concoctions which they wore as hats. One looked from above as though she had a dead cat on her head. The big black door swung in, opened by an invisible hand, and the ladies in their heels trod delicately up the step into the marbled interior. The men followed and removed their hats as though entering church. I thought I would run for a further viewing from the balcony over the hall, even though I would risk being seen. There they were, still in the outer hall; one maid, Freda, received coats and gloves, and the other, Edith, stood by to lead the party into the main hall and to the drawing room to announce their names. As she did so, one man, looking curiously around him, saw me, smiled and waved, thereby throwing me in a quandary as to whether the outside world was, after all, inhabited by so many dangerous aliens. Briefly, I heard my mother's shy 'How do you do?' until it was lost in a rush of voices.

One matter, however, had tested the relationship between the BBC Chairman and the Director General. Even in its youth, the BBC had already acquired from somewhere an old-fashioned attitude to questions of salary increases, tending to wait as long as possible in the hope that legitimate claims for increase would stay quiet under a blessed passivity. At the same time, a blinkered attitude to money was a well-known phenomenon of the church of John's upbringing; and so, even when acting as claimant, John's own approach was complicated.

I always thought that he had a great deal of money: the signs were clear. The occasional lunch in town had always, it seemed, to take place at the Ritz or Claridges, and then at the best table. Perhaps he liked to be seen in these places; and, since he was so conspicuous, there needed to be no difficulty. And then there were two large cars at home, and my mother nearly always received pearls and diamonds for her Christmas and birthday presents. They made her uncomfortable.

Presents for me were often more glorious than I would have chosen. When I was aged eight, and things were disappearing from the shops because of the war, I saw a miniature sewing machine in a toyshop window. I asked my mother if I could have it for Christmas — and I proceeded to look forward to Christmas more eagerly than ever. But under the wrapping of a very large parcel on Christmas Day was a full-grown sewing machine saying Singer, a smaller version of my mother's very splendid electrically driven Frister and Rossman. Over the top of my disappointment, I produced 'Oh' and 'Ah' and 'Goodness' while my father, insensible to real feelings, sat in his high Windsor armchair, his fingertips resting against each other. Then he explained that, because of the war, the Singer factory was no longer producing sewing machines, but that the managing director had found this one for him. There were always managing directors who did the impossible for John.

Back in 1931, John felt that the BBC Board had overlooked his legitimate claim for a pay increase of £750: the Board under Lord Clarendon had agreed the rise and forgotten to implement it. Whitley succeeded in negotiating a rise – but not, as John assumed with some justice, backdated. He would turn their miserly response against them, he said, all his old embedded resentments surfacing, and not accept the increase. He made a statement about the £3,750 that he was owed, and how the Board 'had lost a great chance of making me happy with them'. Temporarily, even Whitley was aligned with the enemy: he would be left guessing while John smouldered silently. Aware of how matters stood, Whitley came straight to the point and, with a winsome candour, again asked John if he would regard him as a friend and now let the matter drop. Then he asked John's advice, most significantly when he invited him to draw up a paper on the responsibilities of Governors. Ahead of him, the Chairman had a meeting with the prime minister on new appointments to the Board. As John wrote up his paper, the quarrel over pay receded. The paper was accepted as it stood by both Chairman and prime minister – and the Whitley Document, as it was called, was required reading for the new Governors for the next twenty years.

Behind this remarkable relationship was surely an attitude of trust. John Whitley seldom, if ever, interfered with John Reith, freeing him once more to act out of his exceptional capacities, treating him in exactly the ways in which John, at his best, trusted his staff to get on with their job, and, for those in positions of most responsible management, allowed them to envisage, expand and innovate as only they knew how. Adrian Boult was given that freedom to usher in contemporary music, for which the Director General had little taste, and to form the BBC Symphony Orchestra, of which the Director General had only limited understanding.

Symbolically, there could have been few more direct signals of this trust than the invitation to John Whitley's wife to become my godmother. But, four years after his arrival at the BBC, John Whitley was no longer a well man. John visited him in his nursing home where he was dying of cancer, and Whitley asked for his ashes to rest for a few moments beneath the dedication in Broadcasting House and then remain overnight in the Religious Studio. Upon Whitley's death, the BBC's flags were flown at half-mast, and all of its correspondence was carried out on black-edged notepaper. For John, it was as though he had lost his father all over again. And with Whitley died some part of the BBC also for John, and some of his power too.

There was a sense in which he never quite recovered, certainly not in relation to the BBC. 'I keep wondering what I'm to do', he pondered in his diary. 'I should like to retire and live much more simply than we do (as of course we would certainly have to!). Living in the style we do does not appeal to me at all, and actually we do not get anything like the value from it we should. There's so much that I want to write, but I do not think I'll ever do it if I'm in a job … I have been such a ghastly mediocrity compared to what I wanted to be and could have been.'[3] It was true that neither John nor Muriel was ever relaxed in the expensive lifestyle which they had set up for themselves. Regularly, my father said how much he would like a cottage in the country with a stream running through the garden; and, since he seemed to be more or less all-powerful, I felt perplexed to know why he could not alter his lifestyle in the way that he wanted. He was the man who could easily conjure up a table in the already fully booked restaurant, and who secured a place for Christopher at Oxford University ahead of 100 others (without consulting the person principally concerned). I did not know that John himself could not understand how he was unable to manage his private life or know at what big task he should next set himself.

But, as his brother Douglas had observed more kindly than his other brothers and sisters, John's intellectual activity, whether in study or in writing, was inextricably tied into action. Even though he had a large collection of books, when John read it was with a view to application. His actor's subterfuge gave the impression of his being far more academically inclined towards study and knowledge for its own sake than was the case. His regular resort to the use of Latin as though to a native tongue was a result of some careful dictionary work and construing; his 'spontaneous' quotations were well rehearsed. As for his being 'a mediocrity', this was a view of himself which was scarcely shared by anyone else, however much they might find him volatile, hyper-critical and given to self-pity, experiencing everything as a personal triumph or a personal insult. Much well-meaning effort was directed towards trying to persuade him of his achievement. But he would not and could not change his view as to his own unsatisfactory progress through life because he was not free to do so. The phalanx of these inner, chastising objects drew his attention continually, and, without the benefit of recognition, preoccupied him with the sad reflections on how far *he himself* had failed. If it was clear to me, as a child, that his idea of retiring was as unrealistic as would be a suggestion that he now set up a newsagent's corner shop, how could he not see it himself?

In 1932, Mrs Snowden proposed the introduction of a staff association. Its purpose was 'to enable the staff to make representations to the Board on any matter concerning their work, conditions of service, status etc.', and to promote the status of women. The use of 'etc.' was something John would never tolerate, ever; and, although less disposed than one might have thought to discriminate against women, especially professionals, John was unimpressed by this move for the emancipation of the junior staff as a whole. Senior staff and many others expressed themselves in agreement also. The squabble died away – only to resurface in 1934 when there arose a rash of press attacks on the BBC. Reporters were intercepted by police in Hedgerley Lane on their way to Harrias House. At this point, John added a night watchman and an Airedale dog to his staff at home. Part of the clamour was for an interview ahead of his address to the 1922 Committee of back-bench Conservative MPs. As he got into his car for the meeting, an office junior handed him a note. She asked him to read it on his way there, which he did. At the meeting, one hostile questioner wanted to know more about allegations of Prussianism in the Corporation, and of low morale. John, undisturbed, murmured that that really was not for him to answer, but that maybe the Chairman would be better placed to do so. Passing him the note which had been handed over in the car, John ensured that this was so.

The Chairman read out the note: 'The undersigned members of staff of the BBC, thoroughly disgusted with the false and malignant statements about the Director General being published in certain newspapers, wish to record their detestation of the action and methods of the newspapers concerned and to reaffirm their loyalty and gratitude to the Director General'.[4] There were

800 signatories to the statement. To a Miss L. Taylor, a junior accountant, a tribute was due for her devoted and painstaking work in gathering opinion. Perhaps she got her reward when the next day's press resounded with cheering headlines. 'Sir John Plays Daniel,' said one, 'but the lions were all tame.' How did the news reach the press, since no press were present at the meeting of the 1922 Committee? The Chairman and the Secretary and another MP – and John himself – played at being press officers for the evening.

Meanwhile, to protect himself against idleness, John announced that he was going to give much closer attention to programmes than he had done. The view which the Controller of Programmes received shortly afterwards was hardly the result of objective research. The Director General made known his opinion of jazz and of the vulgarity of variety programmes: 'Germany has banned hot jazz and I'm sorry that we should be behind in dealing with this filthy product of modernity', he said.

In 1935, his growing gloom was alleviated only to some extent by his pleasure in receiving the honorary degree of DCL from Oxford University. 'It is, of course, the greatest academic honour in the world', he wrote, 'and a very gratifying *imprimatur* from such a quarter on our work.'[5] He took his mother to the ceremony; and she, reports McIntyre, 'was so excited she couldn't eat her breakfast'. He attended the subsequent gaudy at Christ Church; and, when he returned, very late, he found his mother's note asking him to go to see her. To do so, he put on his scarlet robe and velvet hat again and knocked on her door. But, by the end of the year, his mother's life was drawing to a close. His sister, Jean, with whom she was living in Dumfries, telephoned to say that she had had three heart attacks; he could not decide what to do, but Muriel encouraged him to take the overnight sleeper north. Mansbridge, the much-loved parlour maid, was to go into the garden with a torch to pick a bunch of violets. When eventually he arrived with his violets, he was too late. As was usually the case when greatly moved, he started to sound off about the state of affairs in the household and the unsuitability of the undertaker, with the name of the garage displayed on the back of the hearse.

Whether he was comforted by the 400 messages of sympathy which he received, including a telegram from Ramsay MacDonald, the prime minister, it is hard to say. There was little comfort in the letter from his eldest brother, Archie. As a brazen reiteration of the old bitter state of affairs, it said a lot about Archie, who was now at work in the Church of England as Rector of West Halton in Lincolnshire:

> There is somewhere, possibly in moments withdrawn from secular affairs and thoughts of worldly advancement you may recognise it as from religious source, a saying to the effect: 'The first shall be last'. It is a saying you would do well to ponder in view of the Final Judgement – that is, of course, if you believe in God. When I recall Father's intense dislike of the Church of England and of the English Public Schools and your professed affection for him in his lifetime I wonder how, deserting your father's church you call in dignitaries of the Church of England to baptise your offspring and arrange for public school education? It might be well and only fair if you drew the attention of those whose duty it seems to be to advertise you in the press to the fact that Mother had other sons – truly sons, though nobodies – and a daughter, who gave years of her life to devoted nursing of that Mother. Fair is fair, and I do not think either you or your wife have ever sacrificed yourselves either for Father or Mother as Jean has done. I have written remonstrating with the various editors concerned ...[6]

For much of the next year, John was tired, sleeping badly, and depressed. Unaccustomed to the first two of these symptoms, he was under the doctor while at the same time, increasingly, feeling that he needed to leave the BBC. Much of the work he had to do, connected with the renewal of the BBC's charter, he found unexciting. So too was the Ullswater Committee, appointed to look into it.

Clement Attlee, a member of the Ullswater Committee, was a politician for whom John had a great respect.[7] But he showed his hand very much as a left-winger as he tried to put across trades-unionism for the BBC. This, for John, was too close to a political view for comfort: his own political grasp was a loose-knit affair and committed him to neither one view nor another. The BBC had

149

become 'an all-absorbing monster', he noted. 'No home pursuits or interests of one's own.'[8] His work certainly took up all his time; but what had deprived him of family and leisure interests was not the BBC but his own extraordinary cast of mind, which – in his longing to be 'fully stretched' and therefore at work all the hours that he could – originated in some other mysterious world of his own. On Christmas and Boxing Day 1935, he forgot all about his family as he worked on Ullswater. In many ways, his was a single-track outlook in which work offered him his only respite. My mother, for whom Christmas meant a lot, must have wondered when she and the children were ever going to get a look-in.

Over lunch at the Carlton in 1935, he told Marconi, who was a little surprised, how much he had always admired Mussolini for having achieved 'high democratic purpose by means which, though not democratic, were the only possible ones'.[9] Again, restless and dissatisfied with the BBC, and remarking how much he admired Hitler for his magnificent efficiency, he mused that his real calling was for dictatorship.

Professor Asa Briggs could not help noting that John's notions of social and industrial regimentation inclined towards fascism: John made no apology for announcing that he really admired the drastic action taken by Hitler. At home, he liked to draw Muriel's attention to the way in which some of her relatives looked Jewish – with the implication that she did too – as though that were a black mark. I began to think that, in many ways, my father must be a rather terrible person. When he made his loud and public confessions, he was certainly not taking responsibility for them, any more than in showing his emotional nakedness he minded, or was embarrassed about, others being emotionally bullied or themselves embarrassed. I though he ought to mind – or, at the very least, notice.

Having often complained about the BBC's voracious use of his time, he was now announcing to Mrs Hamilton that he was feeling that he had organised himself out of a job. 'This', he went on, 'is very satisfactory in one sense; but I do not know how I shall get on, as I probably can't reconcile myself to slack days.' At the same time, a resolution to this problem was presenting itself: he was asked if he would like to be considered for the chairmanship of a 'vast organisation' and associated directorships. It was Cable and Wireless, with a salary of £20,000. He observed that it was an attractive appointment – but awarded it a negative response. Indecision, amounting to impotence, had taken over; and, when in 1936 the time came for the summer holiday, he was by no means in holiday mood.

Even at the best of times, holidays were a challenge for my father. With his mind occupied with the BBC and whether or not he should leave, he found the prospect of a holiday with the children by the seaside unappealing. Such an arrangement, he said, was 'boring and provincial'. I was four, Christopher eight, and he wanted to go abroad with my mother – after all, he was paying for these nannies and people so that she was not tied down. And the tedium and delay of childhood – he really could not be bothered with it. One might think – not entirely inaccurately – that he had had no childhood himself. But my mother knew that she wanted to be at the seaside with the children. This time, she was determined.

At a place called Thorpe Ness, near Aldeburgh in Suffolk, the sun shone every day. On the edge of the beach, where the sand was dry and loose, was a row of wooden beach huts, one of which was ours. It smelled enchantingly of sand, paraffin and creosote; of towels, sandshoes and beachballs. Brightly coloured things like rubber rings, tin buckets and towelling bathing gowns hung from hooks. In front, wooden steps, well layered with sand, lost themselves in more heaped-up sand. Folding deckchairs, stored in the hut, were very much for the grown-ups. These had sunny stripes on their canvas and a sad tendency to give up being chair-shaped as soon as someone sat in them. With giggles and joy, I saw the nurse transformed from her starched shape to spectacularly flying skirts, lost hat and embarrassed shrieks. 'Oh dear', said my mother, making no move. And then, after much thought, 'Are you all right?'

Now, at last, in sea-going costume and with rubber ring, I ran as though without all speed I would be too late for it all; lest suddenly

151

it would have faded in on itself. But I got there in time: the sea, all unconcerned and rolling its gentle rollers shorewards, had waited for me, the sun beaming down. Into the water, the shallows soon gave way to the more restraining depth, each step calling for a more determined shove to proceed further into its limpid depth. In my rubber ring, I did not so much swim as cast about and, lying on my back, look up at the billowing sky and its forever blue. Then, with the gulls still crying their plaintive cries, I rolled over and found the chuckling ripples all around. Flowing on past me, each carried its own sun glint. Included in their fun, I was nevertheless all alone and, as it were, far, far out at sea.

And then — too rude an intrusion: 'It's time to come in', came the imperious tone. Suddenly, I was among the crowd demanding and insisting that I go somewhere, do something, stop what I was doing and get on with something else. 'I'm not cold', I said; but the magic had fled and the call was repeated, and total disruption was in place. There was nothing to be done but give it all up. After a while, I could get reconciled to the enveloping towel, dry clothes and an extra layer, followed by some plain biscuits, without which, apparently, one would certainly fade away.

The paraffin stove hissed away cheerfully, its warmth drawing forth the excellent creosote smell of the hut. I left my mother happily starting to organise vacuum flasks and sandwiches, because I had an urgent digging project. Seizing my small wooden spade, I ran to the hard sand and dug a hasty castle with moat and, from it, a channel to the water's edge. But the tide was by now so businesslike in its retreat that it was not interested for long in my channel. Lunch was a good idea, and with Christopher I ran up to where the sandwiches were sitting ready in opened boxes. In my haste, I dropped my spade so that it scooped some dry sand onto the sandwiches. I did not think that I had done anything too terrible; it takes experience to learn that there can be no further use for sand-seasoned sandwiches. My father, who had by now arrived from the holiday house, where he had been writing, arranged himself in a beach chair which amounted to nothing more than slats held in an angle by canvas strips, a support which allowed you to half-lie back in the sand. He was wearing his Panama hat, to which he always referred with an odd pronunciation. I later realised that this was an attempt at broad Glaswegian, although I never knew why, or why he found it funny – which, of course, was pleasant enough.

But now he had seen the sand shower. I looked anxiously at him – but he only frowned and made a tutting sound. Then he warned Christopher not to do the same thing as I had done. I began to feel rather terrible. My mother was doing her best to make good the losses, selecting the damaged articles for herself and moving the rest to safety. Christopher bit into his and said it was like eating concrete. My mother told him to Never Mind and handed him another one. I choked back the tears.

But then I forgot the tears in the face of the next difficulty, which was absolutely not of my making or Christopher's. The bathing hut next door had, up until now, been empty; and, as ours was the last hut in the line, the space was clear on that side too. But now a lot of people were arriving and filling the hut next door, and its space, with many of them and their luggage. I knew that, for my father, this would be particularly unwelcome. Therefore, it would be unwelcome for my mother too, and so I felt uneasy about what might happen next. From within the next hut came a blast of sound – with more following. My father spun round in his flimsy chair arrangement and then back again towards my mother. His voice was large and furious – but, even so, it could not have been heard above the people's gramophone.

'What filthy jazz and crooners is this?' he shouted. 'How dare they bring their machine down here and make this damnable noise? I've a mind to go in and smash it for them' – and he started to stand up. 'Don't – no, don't, John', said my mother. 'Don't do that. We'll move our things further away – and I expect they'll stop before long.' 'Come on, Muriel', said my father, as though he had not heard her. 'Come on. We're going back to the house.'

He swept up his chair and a rug, and, glaring at anyone next door who was looking and seeing, stalked off – as far as it was possible on the loose sand and dunes to carry on stalking off – and was soon striding along the lane away from the shore. My mother, the nurse, Christopher and I gathered up wet costumes, towels and picnic things to carry back, hastily putting the deckchairs, rubber rings, spades and buckets into the shed and locking it. I saw one or two of the people looking at us, and all of a sudden the awful noise was stopped. But it was too late: we were climbing up the dunes; the sea's roar behind us was lessening and the shore retreating. I looked back again — the sea was far out now at its low tide, almost silent in its distance below the long blue line of its horizon. Perhaps we had embarrassed it.

We were back at the holiday house. My mother tried to get the picnic going again in the garden, but my father did not want any lunch, saying he was going for a walk. Off he set in lonely rage down the lane. It was a bad sign when he went off for a walk; probably he would not be back for a long time, and my mother would be worried. We did not say much as, out in the garden, my mother, the nurse, Christopher and I ate the surviving sandwiches. But the straight-edged flowerbeds were more than ever severe, and the house, with its sightless, plate-glass windows and high-ceilinged rooms, more than ever forbidding.

For the next few days, my father seemed to be away on his own, saying very little and writing at a table in the sitting room. I heard him say to my mother that he was going back to London. He had said to her — had he not? — that he found the prospect of a holiday at the seaside with the children boring and provincial; surely she would remember that he had wanted to go abroad with her to a hotel. And, since he was paying for all these nannies and people, he could not understand how she was so tied that all they could do was to take a house and have all the servants and nannies on top of them as usual. And anyway, he said, he was going to leave the BBC quite soon because he could not stand it any longer. Two days later, he was still there — and Christopher and I, in uncharacteristically rebellious mood, stuck out our tongues at the nurse when she called us in from the garden.

And then, at last, there was to be an excursion, something that might perhaps lift the general despondency. We were to see inside a house — not, you might think, an enthralling prospect; but, as we drove up the track which led to this particular house, we saw something like a tall tower and, perched high on the top of it, a very small house. Up and up we climbed – the height got dizzy – and then we were inside, looking out across the bunches of the treetops. There was nothing below, apparently, holding us up. My father seemed to be feeling better and was talking away with the man whose house it was and who had made it out of a water tower. It was a tree house, filled with magic, and producing a little of that consternation that goes with magic.

Down on the ground again, a little relieved, we were looking at a post mill, a miniature windmill whose sails were cheerfully circling in the breeze. Great creakings and scrapings came from the millstones, where there was just enough space for the miller to move in and out, feed the hoppers and carry the heavy sacks. He recognised my father, touched his cap, said 'Good day, Sir John – Ma'am', and nodded to us. Soon, my father was speaking with him: he always liked to talk with millers and engine-drivers and mariners about what they did, and they always got on well together. As my mother and father made to go, the miller asked Christopher and me if we would like to see inside. After Christopher had climbed the ladder and had a look, I did so too and saw all these wooden arms and levers, working out of their neat joints, rising and falling and driving a circulating belt so that big metal wheels with ratchets eventually drove a millstone, one stone rotating above the other static one. What had started as corn grains, sliding down a chute onto the stones, appeared in another chute as meal; the miller fetched paper bags and gave us one each, now filled with the ground grain. Meanwhile, the great white sails creaked rhythmically in their comfortable way, on and on, round and round, turning against the blue sky.

That night, as Christopher and I had our supper, and I had scraped my plate clean, I asked my mother who were these people running across this blue and white bridge on my blue and white plate with a blue and white man running after them? The dining room, I noticed, was filled with these plates with bowls and cups and saucers, some arranged on dresser shelves, others stacked up below. My mother said the china was called the Willow Pattern, and there was a story about a daughter who was running away from home with her friend, and her father, who was very angry with them, running after them to catch her and bring her back. Not too keen on angry daddies, I scraped the plate not quite so clean next time and arranged for a blob of pudding to be left on top of the daddy on the plate.

Daddies seemed on the whole to me to be extremely angry people, even when at last they calmed down a little. That night, I dreamed I was back in that very high house, which soon started to walk towards me. I tried to fly, but then I was in the back garden of this house where there was a row of giant vegetables, growing taller by the minute and starting to move in on Christopher and me – huge angry men. They got so close that I woke, unable to move with terror while these fearsome figures were in the room. At last, I thought I could move – that perhaps would shake them off a bit. Somehow I got to the window. I never thought of going across the landing to my parents' room; still less to the nanny's. Instead, and uncertainly, I drew back the curtain a little to look out and away from the terrors of the room. There I saw the dark sky, now becoming pricked with more and more twinkling stars. And then, increasingly drawn to the scene, I saw one large star, far larger and brighter than the rest, shining its steady beam into my room. Here, indeed, was rescue. I leaned against the windowsill, the longer to regard its bright calm light. When at last I could get back to bed, I left the curtain open a little so that the star could go on looking into my room and so that I might get back to sleep.

Still shaken the next morning, I left enough porridge in my willow-pattern bowl to cover over the picture completely. I did not tell my mother of my experience; she might perhaps tell my father. He was being elaborate with Christopher and often gave him a row for keeping his mouth open. And then I must have done the same thing. Perhaps he did not want us around. But neither did he like the house and garden and the other houses and gardens where everyone seemed to be friendly towards each other, playing tennis together. 'We don't know anyone', he said, sadly. 'And nobody speaks to us.' But I knew that they would know who he was and would probably be friendly to us too if he would speak to them. They might have thought that such a busy and important man would want to be left alone on his holiday with his family – and, anyway, he looked fierce.

But, the day after the nightmare, my mother, perhaps sensing something was hard for me, left the nurse behind and took Christopher and me on a visit to the Mere. Here was a large lake, very near to the sea but not joined to it. Around it were large tussocks making up an area which I later learned were salt marshes. As we wound our way from one hummock to another, skirting the black and peaty water between each, I found a tough little plant, on the end of whose wiry stems grew dense sprays of small mauve flowers. More and more peaty cushions were crowned with these; here again was something that reassured. That evening, we were back at the Mere. Now it was dark, too dark to see the sea lavender; but, instead, around and across the Mere hung many coloured lanterns, slung between poles so that, across the water's black and shiny surface, bright colours slid about with gleaming ease. There were lots of people in boats, and we climbed down into ours, small and low in the water. We were rowed out into the night; the water was black beneath the night sky, and my mother was rather nervous. But, as the stars began to flicker into life, I looked for my great big steady planet from last night; perhaps he was away shining down on somebody else. We turned to go back to the brightly lit shore. With each stroke, the oar paused for a moment above the water, drips quickly falling from it and starting to reflect the colours of the lanterns; then the oar sliced back into the water, and the coloured drops were quite extinguished. Next morning, when the lights would all have been turned off, the sea lavender, thriving on its salty turf cushions, would still be there, its flower-heads moving ever so slightly in the sea breezes.

NOTES

1. Reith, *Into the Wind*, p. 132.
2. Shakespeare, *Hamlet*, Act I, Scene 2, line 144.
3. Ian McIntyre, p. 218, from Reith, *Diary*, 24.11.35.
4. McIntyre, p. 203.
5. Ibid., p. 216, from *Diary*, 8.5.35.
6. Ibid., p. 219, from letter of 17.12.35.
7. Ibid., p. 216, from *Diary*, 16.5.35.
8. Ibid., p. 216, from *Diary*, 26.5.35.
9. Ibid., p. 217, from *Diary*, 9.11.35.

10

A Congestion of Kings

OHN REITH and his BBC were deeply involved in the death of one king, the abdication of another and the coronation of a third. The crises, and his requirement to be at the prime minister's side, pleased him greatly. But my delight was in my mother's preparations for Christmas, filling the house with magic. My father stayed disengaged from most of it.

John and the BBC were much occupied with affairs of state in early 1936. In January, the health of King George V was failing; a meeting in the cabinet offices earlier had included John; and now, on the evening of 20 January, Stuart Hibberd, through the BBC's domestic and Empire transmitters, was making solemn announcements at fifteen-minute intervals: 'The King's life is moving peacefully to its close'. Shortly after midnight, John himself gave the final bulletin: 'Death came peacefully to the King at 11:55pm'.[1]

The next evening, John was dining in Downing Street, from where Stanley Baldwin was to broadcast. Their dinner beforehand was jolly: both shared a certain comic twist on life. Whether they were able to make light of John's embarrassment over difficulties that evening with his dental plate is not recorded. Over such an event, he would probably suffer a severe humour failure. I learned, early, never to rely on this frail commodity of his.

As usual, although speaking with less than his usual facility, John responded liberally to the PM's invitation to him to comment on his speech, especially offering the need to embellish it with some magnificent abstracts such as honour, dignity, moral authority and so on, as attaching to the late King. And, well aware of the speculation that was chasing through all levels of society about the association of the Prince of Wales with a certain Mrs Simpson – all most unfortunate in view of her status as a commoner and a divorcee – John further suggested that a supplication to the Almighty to guide the new King would not go amiss. And so Mr Baldwin put that in too, speaking his piece into the microphone in the Cabinet Room, while Mrs Baldwin warmed her toes at the fire.

Not everyone was on such easy terms with John, however. Lees-Smith, the former Labour Postmaster General, liked to make missiles of his statements. Very publicly, he observed: 'The BBC is an autocracy which has outgrown the original autocrat ... It has become despotism in decay ... the nearest thing in this country to Nazi government that can be shown'.[2] He complained: 'If I talk to any employee of the Corporation, I am made to feel like a conspirator'. This last remark was in connection with the old problems for or against setting up a staff association. John asserted that the fair, thorough and democratic investigation which he had conducted had finally thrown out the idea; others claimed that his method was rigged. To such newspaper reports John would pronounce himself indifferent, saving himself a lot of the danger by reading only the social column in *The Times*. My mother knew better, however; and, when I was older, she told me she was sure that Daddy did mind criticism most dreadfully but tried to hide it. Another press report, of which he retained a clearer recollection and which therefore appeared in his diary, compared him with

Baldwin, in that he might regard a crisis 'merely as evidence of his indestructibility'.

A staff association was to be set up after all, as announced by the Postmaster General. Richard Lambert, Oxford graduate, free thinker and editor of *The Listener*, commented that, from this time, the BBC 'became more and more like an extra-mural department of Whitehall: fair, decorous and slow-moving — having lost much of its original *élan*, but also much of its original toughness'. The Director General had moved into some form of personal retreat: 'In fact Sir John Reith seemed largely to efface his personality from the administration and withdraw into a kind of seclusion. We saw and heard less of him than ever before; and it was common talk that he had had enough of broadcasting and was transferring his energies to new fields of work.'[3]

For the time being, the BBC's leader had lost something of his conspicuous resolution, out of which he would urge others towards the distant goals which he saw. It would have been hard for anyone to understand that such a man could be laid low by what were, for him, the many arrows of personal misfortune, against which he really could not help himself.

In 1936, John was still weighed down by the previous year's losses, in particular by John Whitley's death. Whitley had become for John the father he had not had, there having been little fathering in the taut atmosphere of the manse. Added to this, his father's congregation — like any other — regularly made their own incursions and demands for their own particular form of fathering. When John had got over his initial devastation after his father's death in 1919, he found that he could carry on in some sort of equanimity in the company of an internalised and elaborately elevated figure of his father. Precociously affected by the ceremonial, he responded wholeheartedly to the old man's dramatised, pulpiteered self. With the proximities of the manse pruned away, the minister's entry into the assembly of the congregation was impressive: in long and stately robes and academic hood, he followed the opened Bible carried in ahead of him, becoming through all the artifices of drama an ennobled figure, then to rise up into his own high pulpit.

160

This is the stuff of the stage, with setting and role, and the audience – the mute congregation – intent on the minister now sensationally distanced from them. He is the man of God, acknowledging not his congregation's concentration on him but his own aspiration towards the divine presence. As the sufficient vehicle for the Word, he is the more remote, the more captivating; the orator with the mellifluous voice, the commanding figure with the penetrating look. But this was also the man invented by John to replace the one who, as he grew up, could only make such limited space available for him.

But John, despite – or perhaps because of – his difficulties, continued to see himself as one of the elect, the justified, and so had no reason to seek recovery by his own exertions – or indeed, as would many, through the help of their religion. In his own proud and lonely way, he awaited deliverance through a divine intervention of another and more immediate kind: a sort of Recorded Delivery of absolution and action.

As to the origin of his difficulties, I was neither aware nor interested. Other matters of absorbing interest and mounting excitement were rushing up, to the healthy exclusion of the heavy stuff. My mother had a thorough understanding of that great English tradition, Christmas; and, so that it would be properly carried through, she undertook everything, from lavish presents for Christopher and me down to the smallest charm, carefully wrapped, in the Christmas pudding. My father went along with these things as far as he could, although the traditional Scottish celebration was meagre by comparison. He and my mother received hundreds of Christmas cards, all talking happiness and good cheer. He, however, seemed quite to have mislaid this. Although occasionally I heard the name of Charlie Bowser, I was not to know how largely he had figured in both my parents' lives – or that it was his birthday at Christmas time which so upset my father.

Despite Charlie, Christmas spread in and through the house. 'The gardeners are coming in with the logs', I heard. This was one of the powerful signs of the approach of Christmas. The maids were hurrying about, and I saw druggets laid across the hall rugs to protect them from large boots and wood chippings. The garden door was opened, and in rushed the cold grey day as though it had been knocking for some time. Uninvited, it pressed on into the hall and up the stair. Through the open doorway, I caught sight of the dark mass of the yew hedge and the tops of the fruit trees showing above, bare except for a leaf in single silhouette wanly fluttering. Now came the heavy sound of metal on stone, the approach of the gardeners with solid wooden barrows, wheels encased in iron rims pounding the paving stones. At the door, nailed boots rattled, followed by all the grunts, instructions and exhalations needed for moving the logs into the house. As each log was lifted, others shifted and thumped down.

The men came into the house, politely and ineffectually running their boots back and forth on the door mat. A hefty log was balanced on a broad shoulder of each. Now inside, the gardeners' muddy clothes, compared with the antiques and Chinese rugs around, looked incongruous – and strange, too, because the men had left their hats and caps outside, and I wondered at their changed looks. Since I had never seen them bare-headed, I must have supposed that they could never ever be separated from their regular headgear. They stacked the huge logs on either side of the open fireplace in the hall, some laid across the firedogs ready for lighting. My mother went on with her own extensive preparations, and holly glowed around the base of the gallery banisters, down the stairs and over the pictures. Then in came the gardeners again, strung out along a massive tree this time. When, eventually, with more heaving and straining, the tree stood upright in its big two-handled brass pot, it rose up through the gallery to the first floor above. Its topmost spike was level with my eye, and its branches spread thick and dark below. It stood there, silently awaiting the fond attention it would soon receive. For the time, it filled the house with its sweet forest scent.

But I had a feeling, which I did not share with anyone, that it would be nice if some other people – the Naylors: Auntie Doris, Uncle Peter and the boys, for instance – came to join in with it all too. They were so merry. On Christmas morning, I woke to the clatter of the maids moving the great firedogs under the chimney in the hall below. I saw them kneel at the fireplace, crumple newspaper into place and lay kindling wood across it. I watched as the lit match caused the paper to glow and curl – and then, as someone pushed open the swing door from the hall to the back passage, the opening notes of a Christmas carol travelled up, perhaps heard from the wireless in the servants' hall. 'Once in Royal David's City'; its bell treble rose as though to a high cathedral vault – as still, for me, it continues to do every year, as though from some mute and ancient past.

But now the flames were growing and starting to shoot up here and there, licking their way around the large logs which lay across the great stretchers. Then they burst into a satisfied roar with explosions like small guns from time to time, showers of sparks, and more thumps as they shifted position.

My mother played the piano; and, with Jo Stanley, John's secretary, we sang carols. Never consulting a book for the words, John sang a reasonable tenor line. He was struggling to come back from all the scenes of displeasure that had characterised the last few days and now to join in without looking too foolish. One came to recognise the cracking of the ice as he tried, once more, to engage with the family. Still fragile, he was relieved when Christmas was over. He went back to his desk and his diary and, unknown to anyone at the time, recorded his feelings. The children, he wrote, had no use for him. Sometimes he chastised them for this; at other times, he experienced remorse. He wanted to shout at them that he wished they had never been born. He noted that he had already torn up the last of Charlie's letters, of which he had once kept every one until they stopped in 1921. 'I felt sad', he wrote. 'There was an extraordinary affection between us and we shared almost everything.' He supposed that good must somehow come out of it – but, a year later, he was certain that he had no regrets, even though all was lost. His was a fine line in self-deception: his loss had been irreparable.

But suddenly, Christmas or no Christmas, and certainly without my knowing anything, my father was full-bore on the job again at the BBC. The crisis of which the monarchy was at the centre had whirlwinded into life; persons of impeccable decorum, like the King's private secretary, Sir Godfrey Thomas, in a state of distraction, tore into John's office and, as well as unburdening himself on constitutional matters of state, laid into Mrs Simpson as already having a husband anyway, and as also having a voice like a peahen. John ordered up a whisky and soda to help calm him. Then, hugely enjoying the drama, he found that he had to be, for a spell, constantly available to the prime minister's secretary, Sir Horace Wilson, from whose office he came and went at some speed – as did the prime minister himself, causing John to rise ponderously to his feet at every prime-ministerial entry. At last, Mr Baldwin exclaimed that he seemed never to be going to stop, and please not to go on getting up. John said he was sorry about his length, but he liked to show respect – after which they continued with the more pressing matters of the moment. People work well with those with whom they work well.

The next night, shortly after dinner at Harrias House, John was being driven at speed to Windsor Castle, twenty-five minutes away. HRH Prince Edward had specially requested that John be there, by himself, for his farewell broadcast from the Castle, his speech of abdication. John described the scene in *Into the Wind*, quoted here at length because of the merit of the writing as well as the distinction of the story.

> The car passed, recognised and unchallenged, through the Castle archway, up and round to the door of the private apartments. A footman, scarlet-coated, opened without summons; within stood the superintendent and housekeeper. I asked to be taken to the room where the broadcast would be made. A corridor with three rooms in the Augusta Tower – the modest suite which the former King had always himself used. In a little sitting room the microphones had been installed; next door the engineers had their apparatus; at the end of the corridor was the bedroom. Everything was in order, as of course I knew it would be; nothing for me to do but wait; time 9:45.
>
> The housekeeper was lighting a fire in the bedroom: I would sit there and watch it grow. The superintendent appeared in

agitation. His Majesty, he said – and what else could he have called him – was already on his way from Royal Lodge. I knew he was to dine there with his mother and the members of his family. Well that was all right, I said, continuing to sit. But apparently it was not all right by the superintendent; His Majesty would arrive any moment. Well, that was still all right by me. The agitation increased, and, since time was pressing, tactful insinuation had to give place to direct suggestion; would I not receive His Majesty on the doorstep. Apparently he felt himself, with or without housekeeper, inadequate for the purpose. I was minded to tell the superintendent that it was no lack of imaginative courtesy that had set me down by the bedroom fire; that it seemed off, if not improper, that I should receive on the doorstep him who a few hours earlier was the owner; that I was in no sense the host of the occasion. But I let it go; perhaps he was right. At speed, therefore, I returned to the entrance hall – just in time. I wondered, naturally, what sort of mood the former King would be in; how he would behave. He had had some weeks of torturing indecision and suspense; now he had taken unprecedented, shattering action. Was I to adjust face and manner accordingly? In the hurried progress from the Augusta Tower, pursued at increasing remove by the superintendent, I had realised that the question must now be settled. The car was drawing up by the open door. I would behave absolutely normally, as if nothing untoward or exceptional were afoot – just as in Broadcasting House.

He was wearing a fur coat over a light suit, smoking a cigar. A dog emerged next; it went about its own business; I do not remember to have seen it again; have since wondered what became of it; have even forgotten what kind of dog it was – a Cairn or something of that sort. Someone else was getting out of the car now. No one had been able to tell me who, if anyone, would be accompanying. It might be the new King, in which case my position on the doorstep would be odder than ever. It was a man I had never seen before. The former King seemed to be in no different mood from usual. 'Good evening, Reith', he said. 'Very nice of you to make all these arrangements and to come over yourself.' He introduced his companion – Walter Monckton. I knew how much he had meant to his master of recent weeks.

On the way upstairs he asked if all were in order. Yes, I said, and no chance of anything going wrong; everything had been duplicated; and the civil war in Spain had not prevented Madrid ringing up that afternoon to ask permission to relay his talk. That amused him. Some of the furniture in a corner was covered with dust sheets; he was surprised; then said he remembered that some structural alterations had to be made. Presumably he had ordered them himself. . . .

On other occasions he used to have the sheets of his manuscript mounted neatly on bits of cardboard; he had told me that he did this himself. Tonight there was no mounting; ever so many alterations in the script. It seemed he still had some to make, so I went out, leaving him and Monckton at work together. In the corridor I found Clive Wigram, Depute-Constable and Lieutenant-Governor of the Castle; he said he had thought he would just come across. He would not go into the sitting room, so I told him there was a fire and a wireless set in the bedroom; he might like to listen there. It was nearly ten o'clock, I left Wigram in the bedroom and I returned to the sitting room.

At half a minute to ten I sat before the microphones at the table waiting for the signal – the tiny red light that would bring the ears of the whole world into that little room. My voice would carry to the ends of the earth. A thousand million people were there to hear what the man standing beside me was about to say. I thought with quiet satisfaction of the vast and flawless efficiency of the organisation behind the now dull circle of glass. The engineers next door. The control room at headquarters with its innumerable circuits, panels, distributing boards, switches, plugs and lights. All the regional and Empire control rooms and transmitters; all the aerials with their carrier waves vibrating through the infinities of ether. All the links with control rooms and transmitters in a thousand centres overseas. Especially the BBC engineers, in utter competence at their posts. All the ... *This is Windsor Castle. His Royal Highness the Prince Edward.*

I slipped out of the chair to the left; he was to slip into it from the right. So slipping, he gave an almighty kick to the table leg. And that was inevitably and faithfully transmitted to the attendant multitudes. Some days afterwards I was invited to confirm or deny a report that, having made the announcement, I had left the room, slamming the door. It was even suggested that, by doing so, I was not just forgetful of microphone sensitivity, but was indicating disapproval of what was to follow. I had left the room, but no microphone would have noted it.

After the broadcast I walked with Wigram for a little; he was going back to work for a few months to help the new King. Fortunate, I thought, the King and any king who could command such wisdom and devotion of service as Clive Wigram had given. Then, with an 'all-world OK!' from the engineers, I returned to the sitting room, where Monckton had stayed during the broadcast; gave the report to the Prince....

The Prince came to the head of the stairs with me. He referred to his visits to Broadcasting House; he had always enjoyed coming there. He had made great use of broadcasting; it had helped him in many ways; he hoped he would be able to use it again. I could only say I hoped so too. 'Good Luck, sir', I said, coming to attention; bowed, shook hands. He looked up at me and smiled; seemed to be going to say something more. For two or three seconds no movement; then I bowed again; turned and went down the stairs. I felt there was something I ought to have said; wanted to say; could not.

So ended this reign of only one year's length.[4]

The coronation of King George VI and Queen Elizabeth took place on 12 May 1937. Through the BBC, in a way that had no precedent, millions were to be brought directly in touch with Westminster Abbey. The event was subject to promulgation on a scale of which no-one remotely had any experience. Of his own position, John simply said: 'I had had very little to do with it all; approved what was submitted, occasionally made a suggestion; stood by and watched'.[5] His was the quintessential statement of leadership. He did have one great concern, however – not for the engineers, in whose expertise he had complete trust, but for the King himself, famously nervous of public utterances and, having to broadcast to the Empire after the coronation, still trying to master his stutter.

Well ahead of the coronation, a very important person from the Palace, called the Earl Marshal, had agreed that the BBC should have all the facilities it needed for the event. The Earl Marshal, together with the Archbishop of Canterbury, the Lord Chamberlain, the first Commissioner of Works to the Abbey and the BBC's Director General, met in the Abbey to plan. John had been fully briefed, and made a concise statement of requirements. The Earl Marshal asked whether the BBC would also look after filming. Sure-footed as ever, John replied that the BBC would look after it if he liked, but it would not be popular with the cinema industry. The idea was left where it belonged.

After that, at Buckingham Palace, John met the King to arrange rehearsals for the Empire programme of homage. The King went to great trouble over his broadcast as the engineers made playbacks available so that he could work on his delivery. During the last rehearsals, a gramophone record was made to be instantly available in case anything went wrong on the night.

More than a week ahead, all was ready in the Abbey, with thirty-eight microphones inside and twenty outside. The scratches that took place from time to time with the Earl Marshal and his office were understandable in view of the newness to everybody of everything, especially publicity on such a scale. With little warning, the engineers were told that they had to be out of the Abbey by 4pm the day after the coronation. They carried their consternation to the Director General: not even a night watchman was to be allowed, they said, and there was all that delicate equipment, most painstakingly set up. 'I had to come in on that myself', said John easily, with its outcome in no need of mention.

Coronation spirit was at large in the country. It even penetrated the nursery at Harrias House, where pelmets and picture rails were hung with red, white and blue. Across every village green, city square, urban housing development and industrial spread hung flags and streamers. But the BBC's part in the celebrations anticipating the coronation was extremely dignified. There was another in a series of concerts under Toscanini's baton, and a broadcast service of preparation the previous Sunday. The liturgy for that service was assembled from medieval times, and has now become part of the contemporary service. The royal anointing was first mentioned by letter from the Bishop of Lincoln to King Henry III in 1216; and from the *Liber Regalis*, or Book of the Kings, came this prayer, which was used at the coronation of Richard II's wife, Anne of Bohemia, in 1377:

> The Prince shall pray that the providence of God, which has raised him to rule so great an Empire, be pleased to give him justice, piety and wisdom; justice to his subject; piety towards God, wisdom in the government of his kingdom; that, softened by no favour and disturbed by no enemies, he may walk with firm foot in the paths of these virtues.

The Times leader the next day was unrestrained in its appreciation of 'that wonderful service' in which 'Jewels of English from the wisdom and piety of the past proved the stable continuity of this ancient act of consecration'; and there was such music as Milton would have found 'to bring all heaven before mine eyes'.[6] It was, remarked John, another liturgical triumph for Dr Iremonger, director of religious affairs, who was also the narrator for the service in the Abbey. Influential voices were already starting to note that the BBC was creating its own ritual.

For the BBC, the coronation itself went flawlessly. Afterwards, the principal participants gave John their own first-hand account. Conveyed by police car to the Palace that same evening, there they were: King George VI and Queen Elizabeth, until so very recently bedecked – indeed weighed down – with every symbol and jewel of office and regality, and now, as it were, relaxing in their jerseys and tweeds and going over the day in a spirit of 'high delight'. With ample justification, the King was pleased that all that work on his broadcast to the Empire had paid off – no gramophone record remotely needed, even though all concerned might have felt easier for knowing of its existence. And then there had been that increasing concern of which no-one else would have been aware: that, in the hour's interval between his crowning and that of the Queen, the King had found his own crown becoming painfully heavier and heavier.

It was through John's prompting, by way of a senior member of the royal household, that the BBC's chief engineer in charge of everything to do with the broadcast received his special coronation medal at the hands of the King.

NOTES

1. Ian McIntyre, p. 220.
2. Ibid., p. 228, from Hansard, vol. 318, col. 2,370 of 17.12.36.
3. McIntyre, p. 228, from R. Lambert, from the case of Lambert *v.* Levita, p. 303.
4. Reith, *Into the Wind*, p. 268 et seq.
5. Ibid., p. 282.
6. Ibid., p. 280; *The Times* quoted, 12.5.37, with their permission.

11
ℋ𝓜𝓢 Barham

*T*HE 1937 NEW YEAR'S Honours Lists, which included my father's name, avoided the storms which had previously signalled his displeasure when he was omitted. Dinner at Windsor Castle called for elaborate preparations; a new car was also ordered. My father joyfully accepted an invitation to put to sea on the Royal Naval flagship *Mediterranean*; but, during the family holiday, he talked much of leaving the BBC.

The New Year's Honours Lists for 1937 included John. He received a letter telling him that the King wished to award him the Grand Cross Victorian Order 'for his work in connection with him, his father and his brother'. Of this much-coveted honour, John's diary commented that it was 'very nice as not many have this decoration'. To the accumulating list of embellishments after his name, GCVO came second only to Privy Councillor; and the peace and calm that New Year at Harrias House was as welcome as it was unprecedented. The biannual publication of the Honours Lists was something for which my mother would try to prepare herself as one might in response to a shipping-forecast storm warning: emotional low expected, Harrias, imminent; high pressure falling; outlook moderate or poor.

From his aspiring middle-class origins, John was an *arriviste* with first-class capacities and sometime second-class performance. It was shoddy prizes that he lusted after. The Honours Lists, for instance, seemed to be published far more often than at six-monthly intervals, so great were the gusts of fury that tore through the household when they made their relentless appearance as I was attempting to grow up. The trouble was that he had been overlooked; or he had been poorly rewarded; or some useless or disreputable toady of Churchill's had been inappropriately recognised. 'I know my father would have hated to hear me ask for this,' he wrote to Lord Longford when he had become dissatisfied with his wartime ennoblement, 'but could you do something to get me a higher grading in the peerage which previous governments have denied me?' The noble lord either could not or would not, and so nothing more happened.

There were still, however, high expectations to which my mother had to live up – obligations for which she had little taste and for which she prepared with mounting alarm. I found her going gingerly down the stairs, a vision in an ivory gown with a train that seemed to me to cover the length of the stair. 'We are dining at Windsor Castle', she said without enthusiasm. Her aquamarines and diamonds, with which she was liberally hung, glittered enchantingly in the lamplight. She made her way across the hall; and Rufus, the red setter, got up from his bed to greet her, tail wagging eagerly. 'Hello, Ruie', she said and patted him affectionately. He followed her into the drawing room, where a photographer had set up his equipment and was now bowing and my-ladying as hard as he could go. 'What would you like?' my mother asked uneasily. She looked lovely but did not seem to realise it. Already, a picture had presented itself to the photographer's skilled eye. Rufus, sensing a message about her imminent departure, sat himself up before her and offered his paw for her to hold. She grasped it, of course, in her gloved hand, bending over slightly to do so. She was smiling gently and naturally at her faithful friend, even while there was a sudden rush on to move photographic equipment. The photographer covered himself in a black tent, and whirrings and clickings followed. The picture that emerged some days later was to adorn the drawing room for some years to come.

The nanny entered – it was time to go back up to the nursery. In the hall, I saw my father coming down. Unlike my mother, he knew that he cast a rather splendid figure. He wore some amazing uniform which called for knee breeches and funny shoes with silver buckles which I thought looked like my dancing shoes. With this rig-out, one's shoes, apparently, had to be pumps. His, he noted, were adorned with buckles – but should they have been bows? An hour before departure, he had rung Windsor Castle; an answering superintendent confessed that he did not know but would find out and ring back. This he did; buckles was the answer, received with relief.

Against the dark uniform were as many bursts of colour as appear from a summer herbaceous border: glittering medals hung from a row of ribbons; snow-white cuffs and collar and gloves completed the arresting scene. 'Hullo, Marista', said my father loudly. 'Hullo', I said, wriggling and intimidated. He swept by as the nanny and I, she foolishly smiling, waited at the foot of the stairs. 'Thank you', he said absently, and went across the hall to fetch his wife. Then, remembering me, he asked if I liked his uniform. 'Oh yes', I said obediently. He asked if I knew what it was, and, not expecting me to know, carried on: 'It is the Grand Cross Victorian Order – something which only the King himself can award'. Not knowing what might be the alternatives, I fell silent. He disappeared, and I ran up the stairs to watch from the tank-room window for their departure. The Buick was already drawn up at the portico, and Burness stood beside it watching the front door. I waved to Burness; but, if he saw me, he was too busy being dignified and standing to attention in preparation for the front door opening. For a long time, nothing happened. The telephone rang. Windsor Castle again. Not buckles but bows. Then I saw a maid, complete with sewing basket, climb into the seat beside the driver and quietly wait. The front door opened again, and my mother stepped nervously out. Burness saluted briefly and moved rapidly to open the rear door. Behind my mother came Edith, carrying the silk train. My mother climbed into the car, finding it a little difficult as she held up her skirts to do so. She sat on the far side of the back seat as Edith climbed in after and arranged the train at her feet. My mother smiled at her; and, as quickly as she could, Edith stepped backwards out of the car. My father climbed easily in, took off his shoes and passed them to the maid in the front. Then he handed forward two bow ties. He signalled to Burness, now in the driver's seat, to drive on. With a scrunching of gravel and with both parents splendidly adorned — even though one was currently without shoes — they went.

To everyone except John, it seemed at that time that he had reached a pinnacle of power. But, for him, there was still some destiny to be realised. Perhaps he was — as he had always been — inwardly chided by the view of his grandmother, Jeannie Stuart from high Tomintoul, that 'there niver wis a Reith man yet wha hadnae his back tae the wa' (the wall), a view whose insistence for John meant that there were formidable barriers yet to be demolished.

Again, he could not forget his jealous awareness of another. Winston Churchill, suspicious of the BBC's independence, was apt from time to time to speak up significantly for its control by government. But, while Churchill was 66 when he became prime minister in 1940, John had arrived at the BBC at exactly half that age.

A difference between John and Churchill was that the latter, when he at last met his destiny, knew it and was fulfilled. But John could achieve no such consistent recognition for himself, as bit by bit, and with extraordinary speed, the BBC grew under his leadership to be a mighty organisation. He had first expected, as he stood as a youth among the Cairngorm mountains, that his calling would be to something quite out of the ordinary; now, fifteen years on, at 48, he was on the road to its realisation.

Except that he experienced achievement only fleetingly. There were those other voices through which he got the message that he was at best a mediocrity, more likely a failure. Of one thing only, in 1937, after the coronation, had he been certain – and that was that he had to leave the BBC. This he had announced to as many as possible of the passers-by in his life; their instant denial of this strange piece of self-evaluation was probably what he was looking for.

But how did this rampant dissatisfaction come about? He had everything: the most challenging and rewardingly creative job in the country; the plaudits of the many and the admiration of the discerning; a substantial income, a comfortable lifestyle (even if its realisation tended to elude him), a loving wife and two healthy children. What more could anyone want?

A good deal, apparently. Unknown things were missing – things which, still unidentified, the children were to supply, filling up those chasms of emptiness which he faced. But children can only meet an adult's interests in their own terms; dependency, after all, must for the child be one-way traffic. If the terms are otherwise, the child is left feeling inexplicably inadequate, a failure in ways that he or she can never understand, aware only of that insistent perplexity as to how a father's triumphs might in any sense be reconciled with his miseries.

The story of a life, its lost opportunities and its achievements too, must spring from a personal predicament, on whose nature we can only speculate. And so, when John ordered a new car, its purpose was to signal to the outside world that he, John Reith, was a person of consequence. Similarly, having given his wife a single-string pearl necklace, he added to it a second, and then a third string to reflect what others should see as the steady improvement in his fortunes.

One day, a pale blue Wolseley car was parked in the drive. Its front wings were like ocean rollers, and it had a gleaming silver bumper and searchlights for headlamps. This new car was very different from other cars, in that you could travel along open to the sky, just as you used to in the pram. With the nurse, Christopher and I gathered round. My father and Burness were working to lower the canvas hood, and getting on very well together. With my mother driving, Christopher and I were allowed to pile in; the nurse, of course, as well. My mother got into the driver's seat, and after some false starts the huge engine roared into life. I shouted with excitement, only to be shushed by the nurse as my father twitched and sighed. But Burness smiled at me.

We drove through the country lanes at a brisk twelve miles an hour, my father looking straight ahead and apparently content. But I found that my hair kept getting in my eyes. I moaned a little to the nurse, who told me to Never Mind while dabbing away at hers. Despite her hat, my mother had the same problem; and, while she could have preserved her permed hair by tying it up in a headscarf — much in the manner in later years of Queen Elizabeth II when patting her racehorses — my father would have asked complainingly if she really had to tie her head up in a dishtowel.

Harrias House was not grand like other mansions. The wrought-iron gates opened in a large way onto a short drive, and were unsupported by an attendant lodge with watchful eye within. Instead, our front gate was companioned by the potato shed on one side, where the garden's root crops were heaped up beneath wide benches at the season's end, with signs the following spring that they had not lasted the interval. Others that did not last the interval were the tortoises. (My mother referred to them as 'the tortusses' and got criticised for so doing.) They were there to hibernate but got eaten by rats instead. On the other side of the gate was one of Lord Burnham's farms.

And so, even though he did not have a long drive himself, and could scarcely claim membership of the Landed and Titled Gentry, such as might be found listed in *Burke's Peerage*, my father nevertheless succeeded in having many a butlered door at the end of a long drive opened to him, with glittering dinner beyond. In his continuing search for recognition, he had to connect with the scions of those families who had been ennobled for their services to Queen Elizabeth I, or for their more recent prowess in the battlefields of the burgeoning newspaper industry, or who enjoyed the benefits of dollar-stoked marriages of more recent date. If some of these regarded him as an *arriviste*, they also found him an enhancement to any guest list.

It was for John a particularly satisfactory weekend that he spent at Chevening in Kent, guest of Lord and Lady Stanhope, where the other guests were sufficiently distinguished for his happiness: the Canadian prime minister, a British prime minister-in-waiting, Lord Halifax and others. But the man with whom he chose to fall in for an after-lunch stroll in the grounds was the commander-in-chief Mediterranean fleet, Rear-Admiral Sir Dudley Pound. By the end of this gentle exercise, the admiral had pressed John to come aboard the flagship, HMS *Barham*, and sail with her as guest of the commander-in-chief to Gibraltar.

A few weeks later, and one minute ahead of schedule, John's car pulled up at the Portsmouth quayside. Alerted by the flag lieutenant on the bridge, his glass trained on the dockside gate, a prodigious array of gold lace was, as a result, drawn up at the head of the gangway as John started the steep and slippery ascent. There was the Admiral of the Fleet and, saluting next, the Rear-Admiral Chief of Staff, then the captain of the flagship, followed by the flag lieutenant, and the officer and the midshipman of the watch. In due course, they put to sea, and all the little ships and the big ones too saluted with dipped ensigns, the sound of great sirens riding the sea breezes. The quayside, thronged with the waving hands of a thousand of the crew's friends and relatives, fell away; HMS *Repulse* was astern, and they gathered speed into the glittering waves of the Solent.

John was offered the undivided attention of the flag lieutenant throughout the voyage to Gibraltar; he was to move through the ship wherever inclination led and to talk with anyone and everyone to learn all he wanted. He applied himself to his wholly pleasurable task with delight, questioning officers and men with daunting intensity, easily mastering systems and facts. He quickly collected a very satisfying reputation aboard. How well it held when, with little warning, he was handed command of the ship, his account gives no hint. But, in telling his story many times in later years, it was quite clear that there was nothing else that he would rather have been doing. He heard the message to the commander-in-chief:

177

'Sir John Reith in charge of flagship'. But Sir John was in heaven. Then the signal *Disregard* was hoisted; without it, every ship would have followed *Barham*'s movements – which might from time to time have been erratic. The officer of the watch stood down while the happy substitute strained every nerve to alter course from 210° to 180° due south. With the ship's captain standing by, he gave his orders, and back from the helmsman in the wheelhouse came the response: 'Course one-eight-o – *SIR*'.

At evening, they sighted the *Deutschland*. She was returning from the Spanish Civil War, her melancholy task to bring home the German dead and wounded. But the reply was minimal – an acknowledgement and, with it, a request to be excused the nineteen-gun salute due to any ship with the admiral on board. Perhaps this was in deference to the wounded whom they carried.

Early one morning, they passed into the calm waters of the Straits of Gibraltar. For this, officers, men and guest were dressed in white. As they quietly slid into harbour, every ship again saluted the admiral's flag. HMS *Hood* was there, adding thunderously to the noble tumult. *Barham* tied up ahead of her. But, despite the ceremonies attached to arrival, John found Gibraltar a shabby place. Then, under an awning in the ship's bows, he stood before 1,000 men of the lower deck to speak and be questioned about the BBC; and, later, after a large dinner party glittering with admirals, generals and ships' captains, he spoke to a further gathering, their number swollen by civilians as well. The discussion, it seems, was rather purloined by the admirals, perhaps wishing to lay particular claim to their exhibit. Probably he never felt more loyal to, or proud of, the BBC than in such moments when he could publish it abroad and vicariously experience the romance of the tale he had to tell.

But an awful ordinariness descended when he transferred to a P&O liner to return to his office. He had been given a stirring send-off by *Barham*, transferring from one ship to the other in the admiral's barge so that curious passengers leaned over the railings, asking one another who this distinguished personage could be, so splendidly conveyed and now coming aboard. As she put to sea, the liner passed *Barham*; a signal was hoisted. John could not read it, which further depressed his dipping spirits; and so he had to content himself with having an acknowledgement returned. He ended his account of his enchanted days typically: 'I would willingly have stayed on in *Barham* even till the time of her sinking in 1941'.[1]

Later that year, my father decided that he would accompany the family on the kind of seaside holiday which he had already described as 'boring and provincial'. But he would take the opportunity to write his book about his First World War experiences. Assured that we were going to the seaside and that it would be in Cornwall, Christopher and I started to look out for it at approximately Basingstoke. And so, many hours, town centres, main roads and a picnic later, faint and far, and fleetingly too, I saw the blue-grey line of the distant sea. Momentarily stretched between the folding hills, it was quickly lost behind the hats in front and the waving tamarisk beyond.

My father was reading the final directions to the cottage: 'Follow the lane along the shore until the road commences to climb uphill ...'. But the rest was suddenly of no account as he complained about this most regrettable use of the language. 'Commences', he said in angry quotation. 'Can they not use the King's English rather than bowdlerised French? What are they trying to say? The road goes uphill – four words instead of six.' My mother, already starting to move up the offending hill, made no response to this attack on English usage, but unfortunately, instead, passed the drive to the cottage, so that further difficulties followed. Now, with little vision behind except from a very small mirror perched away ahead on the distant wing, she had to slide the car back, avoiding the ditches on both sides. She grabbed the handbrake, roared the engine and wrestled the wheel to steer us at last in between the wooden gateposts. Here, as we scrambled out, was a little white house perched on a terrace, its garden tumbling away before it, and a latch gate opening onto the dunes and the seashore. 'Just stay in the garden – don't go through the gate', came the warning voices as the two of us peeled off and fled down the path and

179

through the bushes. At once, we found a little stream gurgling down the hill and out below the fence, where it had carved a widening route for itself between the dunes and marram grass and then into the tracery of a hundred runnels, fan-shaped across the sand to join the sea.

Many years later on, I likened this flow to George Eliot's opening passage in *The Mill on the Floss*: 'where the broadening Floss hurries on between its green banks to the sea, and the loving tide, rushing to meet it, checks its passage with an impetuous embrace'.

We set about the important task of providing the stream with a dam; my father came and asked if we wanted help; unconvinced, he went away again. No sooner had we created a fine pool than I slipped and fell into it and had to be towed by the hand up the hill to the house, where, with unpacking in full swing, my sorry state was unhelpful. I dripped into more than one expanding puddle before dry clothes could be found.

But the incident soon faded behind hot sun, sand and sea. My father, dressed in an enormous red towelling bathing gown which my mother had made for him and in which he made the short journey to the beach, liked to pretend to be a very old doddery man, bent over and leaning heavily on a stick. We both found this funny, as we were meant to, and he spoke in a thin quivery voice. He liked to splash around in the sea on his back, and would occasionally bounce us up and down in the water – which was fun until it got a bit scary. My mother wore a blue costume with skirts which followed her in the water and then flowed about her as she tried to stand, out of breath from the diligent breaststroke which she pursued in short bouts to and fro. Otherwise, my father spent hours writing in the house, telling the story of his life as a soldier.

One afternoon, my mother persuaded him to come out on a picnic on Bodmin Moor. He preferred her to drive, and she certainly found that better too, what with his uncertain temper in relation to other road-users. Even as a passenger, he would lean across her to sound the horn when he felt that his road space was being infringed. I heard him say to my mother that he had to leave the BBC. And then – there was an almighty smash. We had collided with something enormous. Christopher and I were hauled out from the back by the nurse; and, a bit dazed, we walked down the lane, with Rufus as well. When we came back to the car, my mother and father were sitting at the edge of a field, my father with a wound above one eye being treated by the driver of the lorry with which we had collided. 'I'm sorry about the iodine, Sir,' he was saying, 'I believe it's a bit sore.' 'That's all right,' I heard my father say, 'the more it hurts the more good it does.' But I saw him wince as the kindly driver bent over him with his swab. Then I saw the awful hole in the side of the Wolseley, just where my mother had been sitting. She was very bruised and in pain. When the lorry man drove away – his vehicle, being higher and heavier, would still go – he said he would telephone for a taxi and a breakdown lorry. My father said it was nobody's fault.

The next day turned out very differently. Letters, telegrams and flowers started to arrive. The local telephone exchange reported that thirty-six newspapers had been trying all night to be put through; the telegraph boys cycled endlessly up and down the sandy lane, and the postman trudged up with a bulging postbag. And then came the flowers. Soon there were no more jugs or vases; buckets were filled, and more borrowed from intrigued villagers who wisely painted on their names first. But the reporters and photographers who swarmed into the village were more or less kept at bay by the local policeman; and the local postmaster, when some of the excitement began to die down, very sensibly, in view of his recent exertions beyond the normal call of duty, asked Sir John if he could get a job for his son in the BBC.

NOTE

1. Reith, *Into the Wind*, p. 287.

12

Cast Adrift

*I*N LATE March 1937, the ceremonial to mark the retirement from the BBC of John's deputy, Vice-Admiral Charles Carpendale, carried out with naval ritual, reminded John of his own imminent departure. This was distressing for him and perplexing for others. He did not know what he should do; and, unemployed at home, he brought an unwelcome intrusion into our affairs. Then he did not like the prime minister's wish that he should run Imperial Airways.

It was time for the BBC to say goodbye to Vice-Admiral Sir Charles Carpendale, for so many years John's deputy. He was the man whose sense of elegance in ceremony had graced the change from company to corporation, the BBC's tenth-anniversary celebration and every other event where wit and ease might mark the occasion. He was also the man who could get closer than most to the lonely figure of his chief, even to the extent of chiding him when he became small-minded and petulant. And so, when it came to the admiral's retirement, John sought to mask his distress with a frenzy of activity which would ensure that this farewell ceremony would be unlike any other. It would be carried off in style – in naval style, that is.

It would, for example, draw on the language in which Director General and Deputy Director General had come increasingly to exchange: a pastiche of naval speak, a form of communication which gave at least one of them great satisfaction. Instead of a telephone call, you 'sent a signal', for which you would 'come alongside'. In troublesome times, you were 'shipping it green'. And so, in planning the event, the Admiralty had come to John's aid. Almost certainly, they had given permission for the vice-admiral's flag to be hoisted on the roof of Broadcasting House; and now they supplied two buglers and four bo'sun's mates who, following the admiral's farewell speech, filed on from either side of the concert-hall platform – the first pipe as the admiral stepped off the platform, and the second as he was escorted out of the hall. John was quite overcome.

He was also being forcibly reminded of what to him was his own imminent departure. This was, to him, no less than a death. When the news was broken to the Board, despite their grumblings about his autocratic ways and morbid sensitivity, they were genuinely shocked. He, however, walked as though in sleep, never quite giving up hope that the Almighty, or Mother and Father, would intervene between them, bringing about a great and liberating change to release him from what, it seemed, was the doom that was rushing up at him. For example, Leslie Hore-Belisha, barrister, politician and 1st Baron, at that time Secretary of State for War, was often diligent on John's behalf, and found support for the view that he should be an Under Secretary of State and head of the War Office. But this idea disappeared into oblivion as John, now again disempowered, did nothing to help himself.

At the time of his going, on 19 July 1938, the solid achievement behind him was well known. He was a man acclaimed worldwide, loaded with honours – but obsessed with failure. At the mercy of his own compulsions, he could give no believable explanation to Malcolm Muggeridge, in a television interview which looked back on his life, as to why he had left. Muggeridge pointed out that John was one of the three or four most powerful people in the

UK, yet he had suddenly walked out. John responded by saying that he felt he was going to be, to some extent, unemployed, and certainly not fully stretched. He had left the BBC because he thought there was nothing else he could do there. It was, he said, 'a frightful mistake'. And an implausible one, too. The captain of an ocean-going liner expects to be 'fully stretched' when putting to sea; but, when the ship is full and by, the captain certainly does not see himself as out of a job. Rationally, John had no idea why he was leaving.

He did still need, however, to prove to himself who he was – something that the BBC, for all its headline-grabbing nature, had not managed to do. To anyone else, but not John, it was clear that no position, however powerful and prominent, was ever going to afford him the relief he sought, through which he could prove to himself, to his family and to the world what he could do. He would have to leave the BBC and find another, more glorious position. The journalist and author Graham Greene's interpretation of things for himself is more subtle: 'I would have discovered, I suppose, in Greek literature ... the sense of doom that lies over success – the feeling that the pendulum is about to swing'.[1]

When he finally knew that he had to go, John did not know whether he was walking out or being pushed – and, if he was going, where he was going to. There was, of course, British Ambassador in Washington, an appealingly stagey position to be in. Or he could follow up an opening in the railways, imitating in some part his grandfather and his work on the Scottish North-Eastern railways. In this way, he could have revisited his old engineering skills from the days of his apprenticeship. Had John in later years been able to apply his powers of rationalisation on the railways, Dr Beeching might have lived in vain – he it was who was preferred for the job of railway nationalisation in the 1960s. John could have done any of these things; but, in a personal quagmire, and most vulnerable, he made no move to fight his corner.

'There is a great deal of unmapped country within us, which would have to be taken into account in an explanation of our gusts and storms',[2] wrote George Eliot. Hugh Carleton Greene, as Director General in the 1970s, remarked on John's gifts as an administrator and his performance as an autocrat. But the BBC, he also remarked, in 1938 numbering over 4,000 staff, had grown beyond John's grasp of administrative structures and his judgement of people. John was being increasingly criticised – and my mother, who sometimes understood him very well, saw through his 'don't care' remarks to that most painful minding of his.

Neville Chamberlain, the prime minister, offered John a job that he did not want but did not refuse. Instead, a rather silly exchange took place in which John asked Chamberlain: 'Are you instructing me to go?' The reply came, very reasonably, that he was not using that word. John asked: 'Do you want me to go?' Chamberlain replied: 'This is really too strong a word, but if you went to Imperial Airways I would be glad'.[3] John eventually went to Imperial Airways in July 1938. The prime minister was possibly acting under pressure from the government, which had had enough of erratic brilliance for a while. 'Nothing', wrote one critic, 'became Reith like his leaving the BBC.'

None of these things reached the nursery. But a certain foreboding attached to a visit to London Zoo, rather unexpectedly arranged by my mother. She was not in the habit of taking us up to London, feeling as she did that if children grew up in a large safe house and a large safe garden, with a large safe supervisor and abundant toys, the less said about the outside world, especially in the form of other children, the better. I suppose she feared the big world as its tumult surged around her husband. Anyway, for whatever reason, there we were at the penguin pool, that brand new addition to the Zoo with all its spiral ramps; and there, too, was a crowd of press photographers, apparently waiting for us. Christopher and I had to leave the spectators' area and join the penguins in their arena, now – like them – to be stared at by the crowds leaning over the parapet. Using the buckets of fish which we were given, we were to inveigle the penguins into a wobbling approach, followed by ghastly gulps as they seized the proffered fish. They were very charming as they clustered round with their orange-stained bosoms and sticking-out flippers. But the clicking and winding of cameras and the voracious crowd above were a bit off-putting, especially as I had no idea why they were all there.

John's departure from Broadcasting House, with neither cameras nor entourage, was nevertheless staged for deepest, loneliest melancholy. On the date of his departure, he prevented the planned gathering and presentation and went down in the lift, Muriel with him. She shook hands with Plater, the senior commissionaire; John rushed on in tears. Then a macabre, ridiculous journey round the countryside followed, with Cecil Graves, now Deputy Director General, and Jo Stanley, John's faithful secretary. The purpose: himself to shut down the engines of the high-powered transmitters in Droitwich. Symbolically, he was closing down his own powers.

From then on, in doom-heavy tones, he would tell anyone who would listen, especially television cameras, about his stupendous folly in leaving one of the most responsible and rewarding jobs in the world. This 'one long silent shriek of despair' was the pain of that compulsion under which he had to leave and which he purported to regard as his mistake. From 1938 until his death in 1971, he dreamt, thought, spoke and lived the BBC, but now in almost unrelieved tones of contumely and disparagement. He announced two reasons for leaving: he thought that there would no longer be enough for him to do; and the prime minister wanted him to go to Imperial Airways to run it. How odd that he did not think of a part-time job to do along with the BBC, to fill the hours – or, very simply, to refuse the PM's offer. A whiff of sham hangs around his public reasoning in support of that impulsive, self-destructive route which he took by walking out of the BBC. More truthfully, he did not know why he had done it; nor did he really think he had made a mistake in going. He only knew he had to leave. In the general muddle, he resorted to his practised cry for pity – but this time it was the more excruciating and he the more pitiable. In the spotlight of the public perception, he had driven a knife into the heart of his public persona. Inertia set in.

We have already quoted a journalist's comment on 'that peculiarly Scottish ethic which produces a super ego of terrifying proportions and a view of human experience as an endless assault course'. We can connect John's fantasies of power and position with his lonely childhood, and all those things that followed from the pious predispositions of his parents in Glasgow.

He was more or less rejected by his family. His father, while dis-approving of worldly ambition, was convinced that, among his clever children, John was a failure. He never noticed that John was differently constituted from the others. His mother doled out attention in small doses. When John was young, self-willed and unruly, Glasgow Academy no longer had room for him; instead, he became a misfit at an English boarding school. No-one heard his cry for help: 'If only someone, father, headmaster, anyone, had talked to me', he wrote as he complained about the absence of home life, 'antagonisms and reserves marked amongst us'. But, as a young person reaching adulthood, John's solution was to exempt his parents from criticism and, making of them his inner objects, idealise them. He seemed to need the perfect person, their blemishes sidelined and then obliterated. This is a solution which the psychoanalysts call 'a defence against ambivalence towards the person's internal objects'.[4] It is a solution that promises freedom from guilt – but is hugely brittle.

The more so as John went on to include himself in this false category of perfection. Years later, my mother dared to ask him if he had ever made a mistake. After a suitable silence, apparently giving the matter careful consideration, he gave the answer: 'No'. He had, of course, for the time being excised the question of his leaving the BBC, the alleged mistake to which he had attached very great publicity. But then he never really believed that that had been a mistake.

Because his first family, in the form of his parents, had eventually shown themselves to be imperfect and had therefore failed, he had to find another family that would not let him down – a new and a better one over which he might exercise invention and control. And so he found, or invented, the BBC, and made it his to lead from a position of phenomenal power. But, sixteen years on, he had to turn and hate this family too, because, like his own family, it had gone against him and done him an injury. Meanwhile, everyone – Governors, Chamberlain, Churchill, and most particularly the successor being lined up to take his place – each to John was an idiot.

Once, John had admitted to fear. At best, more than usually prescient on behalf of the BBC and its inborn need for change and development, he was unable to accommodate to the idea of television, even though the BBC could not advance without it. 'A state without the means of change is without the means of its continuation', wrote Edmund Burke. Perhaps, after all, John had to go.

Here, we are considering the possibility that personal hurt, arising from early insult, lives on; and we are questioning the effects of unresolved conflict that, as it makes up the history of a life, contributes not so much to its decisions as to its grim inevitabilities, those things on whose nature we can only speculate. Such hidden motives, emerging from obscurity, assert themselves in the form of nameless inner compulsions before sinking back into anonymity, as unrecognised by the subject as they are inexplicable to the onlooker. From such follows an outcome that nobody seems able to avoid, far less understand.

Clinging to some chimera of power, John had, until asked to desist, interfered with the process of appointing his successor. Instead of Cecil Graves, his deputy whom he favoured – and with whom he must have felt he could remain involved – they chose Frederick Ogilvie, an academic and Vice-Chancellor of Queen's University, Belfast. That John's judgement was perhaps less at fault than that of the Governors did not release him from the charge of interference, to the extent that the Chairman had to tell him that the finalising meeting would have to go ahead without him. Instead, when Ogilvie was in post, a dutiful invitation was sent to him to lunch at Harrias House. Here, his afternoon entertainment was to take part in a tree-felling operation in the garden. Ogilvie, who was one-armed, was handed a saw to help him in his task.

For the second time in his life, John now suffered irreparable loss. Charlie was gone, and now the BBC.

As though in some primitive response to this inner incoherence, and with too much time at home, John had to seek out tasks – minuscule ones – on which to impose his compensatory compulsion for order. My child-sized desk, of which I was proudly possessive, suddenly became a candidate for his reforming zeal, and one day I entered the nursery to find him insecurely perched on its junior chair, his knees sticking up like tree roots above the surface of the desk. He could not understand, he complained, why the drawers were designed so that they did not reach the tops of their respective compartments. I felt drawn into the general air of dissatisfaction. Nor did he think much of their individual colours. Well, perhaps one day, when I had outgrown my desk, I would not either; but just now I had always felt rather pleased by their cheerful look – colours carried their own messages. I was, I somewhere felt, quite into celebrating childhood and had no wish to be hustled through it and into adulthood and its sombre accompaniments.

Anyway, I had my own way of arranging the contents of each drawer; and, even if it did not chime in with some elevated systems theory, I always knew where things were and why they were there – an infection of a sort picked up from the region of my father's own desk. And so, following his rationalisation of my crayons, rubbers, drawing blocks, scissors, scrapbook pictures, *Riding* magazines and so on, I immediately set about the gradual restoration of my system.

Next, he parked himself at my mother's desk, to 'help' her with her bills and accounts. While she rather cherished an image of herself as orderly, he felt that her disposition of an unpaid butcher's bill, a letter from her sister Elsie, a Christmas list of two years earlier and my drawing of a teddy – and much more – all in the same unnerving heap called for his masterly touch, which he proceeded to exert. And so he opened up her household account book to find it three months in arrears – and, because he could not resist adding up a row of figures, he found more with which to upbraid her. Then, in the lower drawers of the bureau, among old account books and letters, he found a dog's collar and some escaped sewing things.

Christopher's desk was in no need of the improving touch, and this was because there was something else to be tackled: Christopher was to be sent away to boarding school. The parents would have argued that they were doing this for the boy's good; it was, however, on John's part more to do with his need for establishment membership, and on hers the impossibility of doing anything other than agree and conform. And so, one day, propelled by the maddening curiosity of the child, I had followed the sound of Christopher's tears into the dining room – where, prepared to feel virtuously superior in view of my tearless state, I could see that here was trouble indeed. Christopher (whom we called CJ) was on our father's knee, where a self-conscious effort at fatherhood was in progress. I had not seen my father trying to be tender with CJ. He was saying things to him about Jesus, but getting little response. This was no place to be, and I went to see if I could find my mother to ask what was happening. 'Christopher is soon to be going away to school. He's feeling very sad', she said, and looked even sadder herself. I felt I should start crying myself because of the general climate, but my curiosity was stronger. 'Why does he have to go away to school?' I asked. 'Can't he just go on going to Mrs Solomon's?' This was the very small local school, which CJ had been attending. He had never seemed to enjoy it particularly, and I supposed – although I certainly could not see how – that the new scheme was to make things better for him. But then all the signals at that moment were of exactly the opposite. And my mother's answer did not make anything more clear: 'It's good for boys to go away to school', she said; but she seemed not to know why this should be so. 'Will I be sent away to school?' I asked. 'Oh no', she said firmly. That was a relief – except that I felt I should support Christopher. It was as though he were a victim of some sort – not that I knew the word – and the fact that he seemed so often to incur his father's displeasure and criticism must somehow be connected. I began to think of the world as in some senses vindictive; I would have to look out for myself.

Not that this was an entirely new idea. Already, I knew well what it was to be the younger and less muscular of two children: to be interrupted in some private dream game of my own with an imperious call of 'What *are* you doing?' And then instructed to carry those logs from here to there, and – no – 'take the other end of the saw. No, *here*, silly.' And so, keen to earn my place in the universe, I did so, with muscles that began too readily to ache taking the place of all those kind fantasies. Christopher, I felt, behind all his busyness and his helping in the garden, had his parents' authority; I, with my dreaming, my splashy painting and inexpert piano-playing, did not.

It was not a happy journey to Sandroyd School, near Cobham in Surrey. At last, I was starting to understand that CJ was going to be left behind; that we would be returning without him, an empty place on the back seat beside me. I was no further forward in understanding why; and, as we went up the drive and saw this most forbidding building at the end of it, I realised that my mother was crying too. I was horrified. I thought that grown-ups did not cry. Christopher was giving it all he had got, and so I could not but join in too. All this was beyond even my father's managing.

As Christopher was trying to say what he wanted to say, the head-master's wife appeared. Mrs Ozanne was covered in furs and false smiles. Suddenly, there was a need to make some show of normality; and, after many uncomfortable exchanges and things said about being happy at school, which had to be quite untrue, Christopher had to go off with Mrs Ozanne. As we drove away, I looked out of the back window to see him, head down, walking away beside the headmaster's wife; she, with her hand on his shoulder, was firmly propelling him towards that ghastly front door. My mother, father and I drove home in distressed silence.

My father, whose forebears had been chilled by the east winds of Kincardineshire and that land's austerity, nevertheless, by his very different route, arrived at predictable conclusions: that work was of more importance than people, of whatever age. Emotionally undernourished, and nursing that forbidding tradition from which he came, he had to simulate rather than experience affection. Life for the forebears at subsistence level held little joy, added to which was Presbyterianism's roots in Calvinism. That meant that any attainment, unless in biblical studies, might well be frivolous. But John, having succeeded beyond the expectations of most, then felt the backlash of his inheritance, and the success which he had won for himself turned on him as though in punishment. He took to rubbishing his own creations as well as those of others.

A few months after Christopher had been sent away to school, John was, himself, away for a long time. To me, this made very little difference, caught up as I was with a programme of governesses who followed one another in and out of the house with the alacrity of a speeded-up movie. John's absence did mean his being spared, for a while, the heavy processes of Paying Attention to Marista. He was away for several weeks cruising in the Caribbean Sea. The Governor of the Bank of England, Montague Norman, had invited my mother and father on a five-week cruise. She, though pressed by both men, had insisted that she could not be away from home for so long, even though Christopher himself was already away.

Even if she had been on board, however, he would still have elected to spend more time with another woman than he should have done, continuing to see her after his return, and, as a result, making of my mother's birthday something of a mishap as — over flowers, crystallised fruits from Fortnum and Mason, and dinner — he explained to her about his 'new attitude to life'. She managed a robust response to the effect that the kind birthday words and gestures were of little account as long as he was flirting with other women. All the lavish gifts for everyone which accompanied his homecoming from the West Indies were because, while deeply sentimental about his family, he would continue his attentions to other women, about which, quite probably, he saw nothing either odd or wrong. My mother went on her own to Christopher's school sports.

John's 'new attitude' to life included a change from his teetotal state. The comments of others showed both relief — that Sir John Reith was able, after all, to climb down a bit — and disappointment that this remote figure, so easy to idealise, could show signs of membership of the human race after all. A teetotaller who drank whisky; a smoker who complained that the habit was dirty and pernicious; a castigator of employees who had affairs while himself being seldom without a flutter of his own; a man who regarded the afterlife with expectation ('we will all be together in heaven', he said, as though this would be as beguiling a prospect for others as apparently it was for him) but who considered suicide; a man who made peremptory demands for salary and expenses increases but refused a share of the profits of the *Radio Times*, which he had started – his views were so contradictory that either somebody is being inaccurate or we are not thinking of the same person. But you cannot confuse John Reith with anyone else. Splendour, pathos and downright wickedness all combined in him – 'a man', according to a review of Ian McIntyre's book *The Expense of Glory* on its publication, 'ruled by infatuation, seeking the big job, the great cause, "conscious of the abilities that almost overwhelm me"'. At one and the same time part of a providential plan and also programmed for calamity, his name has nevertheless passed into the language – and Reithian standards have become the benchmark for today.

NOTES

1. Graham Greene, essay: 'The Lost Childhood', *The Penguin Book of 20th-Century Essays* (Allen Lane, 1999), p. 200, by permission of David Higham Associates.
2. George Eliot, *Daniel Deronda*.
3. Ian McIntyre, p. 238, from Reith, *Diary*, 3.5.38.
4. Charles Ryecroft, *A Critical Dictionary of Psychoanalysis*, entry: 'Idealisation'.

13

The Queen Mary and the Statendam

A PRE-WAR trip to the USA, with elaborate arrangements made for escorting the family from the eastern to the western seaboard, was the headiest experience of my childhood. The return journey, with its night-time war adventures, was memorable for different reasons.

She towered like a cliff above the quayside, the giant letters of her name leaning down from the outward curve of her bow: QUEEN MARY. On the quay, there were a thousand bustling figures, Lilliputians beside her; more moved like ants about her decks. With deeply throbbing engines far below, she put to sea, the massive ropes and hawsers hauled aboard. An agitation of tugs and lighter vessels clustered around. Her siren shuddered into life, a sound as though from long ago to make the airwaves tremble. Launched from John Brown's yard at Clydebank two years earlier in 1937, she was the largest liner in the world – the cathedral of the Atlantic. As she crossed the ocean, each slow majestic downward slide rode deep into the rollers and was followed by a long, unhurried upward climb, the spume furies endlessly chiding her prow.

She was a temporary township of expensive people, lavishly accepting the abundance offered. The evening meal sparkled with diamonds, and a Palm Court orchestra played. One evening, after the soup, the leader came out from among his palm-tree fronds, he and his violin, and bowed their way across to our table. What, he enquired, would we like his orchestra to play? No doubt considering Wagner's *March of the Valkyries*, my father prepared his reply but found that this gracious violin was addressing the young. I spoke up for *The Blue Danube*; my father wheeled round, startled. The waltz floated over the sounds of cutlery, and some nodding tiaras munched in time. But, by the voyage's end, I wearied a little of *The Blue Danube*.

Then our great ship steamed majestically up the Hudson River, and we saw the skyline of the world. My mother was excited and my father taller and more successful than ever. We went up the Empire State Building, at that time the world's tallest, where, like the *Queen Mary*, only the superlative would do for my father. Many sombre men were there to receive us. They came forward with outstretched hands for my father, polite ones for my mother, and dutiful ones for us. The friendly ones pressed on despite my mother's reserve as we trailed through importantly opened doors and sat quietly at best restaurant tables.

After that, we went to the World's Fair in an open-topped bus – and this bus was odd. It had been used only once before, by the young King and Queen on a visit, and people drew back to let us by and stared – we seemed to be terribly important. We had dinner under the night sky among the fountains with their hanging colours; they rose to become a column of brightness dividing the night before falling to nothing.

It was dusk in Winnipeg, Canada, where another urgent group of men were gathered. Disembarking from our train, we followed them in the half-dark, I a little anxiously crossing the high network of railway lines, dodging junctions, cables and hand-operated controls. It was nearly dark in the great engine roundhouse, and spotlights picked out engines like sleeping giants, all still and quiet in their own silent reservations of power.

195

Then, recalled to action, shining pistons were at work in billowing steam and smoke discharged in titanic blasts. There they would be, forging their way through the desert heat of the central American plain, their great bell mounted above and the thrusting cowcatcher ahead.

Then we journeyed across Canada with the Canadian Pacific Railway to western Alberta. To occupy an entire coach is something one supposes to fall to royalty and heads of state. But, since my father saw himself up with them anyway, he attracted the same extravagant treatment. This exclusive coach, with sleeping, dining and sitting accommodation, was the last on the train and opened onto a balcony: you could stand out there and view the Rocky Mountains, rising up to wound the sky with arrogant peaks, blue-canyoned below, clad in black mantles of forests tipping into severe ravines. Gripping its narrow shelf, our labouring engine beat slower and louder; the sound of its bell kicked from side to side of the echoing chambers of the mountains and then on into the next valley as, in the very end of the train, we came on later. Then another engine came to help — and this time, coupled to our end coach, it leaned up against our platform, a great clock-like face peering in a companionable way, with much snorting and hissing. For me, all this was not just little short of heaven; it *was* heaven.

At Jasper National Park in Alberta, a chipmunk was already on the windowsill of our log cabin as we approached. Inside was a bowl of fruit and someone's present for me of a little birch-bark dish. Green grass swept down to the lakeside; and huge trees, in peaks of evergreen like more Rocky Mountains, grew from it. Beyond was Mount Edith Cavell, named after the brave English nurse who had cared for friend and foe alike in the First World War and whom the Germans had executed for helping fugitives to escape. Everywhere there were blossoms; above some, a tiny creature hung motionless, suspended between two small mists: a hummingbird on busy wings.

My mother had a movie camera, about which she became very excited or very anxious or both. With her and her camera, we went out, later than bedtime, to see the creatures. And there he was — a large dark shadow, on his head his antlers like shelves above him. 'Moose', said someone.

196

Another shade moved beneath the trees. 'Elk', said another. We watched them slip away into their own dark velvet world. By the lake, the beavers were too busy to bother with us, dark forms with great rudder tails moving busily below the water's surface, noses and bright eyes above.

But then another chasm opened. It came from nowhere and it came unexplained, bringing with it cancellations, indecisions, foreboding and arrangements. It was called War, and war meant that we had to leave Jasper, that my father had to go back to London. Like luggage, we were back in New York, planted in leather sofas that you could not properly sit in and your legs stuck out in front. My mother perched on the edge of her chair. I hated the flat black hat she wore, heavy and dark like everything else. My father, unusually agitated, never stopped walking up and down. Grim men came and went. Everyone waited; I certainly did not know what they were waiting for. Then, suddenly, my father had gone on board another liner – but we were not going, and it must have been the War that stopped us. Kindly friends swept us up, my mother, brother and me. Jean was the Jeanette of John's youthful sojourn in Swarthmore, near Philadelphia, in the First World War. Jean's friendship had remained, as she promised, constant; and now she and Tom were taking us, first to their seaside cabin in Ocean City in Maryland and then back to Swarthmore where they lived.

In Ocean City, the heat was stifling. Perhaps the idea of a seaside visit was to help my mother through a difficult time following my father's departure. But a clapboard house with gauze doors and a veranda commanding a view of the opposite row of clapboard houses with verandas, and a heat-sealed patch of earth in front of each, did not appeal to her. Looking back, I see a scene such as Arthur Miller painted in *Death of a Salesman*, when the owners of every Studebaker and Chevrolet in each driveway tried with a quiet desperation to counter 'the cavernous Sunday afternoons', polishing and inventing mechanical adjustments. For my part, I stared through the slats of the Venetian blind, watching the sand eddies in the hot roadway whipped into a spinning frenzy by a passing car, subsiding, and then moved along before the breeze into little heaps against the kerb.

The heat waves seemed to tangle with the anxiety waves of the grown-ups. The only voice, which droned on continuously and repetitively, came from the wireless. 'This is the BBC. This is London', it said. 'The prime minister, the Rt Hon. Neville Chamberlain, will now address the nation.' And then – 'we are now at war with Germany'. Well – the BBC was surely my father, and he would be able to turn off Alvar Liddell the announcer and stop the War. But then, I thought later, perhaps he was not anything to do with the BBC any more. And he had left to sail home in a ship called the *Aquitania*. My mother became very quiet, and later I learned of the sinking of her sister ship, the *Mauritania*. Just then, I was more concerned, if possible, to shake free from the attentions of a nanny, whose large bosom seemed in an unwelcome way to bend over every enterprise of mine. Nannies seemed to feel that among the many things they had to correct was the child's view that life was exciting, an endless source of things to be explored.

All the same, outside was unappealing. When we had arrived in Ocean City, towing the nanny, I had followed the roar of the surf to the shore. It seemed that the whole Atlantic must be behind those rollers, easily able in a single primitive surge to carry away all these vending shacks and hoardings, the detritus of petty commerce, all stuck about like litter on the shore. The water rushed through and past the strands of the promenade, welling up hugely among the metallic complex of black girders, stays, angles and horizontals – and then with similar compulsion falling into deep hollows as though sucked from below. 'Don't get too near the edge, dear', called the nanny.

Then, back in Swarthmore, the streets were lit by the splashy brilliance of the autumn maples. In the cooler air, their nutmeg smell filled the garden. But my mother's anxiety about John in London, and us in the States, was long and grey, in contrast to the vehement trees. Tom and Jean McCabe were most solicitous.

And then, three months on, there was John, seated in Uncle Tom's library, beaming pleasure and self-congratulation at having made it across the Atlantic. All his life, his trick was to arrive unexpectedly and to startle people into near-heart failure. His ageing parents had narrowly escaped extinction when he had appeared without warning from the First World War front as they took their holiday evening stroll across a Perthshire meadow. Now, his expectations of a wartime appointment having been dashed, he had set out again for America to bring his family home. 'The fact that there was no job for me was all the fault of that blasted Churchill. If he would let me, I could win the war for him.' The name of Churchill was one I was to hear frequently, learning the particular kind of way in which the name came to be detonated to denote spectacular loathing. 'CHUCH-HILL' was how it sounded; and he would then say it several times more to himself as though to enhance some specific effect.

Frustrated by the barrier that was Churchill – 'they tell me you are difficult to work with', he had growled to John – he had hit on the plan to recross the Atlantic and enjoy the stimulus of the danger of some wandering submarine despatching his ship to the bottom of the sea. He would collect his family and return with them to England, so that together they would 'face the music'. The Atlantic was already a graveyard; but John needed to flout the enemy, the circumstances and Churchill, and also get shot of the chauffeur's wife, who was supposed to cook for him but fussed instead.

Anyway, there at the far end of the library in Swarthmore was John, his habit of demonstrating rare moments of satisfaction fully on the go: his hands were spread out, and his long fingers drummed hard against the bald dome of his head, causing starched cuffs and gold cufflinks all to produce a local commotion. Known as 'flapping', it was a joy to us children because, at least for a little while, there would be no rages to manage. Soon, there was a spectacular 'flap' in progress.

This bravado of his was exciting, and illogically I felt that, if we were struck by a submarine, my father would know what to do and would send it packing. There were almost no other passengers travelling with my mother, father, brother and me on the *Statendam*; it was, after all, December 1939, and it was unusual to be crossing the Atlantic in an easterly direction. Hundreds of families, who could afford to, were fleeing westwards to America to escape the war threat. Under a cloudless sky, my father, for some reason wearing a heavy black coat, strode up and down the decks, conspicuous among the seagulls. I thought he would have liked to have had the captain's job, high up there on the bridge, in command of his own ship.

Change was in the air, however. After four nights at sea, my mother said: 'Tonight we will all be going to bed in our clothes'. I was not sure why. Then there was a lifejacket on the floor beside my bed; but now the feeling that I had had, that our ship was special, that she sailed in a cocoon of safety — that feeling began to drain away. What if we were torpedoed and had to swim in our lifejackets in the icy waters and great waves? Later, I understood that, as a Dutch ship, at a time when Holland was not yet in the war, she was to some extent protected. This explained the gaily coloured lights which, hanging between the mastheads, pierced the night darkness. Giant letters spelled HOLLAND on the ship's sides; the orange glow which they gave off slid about on the dimpled surface of the black water and mingled with the white spume tracks.

When we woke in the morning, still fully clothed, we were entering the English Channel. This was home. This was the journey nearly completed; it was wonderful to sight land. So close it seemed; so beckoning. But what was that? Things sticking up out of the water. They looked like ships' masts. And then, momentarily, as the water surged, the clear rim of a funnel. A sunken ship lay close off shore. As she rested on the seabed, the mast moved with the in-and-out of the waves. Then there was another stricken ship, blown up by a mine. We sailed past one, the evilly sensitive plugs in its perimeter sticking out of the waves and then quickly covered by them again. The newspaper headlines that day read: 'Sir John Reith brings his family home to face the music'.

Darkness came, and there were signs that the liner was dropping anchor. My mother said: 'We are going to get off the ship tonight just in case the Germans find out that Daddy is on board and try to take him away. This way, they won't find us.' She added: 'We would be better not to go on to Rotterdam with the ship'. I was to pack my little red bag with my best things, and we would be picked up by a small ship later that evening.

After a long wait, it was time to leave. We were guided below, leaving behind us the luxury quarters which had been home, and then on down and down and down, stepping into engine territory where the smell of oil was heavy on the air, where metal struck metal and mighty engines throbbed. Men shouted; they caught sight of us – an odd party, seemingly dressed for the Arctic – and shouted some more in friendly greeting. If we went much further down, we would surely be standing on the ocean floor. Suddenly, there was an opening ahead. It was just big enough to see black water rise, and fall away, and disappear. If we were to jump here, where could we jump to? I clutched my red bag, wondering if the dicky clasp would hold and whether my alarm clock would suddenly and inappropriately play its tune, the *Bluebells of Scotland*. Just then, a small vessel shot up past our vision – and as suddenly dropped down again. This was about to be impossible. Even my father was perturbed.

I was surrounded by several large black oilskins. There were men inside them, one of whom asked if he could take my red bag. He threw it expertly to be caught by outstretched arms on the rapid rise of the small deck below. Was I to do that same thing? Not yet, it seemed. The roll of the liner to starboard had exactly to coincide with the instant on which the little ship rose on the crest of the wave before plummeting down into the next trough.

Suddenly, I was thrown out, glimpsing the sea glint in that black gap of turbulence between the two ships – and then into a tangle of black outstretched oilskin arms, roars of approval, and a further downward plunge into the deep recesses of the waves. We rode up again, and there was my mother and then my brother strongly and expertly caught. My father's six foot six inches must have been the most testing of all. Then came all twenty of the embarrassing bits of luggage. They say that, after we left her, the *Statendam* sailed on to Rotterdam; there, she came under enemy fire and was burned out.

The little ship soon cast away from the liner, and we went below, where there was tea and biscuits. There was a rough wooden table, benches, and another hugely smiling captain. But my brother suddenly and quickly slid sideways along the bench. There was no mistaking the signs, and he was quickly up on deck. The little ship was plunging about like a thing possessed. Makeshift seats were arranged alongside the fo'c's'le on upturned trunks; they could be prevented from tipping and so pitching the occupants into the sea only by dint of our never relinquishing hold of the handrail above and behind. The pain of the cold and the fixed position gave way to a penetrating numbness which travelled through my body. The good captain regularly came to visit us, joking easily about the mine that we sailed past. 'The little ships are great at this game', he said. 'They can dodge these fellows no bother.' I looked back at that curved shape, now barely discernible on the water's surface, a thing from hell which we had escaped and which another innocent ship might not. Thankfulness was chipping away at the fear. With no lights to guide, how could our crew have steered clear?

We came ashore at Ramsgate in Kent. Any minute now, the penetrating dark would be relieved with lights. It was one thing having to climb up a vertical pier ladder when your limbs were stiffened with the cold and you had no grip; it was another being quite unable to see it. There was no let-up from the pressing dark.

There followed an interminable wait. It seemed that we were in a coastguard's lookout point of some kind, barricaded in by the luggage and uneasily watched by awkward fellows who adopted alternating poses of retreating embarrassment and mild challenge, trying to figure out what it was about the war that, with no warning, had cast up the BBC from out of the English Channel in the early hours of the morning.

Then there was a move. Burness and Jo Stanley had come, she in these strange times running Harrias House, which was still obstinately stuck in Edwardian times with maids, gardeners and chauffeur, all living in their separate quarters and trying to keep the show on the road. Now, while Burness drove the large black Buick, Jo drove the Wolseley – fully restored after the crash two years earlier. Of palest blue at a time when the few cars on the road were mostly black, it made me wonder – never having thought about such things as targets – whether a German would look down and shoot at this pale wraith travelling towards London, its masked headlights giving off the weakest glow. And so, when Jo, exhausted and unable to see, drove the luggage-filled Wolseley into the Buick, we shot up in terror from deepest sleep.

This strange procession made its way through a deserted London and cleverly on to the Oxford road. At last, the close hedges of the tiny lane showed up; we turned into the gateway of Harrias House and tumbled out into the warm hall of home. Even in the blackout, one could make out holly decked all around and a Christmas tree with bells. Jo Stanley had been hard at work. And, in a half-circle, the servants: all six had waited up and were here to greet and curtsey their welcome. There was Edith, the head housemaid. 'Oh, my lady,' she said, 'welcome home'; and Edith's pretty sister Evelyn said: 'It's good you're safely back'. Freda, the parlour maid, had a ready greeting; and I was especially pleased to see Sybil, who was the nursery maid. 'Oh, Miss Marista,' she said, 'how you have grown!'

14

Old Wuthering Heights

WITH MY father's ambitions for wartime responsibilities thwarted, he was at home more than anyone would have chosen. My mother, like other women, toiled to keep the show on the road; but family relationships were strained.

The ebb and flow of the war, the victories and disasters, came and went well distanced from the domesticities of Harrias House. El Alamein, Dunkirk and Pearl Harbor were names that figured large during the war. Occasionally, I saw or heard these names; but they came as from another civilisation and for another generation. They were never discussed; even the occasional news bulletin did little to puncture the household's preoccupation with the home enterprise or interrupt its attention to the central challenge of outdoing restrictions and beating the enemy.

But the enemy, for my father, often unemployed, was not so much the fascists in Germany as the autocrats of the Services and of Whitehall: Churchill, Montgomery and Mountbatten, against whom he levelled his armoury of invective. From time to time, he received grudging war appointments from Churchill. 'Old Wuthering Heights – there he goes', said Churchill to a colleague. My father wrote to the prime minister, most tactlessly, that he fully appreciated that he did not like him.

John Colville, Churchill's wartime secretary, and later knighted, had an insider's view of John in government. 'He gave the impression of ruthless efficiency, but the efficiency seemed to desert him when, ennobled for the purpose, he entered Government. It is hard to say whether he was worse as Minister of Information or as Minister of Transport, but whatever his failures his achievement at the BBC is a claim to enduring fame. His Scottish dourness appealed to some, who thought it a sign of his honesty and virtue (which it probably was). He loathed Churchill, whom he found insufficiently puritan; but Churchill, who had other worries, took no notice of the fact.'[1] To his diary, his best and dubious friend, John told how 'a crushing, awful and unspeakable remorse comes on me when I think how far I've failed'. He regretted his marriage, he wrote, and he found his children disappointing. But anyone who writes a diary has decided somewhere in themselves that these things will be made public matters.

With little in London to call him there, John and my mother went about their separate occupations in Beaconsfield as though along parallel lines of a railway track. She believed that she could do the work of the six servants – by now all departed – serving three cooked meals a day and maintaining the silly standards whereby every bath and passage was cleaned daily. My father wrote up his diary and the endless letters which occupied his day and which the postman lifted when he made his delivery, as an obligement. He did his accounts, chastised the gardener and sent Christopher to Eton, regardless of its suitability.

Instead of the enormous car in which John used to be driven to the station, a thin little Austin 7 was drawn up at the portico like a sparrow perched on an eagle's eyrie. Meticulously positioned as before, Burness stood looking hard into the privet hedge while the large lordship had to negotiate a huge black coat, himself and many expletives into a hopeless space. With chauffeur and passenger wedged together, and the doors shut with difficulty, it took the exertions of all the Austin's seven horsepower to wobble on its spindly wheels down the drive and out between the disdainful gateposts.

Family conversation was as sparse as ever. You might try, from time to time, to poke in your contribution, only to feel that it had not lodged anywhere. You did not converse with Lord Reith; you listened only. Occasionally, at lunch, he made a statement; but it was more likely to be about the weeds in the path or the bones in the fish pie. Hardly the stuff of dialogue. He was deaf to anything he did not want to hear, and was preoccupied with how terribly he had failed in life, as usual.

But, for the days at home, he had a particular interest and consolation. This was the store cupboard, one of several ancillary rooms set within the many twists of the back passage on its way to the tradesmen's door. Since it was wartime, there were no tradesmen to call there, and the gardener, Clark, cleaned the shoes in the boot room opposite the door. There was no-one to use the servants' lavatory at the end of the corridor. In the store cupboard, my father would survey the shelves packed with jam, jellies and bottled fruit from the garden, the jars of sugar defying the two-ounce wartime ration, and tins of biscuits, fruit cakes and tinned meats sent from America. They arrived in large battered boxes marked 'Unsolicited Gift'. It would never do, in American eyes, for Sir John to have to depend on the meagre allocation of the ration book. In fact, the very thought of his having a ration book was demeaning – a view with which he agreed. And so, bins of meal and flour, pails of pickled eggs and toilet-roll towers all celebrated acquisitiveness in the face of war. This was a room that my father felt had to be kept locked in case the Germans tried to get in, and in immaculate order in case they did gain entry.

Meanwhile, for my parents, both of whom had difficulty deciding things, problems multiplied. He had no job; the young red setter had fits, the pony escaped from its enclosure, and Christopher was not enjoying Eton. But then neither was I making much of Oakdene School, to which

I went from 1940. Life with a governess had given me no idea that there could be so many giggling females on the planet.

The home culture attached no importance to anything that was happening outside its four walls. Who was who, why they were saying what they were saying, and why it was that they should be saying something different; or why, indeed, there was a war and what was happening in it and who was fighting whom – even my father's world, when he was in significant work, stayed behind in London, apart from the occasional enigmatic statement. Not even school, what I was learning, who was teaching, or whether I had friends, were talked about. It was as though a context for living was not to be recognised.

My father said that he would like to join me on horseback; his First World War experience as a cavalry officer would stand him in good stead. He appeared, all dressed up in his officer's uniform, with spurs, and smelling of mothballs. From the mounting block in the drive, he rose up onto Huntsman's high saddle, and, with adjusted stirrups, sat there stiff and straight. Out in the lane, a walker spoke to him. John entered into the exchange, aware, no doubt, of a stage opportunity of a new kind. But Huntsman, unused to army ways, became alarmed, and cast about him uncharacteristically. I followed uneasily on Muffet; but, on the turn into Hall Barn Park, she, perhaps from her own form of equine angst, fled up the hill. Convinced that I could not stop her, I fell off in a hopeless sort of way, sitting up tearfully to see my speeding steed, mane and reins flying, disappearing into the distance. Prudently, my father did not give chase; Huntsman was taking him all his time. Muffet, however, wearied of liberty and allowed herself to be caught. We made our way home dolefully, and the exercise was not repeated.

After tea, a ceremony of scones, sponge and fruit cakes engulfed before a silver teapot on a silver tray, and accompanied by a fierce draught from the cupola above, my father asked me if I would like him to accompany me to feed the hens. Because I never found an answer, he went off to dress up in yet another relic from the trenches: a raincoat which hung in tatters almost to the floor in the garden room. I thought it was enough to put the hens off their lay. There he was, a public figure displaced, Lear among the chickens. But still he had to be rearranging the hay forks, restacking the sacks of corn and poking about behind the sheds. With a saw, he tidied up dead branches on the conifers around about, and evidently found satisfaction in organisation even on this scale.

Then he picked up the handle of what he called 'mein Leiterwagen'. This wooden cart, of which he was immensely proud, he had acquired on an earlier visit to Germany. Not long married at that time, he had nevertheless resumed his pre-war friendship with the Wanner family near Stuttgart and enjoyed the company of the many flaxen-haired daughters – and with one in particular, with whom he sailed up the Rhine. He purchased his handcart and had it shipped to England as a memento of his visit – not that he needed any reminder of Irena Wanner, whose name came up often enough and without difficulty. Occasionally, one such handcart, once a feature of German peasant life, is to be found in a motorway service station, stacked with artificial fruit and vitrified bread.

But when, also before the Second World War, my mother had found herself an unwilling hostess to Herr Dr Wanner, his wife and his beard, she had made loud off-scene objections to the doctor's habit of sitting in his outdoor lace-up boots in the drawing room with its delicate furnishings. It had been Dr Wanner, head of the broadcasting company for southern Germany, who had warned my father of the evils of Nazism – but his diary of March 1933 made it quite clear that he did not accept this view.

> *9 March 1933* Dr Wanner to see me in much depression. He said he would like to leave his country and never return. I am pretty certain, however, that the Nazis will clean things up and put Germany on the way to being a real power in Europe again. They are being ruthless and most determined. It is mostly the fault of France that there should be such manifestations of national spirit.[2]

Even when Dr Wanner was later 'too terrified to say much about conditions in Germany and said he would be shot if he did', John was reluctant to acknowledge the truth about the Nazis, actually arguing in their favour with another German contact in November 1933. It was not until 1936 that he accepted Dr Wanner's tale of the 'awful happenings in Germany', eventually passing private information to the Foreign Office. But still he did not reject the Nazi regime; and, even in March 1939, when Prague was occupied, he wrote: 'Hitler continues his magnificent efficiency'.

But now other matters pressed; my father, more accustomed to commanding than encouraging, said that now I would play the piano for him. Once again, that personal sense in which one was allowed 'to have' one's music was being taken away; my father, while morbidly afraid of thieves, was curiously unscrupulous about others' belongings or affections. I therefore unconsciously presented a piece with which I was not at home, a Chopin mazurka, as being less of a subject for pilfering than some free-flowing piece in which sensibilities of mine were heavily invested, then to be abused. I had a go and then withdrew. 'Very well', he said, very loudly. 'We now know that Marista won't play for us', and angrily barged out of the room.

Despite attempts to disregard the war, one could not stay innocent of its threats. At home, there was my mother's fear and my father's lack of it. In the skies, the massed formations of Allied aircraft flew eastwards to the continent; and, after dark, with their sleep-erasing throb, night-flying enemy aircraft sought their London and Bristol targets. Meanwhile, every window in the house had to be covered in regulation adhesive gauze so that the glass, splintered by blast or direct hit, would not fly. Strips of blackout material were stuck around the frames to prevent escaping chinks of light from becoming an enemy target. Burness, the chauffeur, joined the Home Guard. There was no air-raid shelter at Harrias House other than the kitchen table, thought to be sufficiently large and thick. We would not, in any case, be repairing to the communal shelters built not far away in old-town Beaconsfield. Extinction among home comforts would be preferable. Meanwhile, I carried a persistent image in which German formations overhead, signalled with swastikas like so many tarantulas, fought with the virtuous circles of the red, white and blue of the RAF, brave fighters fending off the enemy action which must surely land on my defenceless head.

And then the war became a noisy thing. In the fierce reality of a single deafening blast and white light, it arrived to rubbish all phoney defences. It even penetrated my father's parasitical gloom. In the middle of the night, there was such a din that I thought I must be dead. And then, although I could not move, I thought I could not be dead because I knew I could not move, and anyway, why did my bedclothes feel like lead? Something shifted a little. I moved, and it thudded on to the floor, followed by more lumps. The air was hard to breathe, and there was a funny smell. I struggled out of bed to see if my parents were there; but the floor hurt my feet, like Brighton beach on a bad day. The air-raid warning began its moaning undulations – I would have liked to have said: 'Oh shut up, I know!' – and I found my mother getting up out of her bed, very frightened, and my father in his, enjoying the racket. He turned out the light, got up and went to look out of the window, and I glimpsed a penetrating orange glow and hard beams of searchlight sweeping back and forth across the night sky. 'That's bombs over London,' he said, 'but ours was much closer.' He spoke with some satisfaction about the Germans and the awful things they were doing; in the circumstances, this was a helpful, if unorthodox, point of view. I said that something had gone wrong with my room, and so he went to look. The light would not work, and so he found a torch. Even its light was dimmed with gauze; but, pointing it in, I could see that what had been the ceiling was on the floor, covering everything in a thick grey layer of dust and lumps. My father asked if I was all right – I supposed I was – and he became more and more cheerful and friendly towards the Germans.

There was another ceiling down in the house, and many others loosened by the landmine, which had fallen in Hall Barn Park a mile away. Its crater was impressive to see, a basin shape excavated, with earth and rubble piled high around it. Harrias House had received a fair proportion of the blast from the explosion, always known to travel in a distinctive but unpredictable way.

My father, who throughout much of the war was unable to find the kind of work of which he was capable, was unhappy. Then, remorseful about my mother, he would rush off to Asprey's, where everyone was obsequious, and come out with an overpriced, jewelled morsel for her. I never thought she enjoyed such expenditure – the feeling was growing that money was not in endless supply – but he felt better, and that, of course, was better for Christopher and me, our mother, the gardener and the dogs. I thought of marriage not as something which in situations like this might break down, but simply as a business arrangement, subject to misunderstandings and occasional satisfactions but needed for managing house, garden and the trail of attendants necessary to existence.

Onto the head of the gardener, Albert Clark, this most decent, honest and courteous man, was heaped responsibility for the garden's multiple failures. Added to this, over-much exchanging with the servants at work was not encouraged; you scarcely acknowledged them or their family if you passed them in the lane. And so I never knew Charlie Clark, the oldest boy, who died fighting for his country, or Alec, who rode his bicycle with his toes out at right angles, or Dorothy, the red-haired girl, who was said to be a talented artist. Years later, when she and her husband met Murray and me, we wondered at this strange way of doing things. Dorothy replied with simple magnanimity: 'Well, that's how things were done in those days'. I thought with embarrassment of how her childhood excellence at the drawing board would, in my received estimation, have carried with it some inbuilt invalidity because it came from the gardener's cottage rather than the big house.

For me, there was another, scarcely articulated perplexity: how was it that this man, about whom I knew so little and who, I understood, had once been one of the most powerful men in the country, was now stuck at home, most discontented, and unable to manage his own coal heap? Later, I read Virginia Woolf on her father: 'He had built around him such a fence of sanctity and occupied the space with such a demeanour of majesty that an earwig in his milk was a monster'.[3] Against such terrible and unpredictable events, my mother was in a state of constant preventative tension.

NOTES

1. Sir John Colville, *Fringes of Power: The Downing Street Diaries*, vol. 1 (Hodder & Stoughton, 1987), reproduced by kind permission.
2. *The Reith Diaries*, ed. Charles Stuart, p. 56.
3. Virginia Woolf, *To the Lighthouse* (1927), by permission of the Society of Authors as the Literary Representative of the Estate of Virginia Woolf.

15

War – Without and Within

M<small>Y FATHER</small> thoughtfully decided against suicide, and this allowed for three ministerial appointments, to Information, Transport, and Works and Buildings, with translation to the House of Lords. But when, through a Churchillian reshuffle, he lost the last of these portfolios, he and my mother became ill. I was to look after them and the house. Then they resolved to move house, but that came to nothing. US Army officers occupied some of the rooms at Harrias House.

During those war years, John told his diary that he was not, at the time anyway, contemplating suicide because it would make things muddled and complicated for the family. This was thoughtful; but, as an alternative, he wished he had never married. The next idea had less finality about it: he would give up Harrias House and its hefty rental and buy a place in the country. The real country, that is, beyond the London orbit and having a stream running through the garden. He supposed that, having failed to mend bridges in his public life, he would now be satisfied doing for a tiny rivulet in rural England what he had latterly failed metaphorically to do in London. His longing 'to be fully stretched' was at odds with his feelings about Churchill – who in turn disliked John. Briefly, in 1940, they were cabinet colleagues under Chamberlain. Churchill still blamed John for 'having kept him off the air for eight years' in the 1930s when he had wanted to broadcast about India. Now, they both personally wanted to win the war. Of course, there were people to speak up for John, both plentiful and powerful, and they wished to see him, now in the national emergency, in a position in which he could truly help to win the war. Among them were Lord Beaverbrook and Brendan Bracken, both close to Churchill. Bracken was his PPS and later Minister for Information. Bracken and Beaverbrook both argued for the use of John's talents. But he, the subject of their endeavours, did little to help them to help him; instead, quite indiscriminately, he disseminated his loathing for Churchill.

At the start of the war, he had been called to see Chamberlain, and had come away unexcited by his offer: to be made Minister for Information. For one who aspired to run the war, it was small beer; *The Times*, however, pointed out that it was those very qualities which John Reith had in abundance that were now needed: grip and drive. But, the paper continued, 'the one doubt about him is whether his long enjoyment of an independent command may have rendered it difficult for him to collaborate in a team'.[1] No comment could more exactly have summed up the hazards which attached to John's time in government, from 1940 to 1942.

John now needed a seat in the House of Commons, for which he was to be returned unopposed for Southampton. Muriel went with him for the arranged lunch, and in the hotel where constituency members were gathering were also several men in uniform. One detached himself, and, holding out his hand, said: 'Hullo, John!' It was Charlie Bowser. John was momentarily 'as a reed shaken in the wind'; he recovered himself, and they exchanged briefly. Charlie was a captain in the Army Service Corps; he was preparing to go overseas.

John was introduced to the Commons in February 1940. The *Daily Telegraph* described his 'granite seriousness'. In a rare moment of cordiality with Winston Churchill, he confessed that he was 'rather frightened of the House of Commons' – to which Churchill made the robust response: 'Not so frightened as they are of you!' Stanley Baldwin told him that 'you come like a new boy at a new school, and you must learn its ways'. He might have wondered how good John would be at learning someone else's ways. By Easter of that year, Churchill was presiding over the coalition government. Then he moved John to the Ministry of Transport, which was a blow to his self-confidence. He complained loudly and absented himself from the Commons when, in June, the evacuation of Dunkirk took place. Churchill made a speech that stood comparison with Shakespeare's Henry V on the night before the Battle of Agincourt.[2] John excluded himself from 'the nation's finest hour'. Then he recovered sufficiently to put his mind to a new scheme: the nationalisation of the railways. The outcome of the cabinet meeting at which it was discussed was inconclusive: Clement Attlee, as Lord Privy Seal, was in favour, and Beaverbrook was against.

John had little patience with or understanding of the processes of politics. When prime-ministerial papers reached him labelled *ACTION NOW* in red type, he responded as though to a personal insult, interpreting it as if the very style which principally characterised his actions, and for which he was known, was now being called into question. In September 1940, London was hideously bombed, and invasion was expected any day. John visited Holborn Tube Station, where 5,000 people had resorted for safety. Here were, he said, 'a ghastly crowd of refugees, mostly horrid Jews'. One might have questioned how beneficial his visit might be. John said that he would run the bomb-disposal squads. Churchill agreed: 'this is your war, you know', he said, rather unexpectedly, and went on to say that he had great confidence in him. Whether he meant it is another matter.

In the Commons debate on transport, John made his maiden speech. 'Bloody good', said Emmanuel Shinwell, tossing a note across the floor to John. The speech had lasted forty-five minutes. But, two weeks later, he was moved on, this time to the Ministry of Works and to the Upper House. He told Churchill that he did not care for either move; that he wanted to stay in the Commons, even after the war, and to be more closely in touch with him, even though, he said, 'you don't like me'. Churchill responded in complimentary terms. John told him: 'I am not happy about either the job or the Lords, but I suppose I ought to take both as an order'.[3] 'Yes,' said Churchill, 'I command you' – and shook hands warmly.

Clough Williams-Ellis, the distinguished and also maverick architect who built the fanciful village of Portmeirion in north Wales, wrote in *The Spectator*: 'Hitler had clumsily and painfully inured [the British people] to large-scale destruction; it was now for Reith to show what dynamite could do when selectively applied in the service of town planning, civic regeneration, and human well-being generally ... Sir John's task to restrain the queue of property owners from pushing past him to set about rebuilding incontinently on their shattered sites – that is a very necessary task that will need all his relentless strength of purpose'.[4]

John had at speed to find bomb-proof strongholds for the cabinet. 'We crashed about looking at steel-framed buildings to the great perturbation of the inhabitants – especially New Scotland Yard', he wrote. He found an alternative meeting place for Parliament in Church House, Westminster. Its conversion was completed in three weeks: 'a triumph of hustle',[5] he wrote. He began to negotiate for the inclusion in his brief of post-war reconstruction and planning; he was developing an enthusiasm for his job.

As he received a deputation of the mayor and councillors from Coventry, their city centre destroyed by bombing, he realised that he did not know what was his authority but that he 'would not have this high-powered civic deputation return to their battered city with a tale of Whitehall gruntings and wafflings, telling their wives that it was all a waste of time and that they had gotten nowhere'.[6] (Not that the mayor and council of Coventry would have used the word 'gotten', an archaism surviving in Scotland and the USA and much loved by John.) If he were in their position, he told the enthralled dignitaries gathered around his table, he would plan boldly and comprehensively, and at this stage not worry about finance or local boundaries. 'In twenty years of

15. Harrias House, Beaconsfield. Marista with her father and mother.

16. Harrias House, Beaconsfield, and adjoining farm.

17. Still towering above everyone.

18. The Birth of Broadcasting. *At a reception given by Oxford University Press and the BBC to mark the publication of* The Birth of Broadcasting *by Professor Asa Briggs. The picture shows (L to R) Mr John Brown (OUP), Professor Asa Briggs, Captain Peter Eckersley, Lord Reith, Mr Hugh Carleton Greene. © BBC*

19. Dressed for the General Assembly of the Church of Scotland, 1967.

20. *With Malcolm Muggeridge, in Kelvingrove Park, Glasgow.*

21. As Lord High Commissioner in the uniform of the Royal Company of Archers, the Queen's Bodyguard in Scotland, at the General Assembly, 1967. Image courtesy of The Herald & Evening Times *picture archive.*

22. Lord Reith Looks Back: *1967.With Malcolm Muggeridge during the filming of*
Lord Reith Looks Back. © *BBC*

23. Lord Reith Looks Back: *1967.* © *BBC*

24. *Marista.*

25. *Murray Leishman.*

26. *Portrait of John Reith. This painting, by Sir Gerald Kelly, is now on show as part of a permanent exhibition in the South Atrium of the Media Centre, Wood Lane, London.* © *BBC*

27. *Photograph by Simon Jones: Marista Leishman standing in front of 'John Reith, 1st Baron of Stonehaven' by Sir Oswald Birley. With grateful thanks to the Scottish National Portrait Gallery.*

coming to Whitehall on deputations,' gasped the mayor at the end of the meeting, 'I have never received such treatment.'

John had wheeled his delegation off to a private room in Claridges for lunch. After it, as they shook hands with the minister and filed out of the room, each was to be seen carrying three daffodils. John had steadily doled out an offering to each departing councillor from the hotel's bowl of yellow blooms, their proud reply to wartime austerity. For John, they carried an eloquent message about the city of Coventry's resurrection. 'Daffodils', he wrote, 'that come before the swallow dares, and take the winds of March with beauty.'[7] His eccentricities were ever honed with imagination – and, this time, with a sudden access of fellow feeling as well. Then, as enemy action rained down in turn on Southampton, Portsmouth, Liverpool, Clydebank and Plymouth, the ministerial visit to their devastated areas followed 'the Coventry model', urging them to plan boldly and think about cost afterwards. On these occasions, his advice was probably without the seasonal flowers. As to the overall effect of such encouragement on the body politic of the nation, we are not told; an eyebrow here and there must almost certainly have been raised as newspaper and other reports reached the cabinet office.

Then he spoke in the Lords. He was authorised, he said, to have planning accepted as a national policy with a central authority; he would pursue the theme of physical reconstruction with a positive policy for agriculture, industrial development and transport, and with some public services requiring treatment on a national, regional and local basis. For the *Architects' Journal*, this was the most inspiring message to have come out of the House of Lords, ever; and the Royal Institution of British Architects made him an honorary fellow. Under him were 1,400 official buildings and the construction of many munitions factories as well as the care of historic buildings. Some people were finding the speed at which he worked rather shattering.

But, as he continued ruthlessly to exterminate any awareness or consideration of events around him, so he made it increasingly plain that he did not have the makings of a politician. He scarcely knew when the current budget was published; and, in his self-imposed isolation, he found it hard to try to understand why he should negotiate with the major parties in the coalition. When he got things done – his principal objective in life – he did so with as few consultations or cross-references as possible. From the Uthwatt committee emerged a bold plan for post-war reconstruction, with legislation for orderly planning, especially in the devastated places, and land held at its pre-war value. But still he did not fully attend to the course of the war: Pearl Harbor in December 1941 passed almost without remark. He was filled with gloom and had a bad Christmas and New Year. Nevertheless, he was to announce to the Lords in February 1942 that his office had an extended remit under the title of the Ministry of Works and Planning.

Then Churchill carried out an extensive reshuffle of his administration, especially in its lower reaches. A courier arrived at Harrias House one Saturday evening. The letter was from the prime minister: 'My dear Reith, I am sorry to tell you that the reconstruction of the government which events have rendered necessary makes me wish to have your Office at my disposal'. Some days later, John got around to his reply; but what he wrote was as dictated by Sir John Anderson, Lord Privy Seal, a kindly Scot who would stand by John: 'Certainly my office and I are at your disposal. It has been a privilege to be associated with the government at such a time. I wish I could have been of more help to you personally on your tremendous and splendid task.'[8] As some were remarking, he was vulnerable because he had no party allegiance and no-one in particular on whom he could count to stand up for him.

Now, in the Second World War, out of work, John was to tell his diary that he was nearer lunacy than his brother Ernest had ever been. (Ernest had had to see out his life in the Crichton Lunatic Asylum in Dumfries.) Then John continued in the same vein to a government minister. For Lord Woolton, whose concern was the emergency of wartime food supplies throughout the nation, this was an unexpected perplexity of another kind.[9] John was telling him – a man he hardly knew and did not like – that he wished for himself that a bomb would drop; and then, as an afterthought, included his family in this act of total elimination. It was certainly noticeable that he did not seem entirely to disapprove of the Germans, savouring the excitement as with louder and closer explosions they hurled things indiscriminately about. But, he confirmed to the flabbergasted minister, his increasing debt was £3,000: Harrias House, with its gardens at which Christopher had worked so hard during school holidays, would have to be abandoned, and in a maudlin way he looked to all the family being together in heaven. Meanwhile, the Almighty, twenty years earlier in constant attendance, seemed now to have moved away, having other things to do.

John's was a personal crisis of the kind which, for him, only work could occasionally contain. And then, because work in itself could never be a solution, his situation was again perilous. He was a one-interest man; he had no hobbies; he could only work. Utterly without self-awareness or any idea that there might be some standpoints of his own which he would be better to adjust, he personalised his catastrophes and woes in one hate figure. 'For one and a half hours I sat opposite him, watching him and his tricks.' If Churchill was aware of this desecrating stare, he paid no heed beyond noting that this man was no team player. And, for John, in whose life there was little space for pleasure and enjoyment, Churchill was a cheerful hedonist and, therefore, the more suspect. The perversity of John's remark 'you never liked me' would be the better for being unscrambled into 'I never liked you', in which form it reached home.

John became very ill. The doctor came often; and, while he tried to look after the physical symptoms, he would have been well aware that his difficult patient was far from well in himself. And then he had two patients: he ordered my mother to bed. Other than me, aged ten, there was no help in the house; and, for one obscurely exhilarating morning, I felt that I could do it all. Never having cooked before, I managed – for around two weeks – to prepare meals (they were often rejected), attend to the animals, wash and clear up. In the morning, I would open up the house and unlock numerous doors; and, in the evening, start the long trek to close it all down. I can only think that domestic help in any form was unavailable. But that is the charitable view. Or was it that John was so short of money — which, unknown to his family, he was — that, after years of extravagance, he could not now meet an emergency? It was when a neighbour intervened that I experienced an unwelcome tide of self-pity.

As well as her exotic name, the Hon. Desirée Butterwick was most sparkling and accomplished, speaking incisively in impeccably cultured tones and 'with that negligent ease of manner which, seeming to claim nothing, is really based on the life-long consciousness of commanding rank'.[10] But, as my father and I were walking one Sunday afternoon down the lane to Little Hall Barn, where Cyril and Desirée Butterwick lived, John, most uncharacteristically, had decided to call. As we approached, Cyril was clearly to be seen walking purposefully down the garden path away from the house in exactly the same way as John himself had more than once retreated from an unwelcome caller. But, of course, only *he* had leave to behave in such a way; incensed, he made his excuses, and we left. Soon, Mrs Butterwick was talking to me on the telephone. No — she did not want to speak to my parents, as she knew they were unwell; but would I come with her to help her with a large delivery of leaflets which she had to do around the countryside? We would be away all day, and in the afternoon she would need to pick up her daughter, Anne, at the station. She drove up to collect me in her battered old car, and off we went, she talking volubly. It was not long before I experienced a great wave of relief at being away from Harrias House and my suffering parents. We drove around Buckinghamshire delivering I know not what. The predicament at home was never mentioned; but clearly Mrs Butterwick did not actually *need* my help but was trying herself to help. We stopped at an inn for lunch and then drove on, finally collecting Anne as arranged. She had evidently been away for some time, possibly starting a college course. As we drove through the gate to the Butterwick home, the front door opened, and a posse of large older brothers came tumbling and harrumphing out of the house. 'How is my little sister?' boomed one, as this mature young lady climbed gracefully out of the old car. Mrs Butterwick said she would be back in a minute when she had taken Marista back to Harrias, and in the meantime would someone please put on the kettle. Over the short distance back, I imagined an apparently ideal life going on within the walls of Little Hall Barn, full of leg-pulling and good cheer — forgetting that Cyril had demonstrated that it was not quite as simple as that. Without difficulty, I nursed a sense of injury as I compared the scene I had just left with the one to which I was returning.

As 'commanded' by Churchill, John had of course been ennobled and made a member of the House of Lords, an event which had passed me by until I heard my mother giving directions to one of the few remaining maids, and saying something about 'His Lordship'. Edith was not wholly startled — after all, she read the *Daily Sketch*, which still reached the servants' hall. I asked my mother about this lordship business, and she said that Daddy was now Lord Reith. Christopher and I would be called the Honourable Christopher and Marista; and she was, as she had been before on account of the knighthood, Lady Reith — but possibly, she said vaguely, this time with a 'The' before it. She giggled uncomfortably. I saw a letter from my father addressed to 'the Hon. C. J. Reith' at Eton, but could not associate to mine, about which I felt uneasy and my father proprietorial, since it was to do with him and not me.

Now my father was to speak in the House of Lords, and we were to be there. As well as being a Lady, my mother had also mysteriously become a peeress — but, because I thought of a pier as something at which a ship would tie up, I supposed that a 'pieress' was a smaller version for dinghies. None of this quite fitted as she and I took our seats in the Peeresses' Gallery, and Christopher, as the eldest son (even though there was not a younger one), sat on the steps of the throne. This looked lonely and uncomfortable; and, despite the thrones and steps, it was just as well there were no kings and queens as well. My father laid forth, apparently effortlessly, to a very silent and attending House; at home, there had been much rehearsing, with the door closed and declamatory sounds coming from behind it.

And then he was back at his desk at Harrias House, totally detached, unaware and writing, himself having become a part of that massive piece of furniture with its leather top and two columns of drawers, all perfectly tidy and running in and out as though on silk. He paid attention to the array of his writing equipment: his glass tray with its red and black pens in their holders and pencil slots; the containers for paper clips and pins, all part of the green glass set; his letter-weighing machine standing alongside. He had seals and sealing wax, candle and matches: holding the stick of red wax in the flame, he would expertly transfer it when at exactly the right consistency to the point of the envelope flap and then decisively impose the seal on the wax — usually his own crest and motto: 'QUAECUNQUE', or 'Whatsoever things are lovely'. Further desk essentials stood on an oak table nearby, in particular two apprentice-piece miniature chests of drawers. He enjoyed these for the satisfying accommodation that they offered in which, with cunning exactitude, one could fit one's stationery reserves.

Occasionally, and rather oddly, John might be found working away with his large wastepaper basket on his desk-top, over the top of which peered Tigger the cat. Neither seemed to find anything unusual in this arrangement; and, although no animal-lover, John had a fond tolerance of cats.

During the war, large houses were compulsorily inspected for their surplus accommodation and their rooms allocated to evacuees from London who had lost everything to the bombs. For John, such a happening was unthinkable, and he set about pulling strings to have American officers from the nearby army base billeted instead. This was a happy arrangement: John actually enjoyed their company and admiring conversation, and the officers were never short on appreciation of the hospitality of my mother's cooking. But she seemed almost to have taken up residence in the kitchen, and, like so many women in the war, was always tired. Added to this, despite appearances to the contrary, money was short. I would have supposed that my father had any amount; that was always the impression. His account books were for his eyes only, however, and so my mother might only surmise what was the case. And she must have wondered how buying a new house would do anything but add to the problem. But now the post regularly brought news of properties for sale. Agents' names — John D. Wood, Savilles and the excellent Mutton, Button and Menhenick — became a feature of the daily delivery; agents' speak was another matter, however. 'This desirable period property situate where it enjoys commanding views ...' 'within mellow stone walls the accommodation comprises ...' — and off John would go, repeating under his breath 'situate', 'enjoys' and 'comprises', with mocking sibilants. The comment of Spike Milligan, of whom John would never have heard, was that 'the cliché is the handrail of the crippled mind'.

Petrol coupons appeared like miracles, and my mother and I would drive away to look at country houses built of ochred Cotswold stone, with hollyhocks at the door and ponies in the meadow. As we entered yet another of these inviting homesteads, I felt, yet again, absurdly sure that my father and mother would not have to go on being gloomy in a place like this; that instead of problems there would be fun. Here, the distant fields of this rolling countryside extended their invitation to roam; wooded lanes with dappled banks bright with speedwell and Star of Bethlehem traced the contours of the fields ... but now we were leaving, and the owners were fielding some desultory questions of my mother's about the heating, the water supply and the many trees, she being otherwise unforthcoming. Realistic vendors knew when they had not made a sale; but I, still hopeful, was agitating back into the car. A glance, and the blue felt hat was apparently pressed even lower on the brow, with an unsmiling look ahead. Here was little hope. 'Well, what did you think?' My question's initial urgency drained away. 'It was awfully shut in. At the foot of the hill, and all those trees around about.' I rushed in with a solution: 'Well, you could cut them down'. She stopped at a crossroads to examine the fingerpost, and, without answering, turned off in uncertain manner to the left. 'The kitchen was dreadfully small and dark, and so was the scullery next door.' 'You could take down the wall in between', I said, against my better judgement. 'And that would let in more light.' But my mother had other realities to resort to. 'The sink was ghastly, and you'd have to take away the lavatory next door.' I had yet to learn that in some situations a solution is the last thing that people are looking for. We drove back into Buckinghamshire. A massive rainstorm broke, and so did the windscreen wipers. Perched forward on my seat, I worked them by hand-twisting the small handle to and fro, changing one aching arm for the other for the remaining forty miles.

One of the very few neighbours who dared to call was known as The Man Smith. This jovial character was usefully without awe of John, and, having one evening received liberal treatment in the house, started out on his bicycle ride home. His course down the drive was so uncertain that, at the foot, he was in no position to make the required left turn but went instead more or less ahead, continuing up the opposite bank – there to be decisively unseated. If my father had any concern for his welfare, it was lost as his shoulders heaved with silent mirth.

But, for my mother, it was her cousin Doris Naylor – Auntie Doddie – who could generate laughter and bustle in the corridors and who could cause Muriel's set expression to scatter from time to time. She became almost merry. In the meantime, I could carry the wind-up gramophone into the hall, and, opening the lid to that dapper little terrier dog with his ear cocked to His Master's Voice, urge it again and again into action with Handel's *Water Music*. Travelling fast on high heels and quick thin legs, Doddie came speeding along the passage, energetically pushing the vacuum cleaner ahead of her. I expected her to rush on, plug in the noise machine next door and make a thunderous din, so that the *Water Music* was newly scored for Hoover continuo. Instead, she stopped, and, leaning on the long suction pipe, listened to the end. 'What I really love is that pa-pum-pum-pa-pum; para-pum-pum-pum-pa-pum ...' And we both laughed at her efforts. 'That's a horn, isn't it?' she said uncertainly.

With Auntie Doddie came Robin and Hew. Robin rode my bicycle straight through the pond and out the other side, where it emerged with punctured tyres and, like him, dripping with weed. In Robin, Hew and, later, Richard, the family humour was heavily invested; even John approved of the boys. But Peter and Doris were under no illusions about John and not all that impressed by him. Unlike others, they could deal without difficulty with his penchant for offloading unwanted possessions into the boot of their car – the Giving Away Cupboard was reserved for unsuspecting visitors – and would firmly take them out again.

But I had experienced Handel's music in a context of shared appreciation; the music that I enjoyed could, after all, be acceptable to others, flooding along like a river in spate. At the piano, doors opened to the Anna Magdalena collection which Bach wrote for his second wife; but, as I experienced melodies moving in to stay, sounding continuously in my head, there followed a certain vagueness about much else. Mine were not 'circumstances in which it was safe to be absent-minded',[11] and it became clear that this musical preoccupation was fairly exasperating to live with. And so, when the Naylor family, to my sadness, had left, I kept the gramophone upstairs and, behind shut doors, heard the obliterating triumph of 'The Trumpet shall Sound'.

After the war, when John was spending more time than was healthy looking back, he wrote to Churchill, by now out of office:

> I have (like you) a war mentality and other qualities which have commended themselves to you. Even in office I was nothing like fully stretched, and I was completely out of touch with you. You could have used me in a way and to an extent you never realised. Instead there has been the sterility, humiliation and distress of all these years – 'eyeless in Gaza' – without even the consolation Samson had of knowing it was his own fault.[12]

Churchill replied:

> I am grieved to receive your letter of January 1 although I am glad you wrote it. So far as my administration is concerned, I have always admired your abilities and energy, and it was with regret that I was not able to include you in the considerable reconstruction of the Government in February 1942 ...
>
> Several times since then I have considered you for various posts which became vacant, but I always encountered considerable opposition from one quarter or another on the ground that you were difficult to work with ... My task in making political appointments in a coalition government, where certain balance had to be preserved, was hard, and I have no doubt that under the extreme pressure of war events I often made mistakes. I am unfeignedly sorry for the pain which you felt which I understand very fully, as I was myself, for eleven years, out of office before the war, during the last six of which I earnestly desired to take part in the work of preparation.

I admired the courage and efficiency with which you made yourself a place and a reputation in the Admiralty, and you were still often in my mind as a candidate for high employment up till the time when I was myself suddenly and unexpectedly dismissed from office by the workings of our political system.

If you think I can be of service to you at any time, pray let me know; for I am very sorry that the fortunes of war should have proved so adverse to you, and I feel the State is in your debt.[13]

It was typical of John that, as he made sporadic and also massive engagements with persons and affairs, achievements following in the shortest possible time – he then collided with the real world, and inevitably his initiative evaporated. He could never learn to do as others did. He might have professed a wish to be more ordinary, but he also relished his oddity and did little to distance his frequent bouts of misery from others' experience of it. But, with his powers and energies intact throughout the war years, it was sad for him and for the country that they were, on the whole, frustrated.

NOTES

1. Ian McIntyre, p. 251, ref.: *The Times*, 6.1.40, with the permission of News International Newspapers; *Daily Telegraph*, 7.2.40, with their permission.
2. Shakespeare, *Henry V*, Act IV, Scene 1, line 250.
3. McIntyre, p. 258, from Reith, *Diary*, 2.10.40.
4. McIntyre, p. 259, from *The Spectator*, 18.10.40, with their permission.
5. From Reith, *Into the Wind*, p. 411.
6. Ibid., p. 424.
7. Shakespeare, *Winter's Tale*, Act IV, Scene 3, line 118.
8. McIntyre, p. 265, from Reith, *Diary*, 1.3.42.
9. McIntyre, p. 272, from Reith, *Diary*, 22.8.43.
10. George Eliot, *Romola*, p. 323.
11. Anna Freud, Introduction to Marion Milner, *On Not Being Able to Paint*.
12. Reith, *Into the Wind*, p. 526.
13. Reproduced with permission of Curtis Brown Group Ltd, London, on behalf of the Estate of Sir Winston Churchill. Copyright Winston S. Churchill, and with the permission of News International Newspapers.

16

The Spy Patrol

THIS CHAPTER is about my mother – a deeply English, rural person of the professional classes. There was a marked contrast between her culture and my father's. A shy person, she nevertheless volunteered to join the local team patrolling for spies. But the sighting of a suspect was understandably disconcerting.

During the war, my mother drove a small wobbly Austin 7. It was unusual to drive a car at all, because most private cars were locked inside garages and resting on wooden blocks. But my mother, who wanted to do her bit for the war effort, could not quite see herself working in a munitions factory with a handkerchief tied round her head, or in the Women's Land Army with hoes and heavy horses. And so she volunteered for the Beaconsfield Spy Patrol and received special petrol coupons for the purpose.

It was with a view to uncovering, if possible, a particular form of enemy action that the local Spy Patrol team was formed. Espionage at work in the rural idyll of the Chiltern Hills seemed almost as unlikely as the government policy of encouraging country-dwelling volunteers to help with the war effort. But the result was that estimable ladies from fine houses – they were the only ones who were not actually at work in munitions factories or on the land – issued forth in flat shoes and bullet-proof stockings and with shooting sticks, 'calling in loud heroic tones as though into a gale'[1] to tell everyone what was to happen during the forthcoming day and spy-hunt.

It was up to the men, of course, to climb into the commuter train or the service uniform. But the intricacies of the social web of rural England were directed and executed by the formidable dames of the shires, working with fearsome competence and effortless superiority from behind pillared gateways and up avenue drives. Their task, they knew, was to keep at bay the threatened erosion of hundreds of years of history, localised around the Great House and its architectural pomps and social circumstances. The reciprocal systems of loyal service to the family by estate workers and villagers were met with the feudal obligations of the aristocracy – those top few among whom there existed an unspoken recognition of social parity. They did see the need, however, to extend their invitation list to include the *arrivistes*, about whom hissed confidences were exchanged: 'the Watsons are very nice; but did you know? – they had actually to *buy* their own furniture'.

> Wealth, howsoever got, in England makes
> Lords of mechanics, gentlemen of rakes:
> Antiquity and birth are needless here;
> 'Tis impudence and money makes a peer.[2]

Joining the Patrol and keeping out enemy aliens was motivated by a residual feeling about the need to back up the men, and also to ward off the change that war would bring about and the depressing possibility that a certain diminution of essentials to living might follow – that one might lose one's second under-gardener to the war, and that the problems in keeping the lakeside lawns mown were getting increasingly worrying. As one owner said despairingly: 'We are even considering fencing the lake – which will be terribly expensive and who is there to do it for us? – and then bring in a tenant's sheep. It's all really rather terrible.' And then there was the sawmill that would probably have to be shut down. 'And', she went on, 'Cook said that the baker was no longer able to deliver here from next month – we are too far from the village.' Neither herself a stately home, nor even having married into one, my mother was never quite 'one of us'. Her family were publishers, her Uncle Will an alarming man who had founded the firm of Odhams Press. And so, while her accents and tastes were Southern Counties impeccable, her lack of confidence in relation to the great houses and her trepidation on approaching their grand gateways made her a sometime visitor only. From her deeply English roots, my mother inherited a dislike of foreigners, braininess and anyone who might threaten that inalienable right to privacy within the high walls and thick hedges of her home.

Her knowledge of class arose from penetrating instinct, and worked out of categories which were then subdivided into further shades of meaning, based on evidence which was usually elusive. There was that ultimate condemnation which too readily pronounced a tentatively introduced acquaintance of mine from school to be 'not out of the top drawer', and which, while herself preferring her ancient clothes at home, condemned others' tasteless choices.

The wartime emergency of departed servants meant that my mother had to take on the tasks of the cook, the housemaid and the gardener's boy, preparing the hefty meals, stewing the chickens' feed, polishing the furniture and taking in the hay from what had been the lawn. All these things she achieved with dogged application and some success, since they came, for some reason, more naturally to her than actually having to exchange with the persons concerned when they had been in post. This process had been painful for everyone, and there was a real sense in which she now found it much easier to get to work herself.

For my mother, being English was the only nationality to be. She could tolerate the Scots, provided that they had been sufficiently exposed to the civilising influences of the English public school and to the acceptable side of London life. Traces of Scottish speech would be anglicised away, and Scotland and ancient family roots visited only from time to time. It was quite out of keeping, therefore, with her beliefs and standards that she should marry a Scot who was curiously devoid of the excellences which she so admired and was replete with an array of angularities peculiarly his own. These were set against a background of a Scottish Bible Christianity, which disapproved of self-indulgent enjoyment and esteemed position, especially that which one achieved oneself. Like Cecil Rhodes, my mother believed that the English were the best people in the world, with ideals of decency, justice, liberty and peace which no other country could match — although she would not have put it like that. Great Britain and her allies would certainly win the war, because virtue on this scale would be rewarded.

Arthur Bryant, the popular historian of the 1920s and 1930s, had a picture of England as a nation of squires, parsons, yeomen and quaint cider-drinking yokels, such as appealed to Muriel Odhams — provided that the yokels were some distanced part of a rustic evening scene outside an ancient timbered Red Lion.

To be brainy, in my mother's eyes, was in poor taste. This was different from being educated; that was an essential, made up of speaking properly and having good handwriting, taste in clothes and furnishings, and manners to match. It was nothing to do with the intellect — in fact, the less said the better. My father had a cousin, Margaret Moffat. Her father was James Moffat, who, as someone mistakenly thought, 'wrote the Bible', which meant that the Moffat translation of the 1920s became the standard alternative to the Authorised Version in Scotland. Margaret inherited his brains to an extent which made Muriel uneasy; one of the first female Oxford graduates, she taught classics at the Ballet Rambert in London, and was a dear person with a masculine voice. She was not offended when yet again you mistook her telephone answer for her husband Frank's. They lived in a delectable eighteenth-century Westminster house under the Abbey's shadow in Cowley Street. Margaret was hospitable, had plenty to say and fearlessly told my father when he was talking nonsense, which he often was, or being a bigot, which he often was. Margaret disconcerted my father and was gentle with Muriel. She had thin unruly hair, and always completed her outfit with large scarlet blobs of earrings and necklace, with handbag to match — all of which, I knew, my mother would dislike. She, in her turn, was quiet and sat stiffly on her chair and under her hat, managing her teacup and cake and hoping that we would leave before John blew a fuse. But this was because she had not quite appreciated how effortlessly Margaret managed her prickly guest. Frank sat quietly observing. A shrewd lawyer, he had no need to speak when there was nothing to be said. Anyway, Margaret had grown up near John in Glasgow's Hillhead; and, while she had found his father affectionate, and said so, his mother was chilling. The less said the better.

Muriel's admiration was reserved for bishops, archbishops and admirals with blue eyes. Admiral Sir Charles Carpendale, John's deputy in the BBC, had been one of these; in his company, she cheered up and became good company herself. But her veneration for monarchy was absolute and unquestioned, including their right to national adulation, heavy cost and extravagant ceremonial. About the absurdity of all this, some people were very clear; the nearest my mother came to criticising the Royal Family was to remark that sitting next to Queen Mary was difficult because she did not have anything to say – and did not even seem to be trying.

Before the war came and enslaved her in the kitchen, my mother had always dressed with studied attention to *comme il faut*. The variations, incomprehensible to me, had each to reflect the nature of the company, the season, the weather, the time of day and the occasion. The 1930s' dress code among the ruling classes was absolute. One day, I found her getting ready for a funeral, arrayed in deepest, darkest black. I pointed out that the buckle on her belt had an ornamental centre of cheerful pink; off I went to find black tape and glue, and then a pair of secateurs for her to cut out from her hat a cheeky feather that had freckles. Even for the Spy Patrol, when she would drive through rural England and never meet a soul, she wore a blue tweed suit, distinguished by age and total indestructibility. She explained of this suit that 'it was very good'. A matching blue felt hat sat flatly on her head. Deeply conformist, she attached a certain godliness to being, as she said, 'properly dressed'. In the same way as, for my father, ultimate virtue attached to systems and order, amounting in the end to a depleted deity, so my mother spoke disparagingly of anyone who dressed tastelessly – her own standards being, of course, beyond reproach. She did, I noticed, look very like Queen Elizabeth, whose picture, along with the King, I had just seen. Like the Queen, my mother had blue eyes; and her brownish hair, parted in the middle, surrounded her rather round face in tight waves to a bun at the back. But one day she spied another woman, three pews ahead of her in church, wearing the same Marshall and Snelgrove silk dress as she. Her red-faced anger and embarrassment simmered away throughout the service and burst into expostulations after it — although whose awful fault it was stayed unclear.

My mother always chose everything I wore, because she knew best and I apparently did not have a view. Unfortunately, I did not wake up enough to notice that I did have opinions, even though they were far below the surface — it was just that they were discouraged. And this, of course, was about many more things than just clothes. But, because in growing up I was inclined to be fat — or so I was led to believe — my mother was sure that there would be nothing in large enough sizes to be found in the shops of Knightsbridge; and so my things, and hers too, were made by a dressmaker who came every morning and whom Christopher and I called The Cromeski. This was not an unfriendly gesture, however; she was young, pretty and very good at her job. Her little boy, who ran about the garden while she worked, and on whom she had to call from time to time from the window, was considered badly behaved, as was her husband, who went off every morning from the cottage across the drive, where they lived, to his nameless job.

In my mother's England, and always beyond question, was the Anglican Church. It was possessed of the same unchanging permanence as The Times, Barclays Bank and Regent Street, in the same way as places with names like Stoke Poges, Sompting and Upper Slaughter stretched back to some stainless past, as ancient as Anglo-Saxon England but without the rude ways of the Angles, Jutes and Saxons. The church, named after the Angles, attracted sensible men and women who drove British cars like Rovers, Wolseleys and Austins to and from the services, and then gently down through the English country lanes. And so, because this was what you did, and was what her father and mother had done and their fathers and mothers, and all the squires and knights of the beautiful English countryside also, my mother went to church. But, at Harrias House, where custom was stronger than conviction, Sundays were problematic. For me, church meant white stringy gloves which had a sort of buzz when you put them on and which also meant that, unless you had a teasel to hold, everything slid out of your grip. Church meant patent leather shoes and white ankle socks; a pretty dress, which you had to keep clean, and a terrible hat with elastic under the chin, which was too tight. From the church gate, our feet munched the gravel up the path winding its way between the bulging yews; louder and louder became the clatter of those prison bells – even the tower seemed to quiver with their clamour. We pushed into the dark interior with its heavy organ sounds and damp smell. We had to sit in the back row – I thought hopefully that this was an escape route. In came the procession of men and boys in white nightgowns with black edges, the men impressed with processing and with themselves, and from the boys a certain rebellion escaping like air from a tyre. Readings, recitations and responses: my heart was in my shiny shoes. I sensed my mother's compliance with the rigmarole, serious and withdrawn under her Sunday dress and coat, and my father's crashing dislike of it all. That emerged in hissed complaints and exhalations which travelled forwards from the back row and caused sections of the congregation ahead to twitch and shift uneasily about.

It was the clergyman's misfortune to be continuously compared by my father to his own father, whom he described in spacious terms and to whom he seemed continually to refer as having 'every legitimate artifice of dramatic presentation at his unconscious command'. And, moreover, since 'the eloquence of his indignation was devastating',[3] there was no hope for any clergyman who aspired to be rector of Beaconsfield parish church while my father was around. He made no allowance for the difference in culture between the scholarly evangelical fervour and pioneering spirit of the Free Church in Scotland, still young as he remembered it in his later years, and Anglican antiquity, here in its English suburban manifestation and with its so very different roots.

On one particularly bad day of drones and incantations, I collected the hymn books and made them into a train on the book board. They shunted well back and forth until I was shushed and my was train dismantled. I had to be resigned to nursing my continuing objection to my shoe buttons, which sat up pert and self-regarding and could be made to hook into one another. My father, meantime, could go on sighing, and nobody shushed him – while God, who was naturally Home Counties, seemed to have an unaccountably limitless swallow for flattery couched in versicles intoned with much screeching and straining at the larynx.

One day, at the age of four or five, I thought I would be Naughty. It was not that my father or mother decided that today we were going to church, with a statement to that effect, but rather that significant tensions and signs were all around. My mother got hotter and more flustered seeing to the dogs, the cat, the rabbits and the arrangements with the cook for the elaborate meal for our return. My father shouted down the stair that yet again that hopeless laundry had completely failed to starch his shirt cuffs and that it was a useless laundry and he could not understand why she did not use another one and had he not been saying this for the last five years anyway. But since, for my mother, problems were by nature insoluble, and had to remain so, nothing was done. Christopher was in his woodyard cutting up logs, delaying as long as possible before answering the Time To Come In call by doing so. But, having decided on a plan, I lost no time and dashed downstairs and in behind the drawing-room sofa. It had vast chintz tulips, and the heavy brocade curtains in faded crimson reached to the floor and gave extra shelter. It seemed a long time before I started to hear voices calling; the nanny entered on fat footsteps and went out again. I always knew she was so stupid. My mother's voice became agitated. A quick light step this time; my father would not miss me, and somehow I did not think he would be angry. Leaning over the back of the sofa, his pride and approval hung on every syllable. Smilingly, he offered his huge hand to take mine, and I felt glad to be found. 'Have you been a naughty girl, then?' Satisfaction had quite overtaken admonition, and together we left the drawing room, two people well pleased with themselves, since it was now too late for church. He went off to his dressing room to exchange all those black clothes for his Sunday down-at-heel, out-at-the-elbow things, and I was again claimed by the nurse, who hustled forwards unloading little rebukes suitable for overhearing and which blew around me like bits of fluff on the floor.

The Church of England was the 'forever afternoon' of the long summer days of the English shires; of wide fields with five-barred gates set in thick hedges packed with bird life. It was the England that lived in timbered houses, their palsied beams bending down to the land from which they grew; that England, too, that inhabited tall Queen Anne buildings, standing high with haughty stare above the umber irregularities of others' tumbling roofs. My mother's England knew not Cleveland, Hackney or Solihull, but, enjoying the benefits of the people's toil in grim industry, disparaged the people who lived in its midst. Her England dressed for dinner, had several dogs and received its minor groceries from a bicycling boy from the village and its major ones by a shiny olive-green van saying Harrods.

Her own childhood place was circled by the South Downs: 'those colossal contours that express the best quality of England, since they are at the same time soft and strong', said G. K. Chesterton. 'The smoothness of them has the same meaning as the smoothness of great cart horses';[4] taut meadow hedges divided them, and village houses sat snugly between them. A church, squat and square-towered, was supported by impenetrable yew trees and an ivied dark. Inside, beyond the oak door's creak, was the musty smell of damp and ancient plaster and the particular silence of the cold recumbent tombs – while outside, over the graveyard wall, a sycamore clump, with leaves so coarse and crinkled that they rattled in the heat, sheltered some drowsy cattle which enjoyed long and tranquil thoughts, their flying tails and stamping feet keeping the flies in predatory clouds around them.

It was from an old manor house called The Homestead that Muriel Odhams was married. The youngest of four, she had already lost her brother Valentine and her fiancé, Gilbert Grune, to the First World War. Hundreds of soldiers, grievously hurt on the front line in France, were being shipped back to England to be discharged at the south-coast ports and into ambulances. But there was a shortage of ambulance-drivers, and the newspapers carried daily pieces calling for volunteers to learn to drive them and do their bit for the war effort. Muriel wanted to reply to the emergency and serve. Her response was to argue fiercely with her father to be allowed to be trained to drive an ambulance. But old Father Odhams, an unwell man, apt to scowl from behind his monocle because of his hushed-up epilepsy, would have none of it. 'What would people say', he demanded, 'of a well-brought-up girl like you perched up there on a box, driving rough soldiers around trying to find hospitals to take them?' An easy catch for convention and for appearances, he was something of a sleeping partner in Odhams Press; his older brother Will was the impatient dynamo of the business.

Harrias House met John's requirements but not Muriel's. Leased from the local estate, it sat in a rather ugly way in an ordinary bit of flat countryside with no views. My mother did make it attractive within, and, because she loved beautiful, conventional and inoffensive things, she filled her house with antiques and with flowers; but she would have loved an old house that was not pretentious and was out of reach of the suction pump that was London.

During the Second World War, as part of the Spy Patrol, she was allocated territory for surveillance: the woods and hills of rural Hedgerley. Miss Meates, from the village, came to join her: she was nice, and eager to help. A child of eight, I went along too. Beyond a rough idea of where we were to go, we really did not know what we were to do if we suspected someone. However, armed with our allocation of petrol coupons and a ration-defying picnic, we drove into the quiet lanes of the Chiltern Hills on such a spring day as gave delight at being out in the country. I watched the cheerful chaffinches with their loud, untuned notes bouncing in the hawthorn-budding hedges, the weightless beech-leaf husks moving about on the air, never quite alighting nor rising either. I peered into the half-lit dark beneath the trees and saw beyond a strand of blue, like a silent tide creeping into land. That swathe of bluebells gave way to carpet drifts of wood anemone at my feet, in bloom now to catch the light and flickering sun before thickening leaves cast a woodland twilight below.

There were few travellers other than ourselves. Those that there were moved silently on foot, or by bicycle, or to the amiable accompaniment of horses' hooves. But, because it was wartime, the peace could be exploded at any time by enemy action clattering across the sky or by army lorries moving through the countryside in droning convoys.

We parked by a field gateway – the Austin 7 was so small as not to be in the way of a horse and cart – and began to walk up the margins of the fields, peering into woods and listening for the cracking of twigs and footfall. But all that we could hear was the cuckoo, 'at once far off and near', as Wordsworth noted. You could not tell from where it sounded, except that it was in one of those beech-tree clumps where silver stems, standing tall on each hillock, were crowned with soft damp leaves like an exhalation. So much exercise and attention, however, stimulated anxiety and hunger in equal measure; it seemed judicious to return to the picnic hamper and to spread it out on the tartan rug.

We drove on. Again, the innocent fields and woods were spread before us, and the air was filled with birdsong. Then, as we started out on foot, we saw a figure seated at the field's edge. On the instant, in confused alarm, we retreated quickly up the hill – but not before we had noticed that the intruder (if such he were) was attending to a large sheet of paper spread out on his knee. A newspaper – or a map? Two middle-aged ladies and a child – we were poorly placed to accost him; and, even if we were able to reach the car by a different route, we would be well within his sight. We, the hunters, now felt hunted; and we scanned the skies for more map-reading, parachute-jumping spies. We assured ourselves that our spy – for such he must be – was so far innocent of our agitated presence.

We navigated two more hills and began to approach our car from a different direction: we had somehow to reach a police station. We saw our man start to move away. There could be no doubt that the sheet he was carefully folding was a map and not a newspaper: you could tell from the way that he folded it. From behind a bramble bush, we watched him walk easily down the field and through the gate. As he passed the car, he turned slightly in our direction and gave a quick wave. A wave to us, whom he had seen and was quietly mocking? Or a wave to an accomplice?

He set out along the lane, for all the world as though enjoying a country walk. As for us, we climbed into the car, turned around and made for the nearest police station. The sergeant looked silently at my mother over his spectacles. Then he pushed them up his nose and picked up his pen. I noticed that it had a relief nib – the kind I liked too. He dipped the pen into the ink unnecessarily often and wrote 'LADY REITH' and her address. At last, he said: 'Is that him what's the Information man?'

This was all very well; but, by this time, our spy would be almost back in Germany reporting on British Intelligence at work. And anyway, what was this 'Information man'? Information was something that in our household did not quite happen – and then I began to think that it was information that my father was Minister for. Because of him, there were no longer any signposts at crossroads. The idea was to confuse the spies; and instead we ourselves had become confused.

But the sergeant clearly felt that his moment had come. Banner headlines in the *Daily Sketch* appeared before him: 'COURSE OF THE WAR AVERTED BY PROMPT ACTION AT RURAL CONSTABULARY'. He looked at my mother hopefully, ready for the flow of evidence. My mother did her best, stumbling over the order in which things had happened. The sergeant wrote doggedly on; his pen developed a squeak, and the corners of his mouth went down. He thanked my mother and Miss Meates gruffly and did not look at me, and we filed out.

After that, my mother did not apply for more petrol for patrols. Instead, she bicycled twice a week to the Burnham Hall to make camouflage nets for anti-tank guns. She joined the committee of the British Sailors' Society which met in Lady Bennett's house. Everyone took along their own contribution of tea and sugar, and on one occasion my mother had to speak at the meeting and make a little report on the money she had raised. Back home, she read her cookery book *The Kitchen Goes to War* and tried to make omelettes with dried eggs.

I brushed the staircase and vacuumed the hall. But I was sad about the picnics.

NOTES

1. George Mackay Brown, *Greenvoe*.
2. Daniel Defoe, *The Time Born Englishman,* Part 1, line 360.
3. Reith, *Into the Wind*, p. 6.
4. G. K. Chesterton, 'A Piece of Chalk', in Phillip Lopate (ed.), *The Art of the Personal Essay* (Anchor Books, 1994).

17

The Navy is Most Grateful

THROUGH the Royal Navy Volunteer Reserve, my father found an outlet for his energies and a relief from his despair. Eventually, he assumed responsibility for all supplies and back-up for the Normandy invasion of 1944. Chairmanship of Cable and Wireless followed, with a world tour. At boarding school, I was torn between relief at being out of the domestic nexus and homesickness; my accident-prone musical precocity frustrated my teachers and me.

For four months in 1942, my father was out of work. I wished heartily for his absorbing employment, something that would create a hygienic distance between us. His company was unnatural and oppressive: would I like him to come with me to feed the hens, or pick brambles (blackberries), or carry in the logs? Did I love him? These were terrible questions, to which the answer was as clear as the fact that it could not be spoken.

He became a Justice of the Peace and, most uncharacteristically, contributed locally by repairing to the police station in

Beaconsfield every Tuesday morning to sit on the magistrates' bench. Maybe other people's misfortunes had a certain appeal. Then he made a move towards getting himself accepted by the Royal Naval Volunteer Reserve. Passed medically fit for sea-going service, he was provided with the navy blue uniform with its navy blue raincoat which made him look, he said, like his own chauffeur. He became Lieutenant-Commander Reith, RNVR. The uniform had angled stripes as opposed to the straight stripes of the Royal Navy; John was 'a two and a half striper', an older man in a young man's job, paid 27 shillings and 2 pence, about £1.35 a day. He was given another broom cupboard of an office on the Finchley Road for his part in Coastal Forces, from which he was asked to speed up the repair of new ships coming in for service.

Sir John Anderson, the Lord Privy Seal, remained his constant ally; he restrained him from attacking Churchill whenever he could, and advised him to put down a marker for himself by speaking in the House of Lords. His motion was an enquiry of the government as to whether they were giving immediate attention to the future constitution, control and management of essential public services. One part of his speech was cheered by their lordships but was heavily criticised by the press. 'Socialism in the House of Lords', protested the *Railway Review*[1] as he argued for a national transport corporation covering all forms of transport by rail, air, road, canal and coastal shipping. A form of nationalisation, he described it, referring to his first contribution to the theme in the early BBC as being a corporation 'not under shareholder control; nor under directors in the ordinary sense; still less under a Minister and civil servants'. The BBC was the first exemplar, British Overseas Airways Corporation another, in which – as certainly was so in his case – was a 'concentration of originating and ultimate authority and power' essentially in one man, he being appointed by the board.

Then, back in his ten-foot-square office, he managed to get the supply side of the navy to become a department of the Admiralty. He got the ear of Admiral Sir Dudley Pound, and marvelled at the experience in which he found himself, a Lieutenant-

Commander, being listened to with care by the First Sea Lord – as a result of which he received a secret communication from the Admiralty. It was 'addressed in that style', he said, 'which never failed to thrill me': 'To Commander-in-Chief, the Nore, Portsmouth, Plymouth Western Approaches, Rosyth, Home Fleet; Vice Admiral Dover; Flag-officer-commanding Orkneys and Shetlands; Rear Admiral Coastal Forces'. It was to the effect that, owing to the increased importance of coastal forces, an enquiry was to be held into all aspects of training, administration and maintenance. This had originated with John; he was, so to speak, making waves. His office moved from Finchley Road to Queen Anne's Gate, where Jo Stanley, his secretary in the BBC and at Imperial Airways, telephoned him from what was now called British Overseas Airways Corporation. Jo was saying that BOAC wanted him back: they had already sent a telegram to the Secretary of State for Air. But, despite this prospect of a return to a reasonable salary, which he badly needed, he immediately turned it down. Perhaps he felt that there was a future for him in the RNVR, even though his application to train to go to sea had been refused on account of age. The enveloping cloud of gloom which had hung about him, as 1942 became 1943, carried on well into the spring as he bemoaned his underemployment. Still trying to accustom himself to having no official car, there he was in the midst of the Oxford Street crowds, towering above them, in his uniform, conspicuous to all and recognised by many, regarding them with infinite distaste, and, as P. G. Wodehouse might have written of him, 'like a pterodactyl with a secret sorrow'. He was, after all, summoning his resolve to board the Underground at Oxford Circus.

Then things changed for the better for John. At home, gradually one experienced an improvement in the atmosphere as something like a rapprochement took place between him and Churchill, the latter writing that he would do his best to find suitable employment for John's well-known energy and capacity – he would like John to be pulling his full weight during the war. In his book, *Into the Wind*, John wrote:

One morning in Queen Anne's Mansions my telephone rang. 'Is that Lieutenant-Commander Reith? Controller's secretary here.' 'Yes, sir', I replied – knowing he would be a four-striper. 'The Controller asked me to enquire if he might come and see you some time today.' My director had picked up his parallel of the telephone on a signal from me; he was agog to hear my reply to this shattering suggestion. I visualised the scene – the Controller of the Navy being ushered into my room – or maybe I would meet him at the front door. He would sit as if for interview beside my table; my chief would presumably remove himself. Utterly improper. 'If the Controller wants to see me,' I replied, 'I shall call on him.' 'Oh,' said the secretary, 'I'm sure he'd appreciate that, as he's certainly very busy.' 'I was afraid of this', said Maurice. 'He spoke to me about you in the Senior the other day.' [Captain Maurice, as maintenance captain, coastal forces materials department, was John's director.]

So, ushered into the presence, I stood to attention just inside the door. Admiral Sir Frederick Wake-Walker, Third Sea Lord and Controller of the Navy, rose quickly, crossed the room holding out his hand – 'Good morning, sir', he said. 'Good morning, SIR', I replied. Emerged from his room half an hour later with a new and incredible dignity; I was NACON 2 – extra naval assistant to the Controller – naval, be it noted.[2]

The first job John was given by the Controller was to examine his organisation and find its flaws – in naval construction, engineering, dockyards, naval ordnance, electrical engineering, equipment, torpedoes, mining, research and development. John was in his element. When his large undertaking emerged in a compendious and well-received report, the Controller asked him to draw up terms of reference for a new department combining Material Duties with the training of non-ocean-going staff. Combined Operations itself had become a vast department under Earl Mountbatten, too big to handle, and it was felt that many of its activities should come inside the Admiralty. Such a department would appoint all technical officers ashore and afloat worldwide and see to the manning and equipping of all bases. As he drafted his structure plan, John mentally put himself in the place of the person who would deliver; his surprise, in due course, that he, a Lieutenant-Commander RNVR, was taking on the job intended for an active-service Rear-Admiral was to some extent simulated. A year ahead of the D-Day invasion, he was Director of Combined Operations Materials. This meant a string of bases manned and equipped, ships recalled from the Mediterranean and all parts for servicing, supplies and spare parts organised, and shipwrights trained – so that, by June 1944, 126 landing craft, 777 major ships and 1,570 minor ones, all of assorted shapes, capacities and assignations, were assembled on the south and east coasts, forests of masts and funnels at every nook and anchorage, drawn up ready to move. His office in the Admiralty kept track of every ship for repair. 'The work', he wrote with no doubt justifiable pride, 'was well and quickly done.'

Meanwhile, back from tours of inspection and, like everyone, short of sleep, John enjoyed working through the night, not using his bomb-proof premises, and finding it less lonely when the bombs were falling, preposterously noting that they were quite companionable. One night, with an air raid in full swing, and clad in dressing-gown and slippers, he stood talking on the pavement with the constable on duty in front of the Athenaeum.[3] Suddenly, the policeman shouted: 'Run, Sir!' John ran. There was a ghastly blast and the crashing of collapsing masonry. As he ran, he lost his slipper. He did not recover it.

For the first time, it became clear to me, in early June 1944, though knowing nothing of the movement of the war, that something very big was about to happen. My father referred with proud amusement to the paper in his office labelled ADMIRALTY – and then also SECRET; or MOST SECRET; and then HUSH! MOST SECRET; and finally HUSH HUSH! MOST SECRET. One Sunday afternoon in Beaconsfield, he stood at the bay window in the study. Rather uncharacteristically holding his spectacles with one earpiece between his teeth, he stared out at the rain as, propelled by high wind, it sheeted across the garden. 'This weather is not very good', he said to himself, but so that I could easily hear. Two days later, the weather was better for invasion. A further two days on, tremendously excited, he was with the Controller in Normandy. He stayed in a deserted farmhouse from which he returned, delighted both with himself and with the blue-check bathroom curtain which he had unhooked as a memento. I made it into an apron for my mother. John Colville, Churchill's private secretary and close associate throughout the war (later to be knighted), had served for a brief spell as a fighter pilot in the RAF, and was returning from the D-Day operation on the same return flight as John and his bathroom curtain. Colville wrote:

> Early in August my two months' fighting leave (extended from six weeks with prime ministerial consent) expired. I made my last operational sortie and was flown back to England in a Dakota which inadvertently flew over Havre, still in German hands, and was welcomed by a burst of mercifully inaccurate anti-aircraft fire. A fellow passenger was Lord Reith, disguised as a captain RNVR. Much better, he said, than being in Churchill's Government. How glad I must be to have got away from him. 'On the contrary, sir,' I replied, 'I am on my way back to him.'[4]

The Controller produced an encomium in which he stated that Captain – by now elevated – Reith had succeeded in the difficult task of preparing ships for amphibious operations. 'He built up a magnificent and most efficient department to which was largely due our readiness for D-Day.' He told John: 'The navy is most grateful to you'.

These blessed words flowed in part because of John's compelling need for work – for prodigious effort with significant outcome. But it was also about the allure for him of ships, the sea and the Royal Navy. He was now being kept sufficiently busy to be unable to worry about being alive. He also had another diversion, having succeeded in securing Joyce Wilson as his secretary. Her family went back to his Dunblane days, she the youngest in a family of four. She was good company – bright, charming and humorous, and an accomplished pianist with a performer's qualification from the Royal Academy of Music. She was also cut out to be a secretary to someone in a high-powered position. Not for the first time, John was deeply unconscious of anything untoward in his behaviour. Invited to launch a tank-landing ship in Newcastle, he took Joyce with him. The management responded by suggesting that she should perform the launching ceremony, to which he willingly agreed.

Not only in Newcastle, but also in Whitehall, tongues were wagging. What John chose not to notice, he did not notice – not even Muriel's feelings when, as happened more and more, Joyce came to stay at Harrias for weekends. It was, as ever it was for John, that while there was one code of rules, expectations and conduct for the rest of the world, for him there was another, totally different, self-selected one. With more than enough on her plate, it was as well that my poor mother could not know, as her husband saw more and more of Joyce Wilson, that ahead lay the purchase of a London flat for John, and, in the same building in Marsham Street, one for Joyce; and that, when it came to a world tour for Cable and Wireless shortly after the war, he of course needed a secretary and was quite unbothered by the questions of protocol which arose at every stop. While the relationship was almost certainly in a limited sense innocent, he seemed to have a compelling need to make a parade of his new and imagined freedoms from the constraints of any form of public fidelity to his wife, she unwittingly becoming the constant figure who had to be rejected in the same way as he, the young John in his days in the manse, had suffered the inconstancy of the disregarding and preoccupied mother. As has been observed by those who study these matters in the field of psychoanalysis, the alienated child sometimes becomes the promiscuous adult.

For my part, I liked Joyce. In a household that too readily succumbed to gloom, she was a cheerful and companionable interlude at weekends. In her mid-thirties, she was good at being young, and she played the piano wonderfully well. Aged 12, and not at all advanced in these matters – there were few opportunities to gain any knowledge of men's and women's relationships – I was arrested by my mother's remark that she did not know where it was all going to end with this friendship between Joyce and Daddy. My mother did not cry; she simply soldiered on with fearful fortitude and a noble, uncomprehending loyalty.

Next, because John had to have a secretary on his world tour for Cable and Wireless, he extracted Joyce from the Admiralty, his prodigious success at pulling strings as effective as ever. As a director of Cable and Wireless, he was aware of how cordially this commercially owned company was disliked in the Commonwealth. He would resign as a director and undertake a diplomatic mission on its behalf, amounting to a world tour. He could, he decided, be 'a minister without portfolio, but with a less silly name' – the real purpose of the mission being not so much 'a question of status with the Dominion Governments, but of my need to be reinstated with myself'.

He did, however, also remark that in regard to his own finances he was 'once more acting stupidly', as again his Free Church inhibitions about earning collided with his fury about his talents and status being insufficiently recognised. He was, as ever, poorly placed to sort out the confusion. Meanwhile, my mother, like John, reluctant to call people by their name, especially their first name, simply produced in regard to Joyce Wilson some kind of sound effect instead.

Paradoxically, John was never more fond of Muriel than when apart from her. He sent her many closely written pages most regularly. His mission was, after all, being undertaken before wartime hostilities were fully concluded and with the consequent extra risks. No-one else was undertaking a world tour about anything. And so, as well as that, Muriel may not have been all that cheered to learn that, once again, he had discovered that 'life was for living', whatever that meant, and that he had bought himself an outrageous pair of bathing pants with 'Honolulu Aloya' printed all over them to celebrate his mood.

After that, what then? Late one night in 1945, my father barged into my room, where I was fast asleep. 'Chuch-hill' – his pronunciation – 'has been pushed out', he boomed. Since this was the form taken by political discussion in our household, the significance of Churchill's removal was mostly lost on me, though I knew at least that my father's thirst for vengeance would be, for the time being anyway, satisfied.

The news of the Japanese surrender in the summer of 1945 was received by the family with scant emotion. But one contribution to its celebration was little short of inspirational. This was the Laurence Olivier film of *Henry V*, which, unexpectedly, my mother took us to see.

> Once more into the breach, dear friends, once more,
> Or close the wall up with our English dead!
> In peace there's nothing so becomes a man
> As modest stillness and humility:
> But when the blast of war blows in our ears,
> Then imitate the action of the tiger ...[5]

Who, one asked oneself, was this Shakespeare who walked the cathedral of the English language and, in liquid eloquence, summoned from words such vaulting emotions as to bestow upon kings their stature, leaders their heroes' deeds and upon humanity itself its 'still sad music'? Behind the lines of this epic film, the images swept on. The field of battle where the English mounted might moved in tense and measured advance, reined in until released into the gathered trot, itself became the surging canter, still contained until at last the explosion of gallop as all those caparisoned horses advanced as one, the bright sky flying with so many multi-coloured pennons, gonfalons and ensigns, the Royal Standard splendidly at their head.

My mother and Christopher and I returned from the cinema. Would I, my mother said, mix the hens' food and feed them? There comes a time in a young person's life when it becomes necessary to leave home. This was it. I wondered how to do it.

A year later, aged 14, I arrived at boarding school with a musicianship that was both precocious and accident-prone, to the teacher's ultimate perplexity. Tension, unrecognised, was setting in with a relentless grip. It took the end-of-term concert to seal my fate in my own eyes as inhibition stifled performance.

Like most of those selected to perform, I practised diligently enough, working away at the Grieg sonata. In the music corridor, every music cell, each with clapped-out piano, was blasted into a tinnient babel as performers from teenies to seniors worked to catch up on lost time. Ominously, the gym acquired massed chairs in rows; and on the day itself we assembled in nervous excitement behind the double doors. First the juniors, who had to be helped by an indulgent presence onto the piano stool, did their one-hand-and-then-the-other-hand show, unemployed fingers stubbing the air. In no time, they were sliding off the stool, to a scattering of smiles and thin clapping. One by one, performers and pieces advanced, every parent mixing envy and triumph with ghastly patience and a looking towards the end. The double doors were opened for the last time by attending prefects – and there, on all three sides, I saw the consuming crowd, my father a black mound in the midst, instantly conspicuous. This was do or die. A reasonably good start: I liked the Grieg.

But this false dawn led to the testing grounds ahead where the music suddenly had to flow rapidly. For this, there had been an accumulation of the teacher's pressure, worked on with diligence and tension in equal measure, the musical excitement the ultimate trip-wire. I stopped, fingers fused. I would go back. But the chasm opened as before; it would have been easier to persuade a terrified horse to jump a gorge than my hands to cover the notes. I gathered up the sheets and left, the doors already opening for my predicted and mortified exit. There was as much hope of my performance becoming reconciled to an audience as of the polarities bonding.

When I left school at the age of 17, my father's next move compounded the problem. I was to have lessons from Dr Frederick Jackson of the Royal Academy of Music. My father could hardly know that the last thing I needed was more lessons, especially those in which he had a stake. And certainly not from a high-powered teacher and performer in a setting to which only the most promising pupils gained entry. My childhood was already a heavily instructed one. My parents, in their different ways, were controlling, so that music for me was left in a state of being offended.

What I needed — and what everyone needs in a similar position — was freedom and encouragement.

The self-taught pianist Alfred Brendel attributes some of his extra-ordinary international success to his 'not being hindered or damaged by teachers'. More and more, we need to rediscover that 'education', when connected to its Latin root *educere*, means to 'lead out'. 'It is not instruction but provocation that I can receive from another soul', quoted Freeman Tilden, the great American communicator of environmental awareness.[6]

Hard as it would have been to put into words, there was a real sense, I knew, in which, as a child at home, I had not been able to 'have' the music that beat and sang within. This was scarcely, one would have thought, a matter for pilfering — and yet indubitably so. It was, after all, with alarm that my mother perceived that music was coming to mean a lot to me. She very much wanted it to be tamed into something safe and ordinary like hymn tunes, 'songs my mother sang', and Gilbert and Sullivan. My father, however, did recognise something going on — but not his own unconscious need to plunder and embezzle it. I was to realise in some sense that what I had was not wholly acceptable in one quarter and was ripe for acquisition in the other.

The headmistress handed me a small cutting from *The Times*. 'The Reith Lectures', it said, were being founded in honour of Lord Reith and in recognition of his contribution to culture and national life. I knew that he would feign an immense unwillingness to sanction them and would come as near as possible to blocking the honour without actually effecting it. I also knew the schoolgirl's desire to swank about my distinguished parent as a way of standing out from the general crowd.

It was Christmas 1949. My mother and father were invited to a carol service in St George's Chapel, Windsor. I was included in Canon Alec Vidler's invitation, and I took with me a fair measure of fright. After the service, there was to be a gathering in the canon's residence; and, even though school was now behind me, I had learned few social accomplishments within the confines of its cloistered regime that would give support at such a moment. My father went, as ever, what he would call 'tidily dressed': 'I always wear a hat whenever there is a chance of guards or sentries saluting', he said, regardless of the fact that he always wore a hat anyway. He also claimed that he only liked parties in which men bigger than himself were present. But, because he seldom recognised anyone as such, one might conclude that he only rarely enjoyed parties.

The genial canon was a large man, a study in black and white. His black shirt with white tie toned with his black beard with white rim. His good friend was that engaging wizard of a man whose large and very public talent people loved to hate: Malcolm Muggeridge was seen as being spicily wicked, a man whose wit made him a national figure, even in the days before television had worked its way into the consciousness. Now, over the heads in this large and crowded room, John saw him enter. Wherever it was in his hierarchy of the greater or the lesser hate figures that John had Muggeridge placed, one thing was now certain. John was fighting his way to the far end of the room, and, parting the curtains, hoping to make good his escape by this improbable route. It was obvious to me, and no doubt to many others, as the curtains heaved and bulged, that he thought he would escape by the window; but, in common with most decent castles, Windsor had its own moat, which, designed to delay entry, would now prevent exit. This had rapidly still to be achieved, and by the more conventional manner, though with much pushing past tight groups apparently locked in fascinating exchange but in reality becoming more and more aware that something bizarre was going on in their midst. Conversations languished; glares stolen became unashamed stares as the Right Honourable the Lord Reith of Stonehaven, PC, GCVO, GBE, LLD tried to flee that gnomic regard that watched him steadily from across the room.

Paradoxically, as in time Muggeridge so succeeded in gaining John's trust as to work with him on a series of acclaimed televised interviews, he, more than anyone, came to understand his strenuous and contradictory subject, to the extent that he found him, 'in a weird way, loveable'. He went on, as we have remarked, to ask: 'How can this man continue to convey an impression of greatness despite so many intimations of littleness?' No doubt he was remembering that exceptional display of littleness at Canon Vidler's party.

NOTES

1. *Railway Review*, 26.6.42; McIntyre, p. 269.
2. Reith, *Into the Wind*, p. 468.
3. Elite and ancient gentlemen's club off Pall Mall. Election for membership much sought after.
4. John Colville, *Fringes of Power* (diaries). Reproduced by permission of Hodder & Stoughton Ltd.
5. Shakespeare, *Henry V,* Act III, Scene 1, line 1.
6. Freeman Tilden, *Interpreting our Heritage*, 3rd edn (University of North Carolina Press, 1977), p. 33, quoting R. W. Emerson.

18

No Longer a Monopoly

M Y FATHER exerted himself to defend the BBC's monopoly, even though commercial television was well on the way. He wrote his autobiography, *Into the Wind*, interfered with my musical initiatives and pursued my university career with daily letters. When I was appointed to raise a large sum of money within the Church of Scotland, his old insecurities surfaced in relation to Lord MacLeod of Fuinary, for whom I worked. My father listed his seven most hated figures – among whom was Murray Leishman, whom I would marry.

Malcolm Muggeridge found John rather stupid. Or so he said later to John's oldest granddaughter, Iona. If he meant that John was emotionally stupid, he was right. Lacking subtlety in regard to others, John was tone-deaf to dialectic and discussion because there was no way in which he could significantly tune in. He might claim 'to be a good judge of character'; but deep-level listening was not his.

When he had a passionate concern for an issue or a topic, it was because *he* was the topic, but disguised as public-service broadcasting or the rationalisation of a service – or, that *summum bonum* of all endeavours, efficiency, regardless of whether the subject was Imperial Airways before the war or New Towns after it. But he had a natural logic with which he could penetrate to the essential argument and carry on to the planned outcome, no matter how great the subjectivity mixed in with it.

But now, in 1951, the government was putting forward its plans for commercial television. The BBC's monopoly was about to be fragmented; and so it was with more than logic that John led the opposition in the debate in the House of Lords. A parliamentary correspondent wrote: 'Nothing quite like it has been heard in the House of Lords. It was more like the utterance of a prophet, and it was clear from the faces on the Government front bench that prophets are an embarrassment to them.'[1]

The departure of Sir William Haley as Director General more or less coincided with what John called 'the smash-up of the BBC'. Haley venerated his prickly predecessor and had succeeded in drawing John into a closer relationship with the corporation than he had had since leaving. It also opened up a minefield: 'It was, of course, Reith's passion for the smallest detail which lay at the root of the trouble. The itch to get his fingers into any aspect of the BBC's activities was uncontrollable', says Ian McIntyre in his biography. It says much for Haley that he could challenge John: 'If you could only realise what a towering legend you are!'

But John, claiming that he was more used to being under-estimated than overrated, was, in the circumstances now facing the BBC, backing off from Haley's intense protestations of friendship. And so it was I, rather than John, who rather oddly was brought in to accompany Haley on his round of farewells in Broadcasting House. The pair of us, awkwardly and with scant conversation, lunched in the Governors' dining room. I found it difficult to rid my mind of a journalist's remark that the DG was the only man he had ever met with two glass eyes.

John was now writing his memoirs. He had concluded the part-time job which he had been enjoying as chairman of Hemel Hempstead Development Corporation, having found within himself a natural aptitude for town-planning. This had been recognised with a Fellowship of the Royal Town Planning Institute. Now the urge to write, 'of which he had been vexatiously aware' throughout his working life, was no longer going to be satisfied with his daily diary entries. And so he occupied a small table and chair in the sitting room of the Blue House.

The Blue House was two attractive fisherman's cottages made into one and made available for summer holiday letting. It was one of several clustered round the harbour of Portmahomack in Ross-shire; and, because John liked it so much, two summers were spent there, despite the distance from Beaconsfield – and despite, too, the bad start to the first journey, when the overloaded car, with all four of us aboard, had sat down on its brakes and refused to move. The subsequent unloading and halving of the baggage was something about which you might have a private giggle at the time, or refer to later with care.

But John was in a sufficiently equable frame of mind to pursue his writing, ordered as ever in his doings. His fresh paper and his completed writings were in neat piles beside him, along with his pencils, rubbers and gold pen. You could no more have imagined John Reith without his gold pen than you could consider Hadrian without his wall.

Perhaps because the fishermen were taking Christopher out in their cobles to fish the salmon nets, he invited them in for a dram. Six or so piled in, John at his most genial, the men becoming more and more at home. John's writing, however, for the typing of which he had again recalled Joyce Wilson, was not without its critics. The chief reader for Hodder & Stoughton commented on the author's prose style: 'It is enough to make the Brothers Fowler turn in their graves'. John was surprisingly accepting of this remark, reducing by a small percentage the number of sentences which were supposed to make do without their grammatical subject, their verb having to do the work of both. *The Spectator*, impatient with the prose style, described it as 'a series of short snorts'.

As for me, I found refuge with my oil-paint box in my bedroom upstairs. It had been given to me one Christmas. But it had had to be, my mother explained apologetically, second-hand – such things were nowhere to be found after the war — and it was a little damaged. But inside the polished wood case were tubes of paint in their compartments, with names like burnt umber, burnt sienna, crimson lake, terre verte and chrome yellow. There were two much larger tubes of black and white and a small bottle each of linseed oil and turpentine. And then there were brushes, all elegant with long pale varnished handles, some broad and flat and in a series of sizes, others fat and round. From lessons at home, I learned to find my way through the processes and on to the oddly resistant canvas, now resting on an easel rather than lying flat. It was in many ways an intractable medium; colour in such volume and so massed had to be practised long and hard before it could be cajoled into even a remote representation of some scene or object. The technique was about effect rather than precision.

From a neighbouring farm had come a great bunch of sweet peas, from which I selected four blooms. I opened out the paint box on the bedroom floor and spread everything round about it, at the same time adjusting to the absence of the easel. Before long, after a pencil sketch, red, mauve, crimson and white blooms started to live and grow under my brush. This was exciting and absorbing. Then there was to be a drive to Tain, where, apparently, there was shopping to be done. All the time, as we moved about the tired little streets and drab post-war shops, they looked to me neither tired nor drab. When there is an inner excitement, the most mundane objects and surroundings can assume a gleam all of their own; even the sign saying No Right Turn looked good.

By now, I was preparing for university — and, having been given, as Ian McIntyre notes, a 'generous supply of Reith genes', no sooner had I fallen into some kind of fragile understanding with my father than it was explosively blown apart. When it looked to him as though I was about to leave home — I had arranged a few days' holiday youth-hostelling with a friend — this was to him a delinquency, an estrangement acted out. How one was to enter the adult world without leaving home, unless as a sad case of arrested development, was puzzling to me. And so now, as I was about to depart on holiday, cycle frame straining under the load, he, eschewing a farewell, repaired to the chicken run, where a cackling consternation erupted. Perhaps he thought I would join him among the squawks and feathers and say how sorry I was, and that I was quite wrong to go off and – horrors! – stay in youth hostels. After all, if I wanted a holiday, he would find a good hotel and pay for me there. And anyway, I should realise how much he could help me if only I would ask. Help me to do what? If I was to be Head Wren, it was hard to see how I could do that without first leaving home.

There were consolations, however. The parish church organ beckoned. At the console, the button's press yielded the creaking of the expanding bellows. Centred on the organ stool, I saw the console climb in cliffs before me, the ivory draw-stops clustered round, and the pedal board fanned out at my feet. I felt like a ladybird on the bridge of an ocean-going liner about to cast off. Here, this great creature surrounded me, attendant on my command. Diapasons and, stacked behind them, serried rows of brass and wood windpipes would yield the trumpet's snarl and the reedy oboe, then to explore the high vaults; my feet would stride the pedal notes, the bourdon would speak and a toneless shudder would emerge from the earth's kernel.

This private world was not to be. My father, for whom music was either 'magnificent' or nothing, decided that this was after all to be the field in which I was to excel, and that he would intervene to ensure the outcome. Arrival at this particular summit would take place magically and without pausing in the rut with the rest. Some footholds on the musical path upwards would, however, in my case be provided, by the simple device of arranging for me to meet some of the distinguished souls already there, whereupon, as in broadcasting, some amazing form of transmission would occur.

Accordingly, we started at the very top. On the musical pinnacle sat St Cecilia herself. But she was reluctant to leave her stained-glass window, and her surrounding maidens continued copiously to drape their long hair about her small positif organ. On to mere mortals. Sir Thomas Beecham was disliked by my father because the conductor was unalarmed by outsize egos and liked to tweak them with his wit. And so I met Sir Adrian Boult. Boult had insisted on sustaining a friendship with John long after BBC days, his usefully humorous take on life contrasting with, and sometimes helping to extinguish, the pyrotechnics of the other. And then I met Sir William Mackie, organist of Westminster Abbey, no less. High up in the organ loft of the Abbey, suspended, as it were, in a cocoon of light, this gracious man waved me into his position at the organ and gave me some outline directions. He waited by, smiling. My father stood behind, adding to the number of gathered gargoyles. But I had only one need, and that was for all the nine centuries of masonry and glass to fall, directly and immediately upon me.

After that, I was trundled, or rather chauffeured, to the workshops of the greatest (he had to be the greatest) of British organ-builders, Father Henry Willis III. He was an ancient, tiny man with a young person's cheer and the alacrity of a hummingbird flitting from blossom to blossom as he moved through the intricacies of the rebuild of a cathedral organ, spread out on his workshop floor.

I felt like the poet John Betjeman: 'Failed Divinity — was nothing to be done?' A paper by Sarah Nettleton called *The Internal World of the Musically Gifted Child* has this to say: 'Music is experienced as always having been there ... sound and its effects are not an acquisition but the experience of a function which music once had for us all and which we have retained. Music, it seems, can reach back to a primary timelessness, to pre-verbal memories ... It expresses feelings in a non-mediated way, directly.'[2] There was still something that could not be plundered, I felt.

At the University of St Andrews, among the many anxieties of being a student, were new delights to be realised by plucking up courage to engage with the life of this ancient Scottish university. But opportunities were available only to the extent that, step by step, I could detach from home. This was not made easier by my father's almost daily letters and regular telephone calls also. But, still, horizons opened out, whether in lecture theatre or in coffee shop. Or in the Chapel choir. In Cedric Thorpe Davie, we had a gifted choirmaster. One day, in rehearsing the Fauré *Requiem*, we sopranos crash-landed on high A. Cedric buried his face in his hands, and then, regarding us through a managed impatience, appealed to us. 'Look', he said. 'You're a seagull alighting on a tall flagpole. You don't scramble up to reach it from below; you drop down on it from above. In the same way, you are going to drop onto this high A.' And then, with annoyance and inspiration mingled, 'SING! Sopranos', he cried. Reassured, and connecting with the thrill, we landed sweetly on our note.

But, back in London, where my parents had moved to a unique flat in the medieval Lollards Tower in the precincts of Lambeth Palace, my father's desolation at my departure to university, I learned afterwards, was dislocating normal behaviour, as again he tried to befriend various young women. When in due course I got my degree, in English and Philosophy, I knew that I could never again return home.

In 1950, the Labour prime minister, Clement Attlee, had offered my father the chairmanship of the Colonial Development Corporation. Although John had quibbled and delayed about pay and conditions, he had taken on the job with quiet joy – which had then to be even more controlled, since he was the subject of an *Observer* profile:

> In its long history, the British Empire has owed a great deal to a few men of genius. They were not easy men, nor were they the type that succeeds in the give-and-take of our domestic political system. But it was men like Raleigh, Clive, Hastings, Gordon, Livingstone, and Rhodes who made ours the most successful of the empires of modern times ...
>
> Where, in our mild, modern community, could one find a man possessing the technical and social standards of today and the peculiar cast of mind of the great imperial pioneers? In selecting Lord Reith to be Chairman of the CDC, Mr Attlee has shown great insight of the man and the job ...[3]

John, however, along with Churchill, was not the only giant abroad in the land. The Very Reverend Dr George MacLeod, Celt extraordinary, mystic, patrician and rebelling minister of the Church of Scotland, was nearly of an age with John and had grown up in a grand house in Glasgow, a few doors away from the Reiths, who, by comparison, lived more modestly a little further down the hill in Lynedoch Street. George MacLeod's family were very much of the Auld Kirk, with a long line of distinguished ministers stretching far back. The young John Reith found much to envy in all this, and leaned from his window of a Sunday morning to assure himself that more carriages drew up at his father's church than at the rival show up the street.

Now, in 1958, here they were, together in the sitting room in George's house on the island of Iona. The Iona Community was George's foundation, and its minister and lay members worked together to relate politics and practicalities to the Gospel. George had recently been made a member of the House of Lords; but this elevation did nothing to counter the disarray in which he and his spirited wife, Lorna, lived. The fire was not lit, nor had the ashes been cleared out from the night before. George, moving about restlessly before the fireplace, flicked cigarette ash in the general direction of the grate; but he left it so long that the ash curled over and tipped partly down his jacket, already well signed from earlier deposits of smoking and dining. The disordered furnishings, insistently used, nevertheless retained a surviving hospitality; an unpredictable number of guests travelled in and out of the house.

Now John and Muriel were among their number – reluctantly so, no doubt, and only because I was organising a fund-raising campaign, chaired by George, for the Church. There George was, an inbuilt contradiction, uncomfortable to be with, but also the best of company – the uncompromising centre of any gathering in a way that his contemporary was unable to match.

Ian Mackenzie, one of the then increasing number of ministers around the Iona Community, on the island rebuilding the Abbey, wrote of George as 'a romantic adventurer, a Celtic word-spinner, a mystic, a poet, an entrepreneur, a warrior, a seer'.[4] And he was also the Great Communicator. On platform, podium or pulpit, however massive the building, it was as though, from this orator, lightnings and energy coruscated to enflame the intervening space and assail each and every one of the assembled multitude. No-one had experienced anything like this. They may have known that his would be no limping phrases, no tired metaphors stranded like jellyfish above the high-tide mark. Clichés would have been strangled at birth; the audience prepared for a performance – but, instead of enjoying it, they were shattered. Afterwards, they moved out as one, silent, concussed, nursing so many political migraines. George, an ordained minister, was concerned for the here and now more than the hereafter; for the national and the international emergencies of living and for the people who do not prosper. 'The defeat of soil erosion is a more imperious need of God than a ministry in some dormitory town where the whole guts of life is catered for by the secular and the dog collar surrounds a yapping voice that is left to talk about the spiritualities which are now so attenuated ...'[5]

I reflected that these two men, who had known of one another for long enough, had never sought one another's company. Almost certainly, John was disconcerted by George; he was, after all, unused to people who were completely unafraid of him. And George's abrupt, declamatory style was apt to connect more with what was going on in the images of his mind than with what anyone else may have thought or said. John was not the first to be blown off course by George. After George's idiosyncratic perceptions and imaginings, John's assertions were apt to sound more like so many preliminaries to a good document without a project behind it. For John worked in immediacies, most of which were filled by his image of himself inhabiting such issues as monopoly, dictatorship and independence. Again efficiency, that bastion of order and logic, became, in his view, a celebration of some ultimate aim which he had nevertheless anticipated. It was as though, supported by his personalised view of the Almighty, he did not have a beyond, a distant aspiration, a commanding view. All of his aspirations – visions, even – of the best and greatest ends of broadcasting were visited and inhabited by his ferocious ego, crowding in and obscuring. He, who found it hard to love anyone other than out of self-love, had, however, his highest ideal, and it was for the BBC: that it should retain its monopoly and its standards; indeed, that he should one day return to claim his nearly dictatorial rights. It was small wonder that the conversation between George and John fast became like something the dog had brought in and intended to bury when he had time.

I was on the island ostensibly to plan further for the church-extension campaign. I quickly learned, however, that, for George, detail was a bore: airborne in his thoughts and images, he seldom landed to explain himself. Abruptly, I was told to 'Follow me', and he climbed the stair out of the Abbey and stumped along the corridor and through the refectory. There, as it happened, the Community members at work on the buildings were enjoying a break. Normally, there would be nothing odd or different about this; but this was no normal set-up. The Iona Community was a bastion of male exclusivity. I enjoyed the experience as I walked through the friendly crowd. Now, at a desk, George started in characteristic vein: 'If Boots Cash Chemists were to open up a new branch once a month for ten years, it would be thought a miracle of business achievement. That is what the Church has done; it has raised £3 million since the war to open a new church once a month for ten years.'

He dived into a mountain of papers on a laden table beside his desk and amazingly drew forth a letter from the clerk of a rural presbytery in the west of Scotland, who asserted – with some justification, I thought – that Dr MacLeod had to understand that his members worked in rural areas of declining population and with falling church rolls; that income was diminishing and that – and here George continued as though still reading from the letter – 'when I am preaching and wishing to emphasise my point by pounding the cushion on the lectern, the dust that rises from it is so thick that I quite lose sight of my congregation'.

I had met Murray Leishman at St Andrews University, and we were now engaged. Photographs in which we walked cheerfully into the future appeared in the press. We were happily dressed in polo-neck sweaters; but a sweltering telegram from my father reached Murray: 'Can Mr Leishman not learn how to dress properly, even if only as a Minister of the Gospel?' This was, of many taunts, one too far, and he sat down and wrote a cracker of a letter back. He showed it to Rev. Dr Bill Smellie, minister of St John's Church in Perth, where we were to be married. Bill, a wise and steadfast friend, praised the letter warmly. 'That's a splendid letter', he said. 'Now – put it in the bottom drawer of your desk, and have a look at it in a year's time. Remember – you can afford to be generous. After all, you got the girl.' The letter did not go.

But John's behaviour became stranger than ever. 'He continued', wrote a journalist, 'to occupy himself with a succession of compliant women, all of whom he wished to befriend and dominate. When a relationship ended in tears he was vitriolic, excising the fallen favourite from recognition or forgiveness. One was his own daughter.' He was regularly to be seen with a certain Dawn MacKay. He took her to see Noel Coward's *Waiting in the Wings* and to expensive restaurants. They travelled by sleeper to Edinburgh, from where they went to call on her god-daughter in Perthshire; and, at weekends, John was a regular visitor to the MacKay household at Finchampstead in Berkshire. When enraged, he would smash his coffee cup – but still they had him back. Our wedding date announced, he made a great parade of his intention not to be there, 'Marista', he said to the MacKays, being 'no daughter of mine'. 'Good gracious,' Dawn exclaimed, 'Lady Reith must have been carrying on with the milkman, then.' But such doings reached me indirectly, or not at all, as my birthday and our engagement passed unacknowledged. To those who would congratulate him on our engagement, he replied that 'it was a matter of distress to other members of his family'. But, as George MacLeod remarked, 'only the fourth person of the Trinity would be good enough for a daughter of Reith'.

John, in 1960, was more or less occupied with directorships of British Oxygen and Phoenix Assurance, and also with the liquidation of the North British Locomotive Company (NBL). He had to put up with being deputy chairman to Tom Coughtrie's no doubt entirely able chairmanship of NBL; but he retained a possessive hold on any organisation with which he had had an association. It was, after all, with NBL in Springburn that he had served his apprenticeship fifty years earlier. John was startled one morning, as he appeared in the boardroom in good time for a meeting, to find that I had preceded him. I wished to challenge the absurdity of his carry-on about my engagement, and in a way that was more effective than words exchanged. Verbal communications tend to have, in such circumstances, their own built-in degeneracy as passions and irrationalities take over. The astonishment of other arriving board members was also useful. After that, I drove into Glasgow to pick up the day's work in the office.

In the midst of the wreckage, John had, through some astute moves by Hugh Carleton Greene, now Director General of the BBC, mended some fences there. Greene, seeing choppy water ahead for the BBC, found it useful to have Lord Reith on his side – if for nothing more than to forestall his firing-off at random and in some regrettable direction against the BBC. Various BBC events opened up to John – to which, deserting his wife, he took Dawn. The BBC, still scarcely out of the shadow of the stern prophet of old, must have found this new style perplexing to say the least; some, perhaps, remembered the story of Peter Eckersley and wondered why they had striven so hard to live up to Reithian standards if these could so easily cave in.

Secure in one another, Murray and I could not experience remorse as the sounds of distant cudgels thrown, libels uttered and coffee cups shattered reached us indirectly. Murray's parents, Bobby and Gladys, kept their shock to themselves and were in kind, generous and celebratory mood throughout. John had asked BBC Scotland's Andrew Stewart to make a few enquiries about Bobby Leishman. He found he was deputy editor of the *Evening Despatch*. The wedding was fixed for 3 December 1960. Murray's sister, Muriel, and her husband Eoin marked the engagement with warm hospitality. They heard some of our story almost with disbelief. As for John, he might be at the wedding. Or he might not. Whatever he decided, problems would abound – we were not terribly bothered. But we held out another olive branch. Knowing that he would spurn the offer of an arranged meeting, we arrived at Euston station early one morning and waited by his car and his chauffeur. As he got off the overnight train from Edinburgh, as usual excluding the scruffy public from his gaze and looking as if he had had bad news in 1889 and had not got over it, he failed to see us. Philips, his chauffeur, said: 'There is somebody here hoping you will recognise them, my lord'. Philips knew fine what was going on. I said 'Hello', and introduced Murray, who had to hold out his hand for a long time before the salute, with glare attached, was returned. He noticed my engagement ring and later wrote it up in as unflattering tones as he did his future son-in-law. But the row over his signet ring, which I had taken off with some finality, was to run for the next six years. Such pachyderm prejudices as these could do nothing other than fuel our detachment, the solidarity of our friends and, among the closest of them, a certain relieved merriment.

At Bill and Chrissie Smellie's hospitable house in Perth, we watched the John Freeman interview with my father. There were two things about this interview, neither of which was evident: that he had been deeply afraid of the interview, and that Dawn MacKay was watching on a monitor next door. But that he was a rogue, up to his tricks and his subterfuge again, was transparent to us all that night at the manse in Perth. 'I was more impressed by the performance than convinced by the person', Murray remarked.

But there was a price to be paid. A childhood epilepsy was to recur, and I woke to find myself in hospital, remembering nothing. Then, with Murray there, recollections here and there began their gentle and random assertions, and with them came feelings of infinite comfort and assurance. This was not to be like last time, against the world alone. I could leave hospital; for the consultant, this further epileptic attack was 'idiopathic', or, in layman's terms, a safety valve operating out of fearful pressure.

Another aid to recovery was this letter from George MacLeod. He was heroically trying to carry on where I had suddenly left off in the church-extension game of visiting presbyteries.

Dear Marista,

Of course I passed that document to you when you were well. I am so sorry to have bothered you with it. I am quite well again.

The Highest flight of my visit was to Kirkcudbright Presbytery where I went alone, collecting cards springing out from all corners of the back seat. (By that time three thousand, originally ordered, had been refused by ministers all now in mental homes after seeing their Sessions). But I brightly arrived at K. and asked the way to St Andrew's Church. This was at a side street and turned out to be a Roman Catholic Church (the time was five to three): not even, I supposed, the Roman Church had come in on the scheme, I realised they were all waiting for me at Newton Stewart! I got on the 'phone to the Police there, but the constable said it had little to do with him. I told him I thought that criminal negligence, but he failed to get the point. A sergeant took over and agreed it was an arresting situation. He promised to bike to the meeting and at least hold the Convener in communicado till I arrived. I hurtled across to Newton Stewart at my usual desperate thirty miles an hour (fifteen miles away), and arrived to find the entire meeting sitting immobilised and silent. The dust that had fallen from their moustaches positively littered the room. They gave me the impression – never yet entirely disproved – that they had been sitting there since you addressed them last February. I rattled off all my best stories, each of which fell like wet bits of chewing gum sprayed around my feet. I put the cards, in correct numbers, on the chewing gum, and left with the Convener, who was not taking the cards himself as he had discovered dry rot in his Bible. I have every reason to believe the whole meeting is still sitting there. Operation last meal will shortly be enacted unless their wives discover in the course of the next fortnight that they have not in fact come home.

As regards the rest, innumerable people sent their good wishes to you.

Once I had sufficiently recovered, I set about encouraging my mother, now permanently at Christopher's farm, to send out wedding invitations and arrange a meal at the Station Hotel in Perth. Absorbed as one is in one's own marvellous affairs, I felt unsympathetic to her general reluctance and gloom. But sandwiches and a pot of tea was hardly, in my view, a wedding feast; and, with backward looks about the cost, I wheeled her along to the hotel and managed to get an ice-cream to accompany the teapot.

It must have been hard for Christopher to have me staying at that time at the farm. At a particularly contumacious moment, I left the room and retired to the kitchen, there to do the washing-up. I shut the door before bursting lustily into song, no doubt rehearsing the cheerful Handel melody that lay ahead on our wedding day. But the door flew open. 'Don't you understand how perfectly *ghastly* everything is? How can you possibly *sing*? It's all your fault', said Christopher. At which point there came a further delivery of wedding presents to add to the intruding heap in the corner of the kitchen.

But, if Muriel had had a hard time with her husband, there was much more ahead. *Quem Deus vult perdere, prius dementat* – whom the gods wish to destroy, they first drive mad – as the Latin hath it. In addition, there are those around who are sorely tried in the process. Of Barbara Hickman, more was asked than should ever be required of any human being. She had come as a junior secretary to John under Molly Cotara, his secretary in CDC days. She returned to work for him in early 1961, and was at once told that she would find quite a change in him since she had worked for him last. He trotted out his famous dictum as to what life was for – to which was now added that it was also for loving. Not long into the job, she found herself not only typing out chunks of his diary which were intended to relive his feelings for Dawn MacKay, but also having the content discussed in preparation. A section of the diary was kept locked in a briefcase, with detailed instructions to Barbara as to how she was to gain access to Lollards Tower to secure it in the event of his death. (In his old age, my father wrote to *The Times* seeking advice on the destiny for his diaries. He wanted the public to exert itself on his behalf and, feeling sorry for him, work away to find solutions to a problem that was not really bothering him at all. He never had any intention of heeding what was fed back to him from a range of racked brains and sympathies extorted, and enjoyed the continuing life of the problem and the strong possibility that Christopher and I would fall out over it in due course. He nearly got his way.)

The question of suicide was not one he spared his young secretary, as she found herself carrying ever more of his emotional load. She booked dinner tables, conveyed ambivalent messages to Muriel — to which she strongly objected — as to why he was delayed that night, and bought theatre tickets, all in British Oxygen's time. If she had a conscience, his did not bother him as he lived his obsession with Dawn MacKay and the resulting mayhem which surrounded it. In later years, Jo Stanley made it her job to edit out much of the Dawn MacKay material — although not the section on the time when, with her, John wrote that he was sexually aroused — from which Barbara had concluded that they had not, after all, had sexual relations. Not that anyone else, in the enlarging public who looked on at his infatuated state, would have shared her view. She was probably right.

Dawn MacKay remained usefully unaware, it seems, not just of how things were being perceived, but also of the effect on his family, especially his wife and son. She was having a good time meeting people, going to places she would not otherwise have done, and receiving expensive gifts; but she was also perceptive: 'I don't think I was altogether real, you know. I was a sort of fictional being, a fantasy composition of things that he had always wanted, bits of what he would have liked Lady Reith to be, of what he wanted Marista to be, only I didn't have Marista's brains ...'[6] After one of his more outrageous outbursts, criticising his wife as being 'no suitable consort for me', Dawn reasonably enough asked him why he had married her. Even she was taken aback by his answer: 'Somebody else that I didn't particularly like was interested in her, and so I thought I would see if I could cut him out'. He had always enjoyed shocking people, untroubled as he was by scruples of any kind.

Dawn MacKay was private about the work she did for the telephone Samaritans; and now her skills and experience were to be tested. John telephoned her in the early hours when she had just got in from a ball. He was in a great agitation. He was alone at Lollards Tower, and told her he had a gun in his hand. 'I didn't *think* he would commit suicide, because I thought he was too arrogant,' she said, 'but there was always the danger of a dramatic gesture.' After the best part of two hours on the phone, her Samaritan repertoire exhausted, she finally said: 'Well, if that's what you want to do, it's perfectly easy – just pull the trigger'. There was a tremendous crash at the other end of the line. She thought: 'Oh, my God!' – but all that had happened was that he had dropped both the gun and the telephone, and that was the end of it. The next day, her father rang John and said: 'You'll kindly get into your car and you'll come down here'. He drove down, meek as a lamb, and handed over the gun.

Barbara Hickman was always clear about the involvement of the whole MacKay family in the Reith affair: of how he drove with them on their visit to Orkney and how he regularly spent weekends with them at their home. John would, she told me, stay late at the office, not because there was work to do but because he hated to go home to Lollards Tower, complaining of the loneliness. Muriel was at Christopher's farm in Perthshire, probably more at his insistence than out of her own conviction as to which of the two men, husband or son, she should be caring for. She would probably have chosen the first, had he consented. As it was, with Philips waiting outside the office until almost midnight to drive him home, he would then go and walk to and fro on Westminster Bridge, considering the parapet. Then he had appendicitis; he would not allow Muriel to come down, and Barbara visited him daily. He almost forgot his forty-fifth wedding anniversary, for which Barbara was despatched to buy a brooch for Muriel.

His tenuous connections with the world of work suffered a further blow when the British Transport Commission offered Dr Richard Beeching the job of rationalising the railways – a job that John coveted. Pathetically, he got himself a lunch with Beeching to say that he would be glad to help him in his task if Beeching could find a position for him. Beeching said neither Yes nor No, which meant No. Observing him at a meeting, Richard Hoggart described 'the towering and anguished-looking Lord Reith [who] spoke as though his words were being cut out of granite in a thunderstorm'.

My mother and father had spent Christmas 1960 at Christopher's farm. Murray and I, lately returned from our Norwegian honeymoon, basked in the cheerful illusion that the feelings of benevolence which we were experiencing towards the world in general would act in a soothing way on its more contumacious aspects. It would be a pity, we thought, not to call in just briefly at the farm, and, if not to wish them a Merry Christmas, at least to acknowledge a common recognition of the day. As we began to negotiate our way into the tiny dining room of the old farmhouse, where they were in mid-turkey, John shot up from his place as though detonated. He could not have looked more startled and appalled had Hamlet's ghost popped up into the empty space opposite. Christopher's housekeeper, the feisty Kathleen Johnstone Brown, said to Murray, as we made our getaway not long afterwards: 'My lad, you were never nearer death'.

In Ian McIntyre's biography of John Reith, *The Expense of Glory*, the indexed entry for Murray is: 'Leishman, Murray, Reith's loathing for'. The reference would have done credit to Hazlitt's essay 'On the Pleasure of Hating'. 'The spirit of malevolence survives the practical exertion of it ... There is no surfeiting on gall: nothing keeps so well as a decoction of spleen. We grow tired of everything but turning others into ridicule, and congratulating ourselves on their defects.'[7] But, even had John read this, it would have taken more than one of the greatest essayists in the English language to dislodge him from the growing range of his aversions. He went on to reshuffle his seven original hate figures, placing Murray higher up in the priority placings. Earl Mountbatten retained seniority: 'a playboy, fraud, counterfeit'; Anthony Eden was 'a hollow third-rater'; and, as for Hugh Dalton, 'he couldn't have been more civil – nor less sincere. And then Mr Leishman, whom we all so much dislike.' But Murray and I were too happy to notice. And, if we had needed encouragement (which we did not), John Reith could not have found a more effective method.

Among the many who have commented on John, Malcolm Muggeridge came nearest the truth. His was a more original and agile mind than to adopt one view of John's weird temperament and near-psychosis, content with neither a picture of flawless power and eminence nor creeping degeneracy and rancour. Instead, he worked out of his own enthralled perplexity about John:

> He gets little satisfaction from being told that as a result of his reign at Broadcasting House he has made his mark on the times as it has fallen to few men to do. 'What sort of mark?' he grumbles. His pride is very great. If you taunt him with the absurdity of ambition – for instance regretting not becoming Viceroy when the Indian Empire had itself disappeared and all traces of its Viceroys with it – you suddenly realise that he seriously supposes it wouldn't have disappeared if he had been Viceroy.[8]

Muggeridge was arrested by by the power of the man as well as by his trifling with life; irreconcilable opposites contended within him. John Steinbeck called it the greatest story of all: the story of good and evil, strength and weakness, love and hate, beauty and ugliness – these doubles are inseparable, he said. Looking back on John Reith, one sees this observation embodied, as with it one considers the catastrophe of personality and the unredeemed legacy of family.

NOTES

1. Ian McIntyre, p. 309, undated ascription.
2. An unpublished paper by Sarah Nettleton, with her permission.
3. McIntyre, p. 303, from *The Observer*, 19.11.50, copyright Guardian Newspapers Ltd, with their permission.
4. Rev. Ian Mackenzie, from *The Scottish Review*, Spring 2002, with his permission.
5. From a letter, MacLeod to Reith, 1960, in the author's possession.
6. McIntyre, p. 345.
7. McIntyre, p. 352.
8. From an article which first appeared in *The New Statesman*, 3.10.69, with their permission.

19

Adequate Circumstances at the Palace of Holyroodhouse

*I*N 1967 and 1968, a ten-day viceregal appointment to represent the Queen at the annual General Assembly of the Church of Scotland entirely suited John. All had to bow and curtsey to Their Graces, who were accommodated at the Palace of Holyroodhouse with a retinue. He had to make meaningful speeches, dress up in various uniforms, parade, and open all manner of enterprises.

'For once,' wrote John in his diary, 'I found myself adequately circumstanced.' He had been called upon to act as Lord High Commissioner to Her Majesty the Queen, representing her at the General Assembly of the Church of Scotland, and living in one of her palaces for the Assembly's ten-day duration. He would be a kind of viceroy. He would need a retinue, and he would need to dress up in every kind of outfit to which he could reasonably lay claim. The Royal Company of Archers, for instance, a body formed in 1676 by 'an influential Body of Noblemen & Gentlemen' as the Queen's Bodyguard for Scotland, had its bonnet enhanced with a high feather. Whatever he wore, it would be hung with medals; he himself, throughout the Assembly, would be addressed as Your Grace. His every move would produce bows and flutters of curtseys – all of which were acceptable to John.

In fact, becoming a stage sovereign was something into which he fell so naturally as to suggest that he had been waiting in the wings for someone at last to recognise the self-evident and to act upon it. And so, when the call came to move into the Palace of Holyroodhouse, he was at once on the job, working with his Purse-Bearer, manager of the elaborate programme for the Lord High Commissioner and his lady, Her Grace. Together, the two men appointed aides-de-camp (ADCs) and a chaplain. At this point, because otherwise tongues would wag, John could not avoid appointing Murray (his son-in-law) as chaplain, and me as Extra Lady-in-Waiting. They drew up lists of those to be invited, thought to be distinguished and influential in terms of responsibility and high office, lineage or personal achievement, both in Scotland and beyond. Some would stay at the Palace; others would attend one of the formal banquets. The Lord High Commissioner and Purse-Bearer worked on the speeches and procedure when His Grace and his entourage would actually visit the Church's General Assembly, convened in its Assembly Halls on the Mound near the top of Edinburgh's High Street. They arranged for the many public ceremonies to be enhanced by His Grace's attendance: the hospital wing opened, the battalion harangued and the regiment closed down. The robed Academicians of the Royal Scottish Academy were to be met and addressed, and luncheon arranged with the Corporation of the City of Glasgow, traffic stopped and police outriders laid on.

His Grace's programme at Holyroodhouse would start very properly with the Ceremony of the Keys. In setting the tone, my father would ensure that everyone would realise that things this year were going to be done as never before. Into the Palace courtyard, up the stairs and then into the Throne Room processed the Lord Provost of Edinburgh and the councillors, their ponderous robes and grave looks masking inquisitive glances at the numbers of the great and the famous now making graceful adjustment to being part of a crowd looking on rather than, as was their custom, taking centre stage. Anyway, they were most curious to know whatever was going to happen next.

Modest earls looked across at the portraits of their ancestors gazing sightlessly from the wall opposite, and an Hon. Sheriff Substitute considered whether, in the event of the Purse-Bearer again forgetting his name at the introductions later on, he would dismantle him publicly and draw attention to his annual amnesia.

The Lord Provost climbed onto the dais in the centre; and, as he did so, the band in the courtyard below crashed and thumped into life, which meant that the viceregal procession was approaching. The throng within, peripheried around the Throne Room walls, stiffened and eyed the entry for the arrival of Their Graces. Instead of the muffled tramp of the regular step approaching — the carpets were too thick for that — they heard the rustle of women's silks and the metalled sound of the ceremonial sword. First came the Purse-Bearer, Sir Alasdair Blair, with the tall carriage and looks of the natural soldier in ceremonial rig. His Grace came next, resplendent in the uniform of the Grand Cross Victorian Order, so large as quite to obscure his wife, Her Grace, coming timidly behind, never one to make an entry of any kind, but looking very beautiful in an ivory satin gown, hung with a profusion of aquamarines. After her came ADCs and a rivulet of ladies-in-waiting and extras in long dresses. Their progress round the room was marked by the responsive ripple of bending bows and dropping curtseys travelling through the spectators as they passed by. Everyone was coated in the reverential hush created by 'Kings and Queens ... playing their stately farce', as Robert Louis Stevenson said. Then the procession moved towards the dais, where the keys of the city were to be ceremonially handed over. His Grace stepped up. His GCVO uniform was crusted with decorations. He glared down at the Lord Provost, who thought that he had never seen such a look overhung by such brows, and was a sparrow inadvertently strayed into an eyrie and eyed by a golden eagle within — 'a giant with but a single idea' (though Coleridge was describing the beam engine at work at a lead mine in the Scottish Borders).

The Hon. Sheriff Substitute decided that, when the time came, he would embarrass the Purse-Bearer.

The Lord Provost made a speech and handed over the keys of his city on a velvet cushion. His Grace bowed briefly and received cushion and contents appropriately. And then, with even greater symbolical straining, he graciously returned them to the Lord Provost for safe keeping – it being clear to everyone that, unlike the old way, when one had to rouse the town guard, negotiate credentials and have him fit his ponderous key into the lock of the West Port, entry into the city today is a prosaic matter of sitting in a queue, motionless, as though in a car park.

A little light on historical detail, His Grace had, nevertheless, no difficulty in pushing back the dramatic frontiers of the occasion, intoning with such words and delivery as would properly reflect antique ceremony and regality. The rolling Rs cascaded like a Highland river in spate as he announced his 'returning to you, my Lord Provost, the keys of your own incomparable city'. The Lordship and councillors looked thoughtful; but many people there that afternoon were to find that, in later years, they had remembered the torrential phrases of significant oratory.

In the evening, with the guests again perimetered around the Throne Room, the Purse-Bearer accurately introduced ninety-nine of them to His Grace, forgot the name of the Hon. Sheriff Substitute, and was publicly and noisily bitten. At a less conspicuous moment, he and his wife accepted me, the Extra Lady-in-Waiting, as escort out of the Palace, and the two spaces at the banqueting table were discreetly lost.

The prime minister, Harold Wilson, and Mrs Wilson arrived later in the week, the climax of intense police activity. The guests for dinner and overnight stay had already moved into the Palace; and, now gathered in the drawing room, the prime minister appeared in their midst. In the unaccountable absence of the Purse-Bearer and the Lady-in-Waiting, I, unprompted and unrehearsed, had to move into action fast and introduce the prime minister to all the recently arrived guests, whom I had only just met. Already, habituated as they were to the ways of formal gatherings, they had lined themselves up for the purpose. This time, there was no Hon. Sheriff Substitute to upset an applecart, and we got safely to the end, all those names and faces instantly printed on that computerised brain which reliably served the prime minister. But, at the end of the line, I had to resist the urge to collapse, exhaling inelegantly, onto the nearest Regency chair.

In later years, when Yehudi Menuhin came with his elegant wife Diana, his world fame and his own retiring nature, his interest was as to how our daughter Martha was, who he had heard was unwell. But, back at the Palace, His Grace would have Yehudi play before the company. I was despatched to Yehudi's apartment, where, doing his yoga, he was upside down as I delivered the message through the closed door. Since you cannot refuse even a surrogate royal command, he played – but he was most ill at ease, and needed all Diana's encouragement. Playing to order, even for the greatest, is not on. My own minuscule experience, when inappropriately commanded, bore this out.

I cannot but associate the whole Holyrood pageant with a remark made by the late Roy Jenkins on his experience as Chancellor of Oxford University. It was, he said, that of 'impotence assuaged by magnificence'.

One senior divine, known for his devoted service to ancestry and position, complained about the arrangements that were, one afternoon during the 1968 General Assembly, to expose His Grace to the annoyance of small children visiting. Because I was the children's mother, and Her Grace had specially asked to see them, the arrangement would stand. My response was suitably robust – as indeed, to his surprise, was that which greeted the grandfather in question. He met his grandchildren in the Palace cloisters. In full regalia, this time of the Royal Company of Archers, feather stretching up a further eighteen inches, he bent down to his six-year-old grandson. 'Well, Mark,' he said ominously, 'what have you got to say to me?' The boy looked steadily up at him. 'Well, Grandfather,' he said, 'how can I have anything to say until you have asked me a question?' At this sturdy approach, a sudden engagement called His Grace elsewhere, his entourage hurrying along behind.

Then it was my turn to withdraw. This time, a well-known headmaster and his wife suggested that we have tea together, declaring themselves to me as recipients of special confidences of His Grace and entrusted with his personal tribulations – of which, I was about to be informed, I was the centre. I began wearily to count up all those whom I knew to have credited themselves with being – so they understood – thus uniquely entrusted with his confidences: people in whom he had little interest, whose admiration he enjoyed while despising their sycophancy. Now, in the 'obsequious tones of the pompously inadequate', as the Scottish poet Maurice Lindsay said, and with ghastly kindness, Mr and Mrs Headmaster would help me to realise that I had hurt my father deeply when I had left home, disregarded his advice and got married. Perhaps they thought that, with their help, I should walk out on husband, family and home and say sorry to Daddy. What an extraordinary effect he had on people, so that otherwise responsible beings were unaccountably deprived of sense and reason and, losing all judgement and courtesy, launched in. It was all so familiar.

John's family had always been at war with itself; from early days, he had started to practise standing up for himself in the face of so many older brothers and sisters. Bad temper flared up readily; and so now it was not long before Purse-Bearer and Lady-in-Waiting were meeting urgently to try to prevent His Grace from belittling his wife in such a public way as to make everyone wonder where to look. In their public life together, she expected – but did not necessarily experience – the woman's prerogative of moving first through a doorway; but now she forgot that his position as Lord High Commissioner overrode custom. He grabbed her shoulder as she moved ahead. 'Can you not remember, woman, that I go first?' This was terrible, and the escort began to think longingly of the *real* royals, who, had a chandelier crashed before them and an ADC disappeared in the wreckage, would have kept going with unperturbed and stately pace, diverting minimally, effecting an automatic reference to the section of Debrett concerned with collapsed chandeliers.

'A remarkable man, His Grace, don't you think?' said the Solicitor General to me, amiably offering a conversational opening. We climbed into one of the immense black and gleaming limousines which made up the traffic-halting processions needed to cover the distance between the Palace and the Assembly Halls on the Mound. As we did so, I noticed an incipient emergency. 'Tell the ADC his flies are undone', I hissed to

Murray. 'Have you met His Grace before?' pursued the Solicitor General. I looked out at all those High Street buildings 'in their most admired disorder', as dear Robert Louis Stevenson said, with a gable and some crow-steps printed on the sky. I made a laconic reply: 'Once or twice — yes. He's my father.' The aftermath to this outlasted the brief journey, and over disembarkation and the next procession a sober-faced control had to be exerted.

20

Vex Not His Ghost

FINALLY, my parents moved house from London to Edinburgh. They drove from their grace-and-favour house in Edinburgh's Moray Place to receive the Order of the Thistle, the Scottish equivalent of the Order of the Garter, in St Giles' Cathedral. My mother was delighted to see her grandchildren; my father was cautiously intrigued. But a fall was, for him, the end. In due course, the memorial service in Westminster Abbey was attended by many from the BBC. His ashes were interred in the graveyard of the Old Kirk of Rothiemurchus.

As an old man, John seemed to have learned nothing from his youth, least of all the blessings of change and the cultivation of helpful attitudes. 'He had saved up for that festival which was never to be', said Stevenson, so that in his seventies he still saw himself recalled to the BBC. His was 'that hysterically moving sort of tragedy that lies on the confines of farce ... a combination of calamities nonetheless absurd for being grim'. He seemed never to incorporate the blessings and successes of much of his time

279

at the BBC in any way that might sweeten his subsequent career or make him the more pliable and thus available for the tasks of national importance that were queuing around him looking for candidates with the capacities which he had.

But now, in 1970, and with little in London to detain them, Muriel and John moved to Edinburgh, having been awarded a grace-and-favour house, the Queen's gift, in Moray Place. No doubt John's lawyer, Joe Burrell, had been sleuthing on his behalf. But the elaborate fittings that my parents installed, and the changes made, left them both much weakened.

Their grandchildren, who were fond of their grannie, would come with me to see them both. She was so affectionate, and they could make her laugh. She hung up Iona's painting in the kitchen and made tea for everyone. Grandfather remained sensibly at his desk, and all was peaceful until he found he had no stamps and flew into a rage. Trying to make myself heard — he was by now profoundly deaf — I said that Martha and I would go out and buy some. On our return, Martha carried them in and put them down fearlessly before him. 'Here are your stamps, Grandfather', she said. He was not so deaf that he could not catch the five-year-old's bell treble. He saw the stamps and the eager face looking into his. 'Thank you, Martha', he said, with an effort remembering her name. 'Thank you very much.' And then, rather elaborately: 'That was very kind of you'. Perhaps he did not need to be so afraid of children after all.

John was made a Knight of the Thistle, the highest decoration awarded to a Scotsman, the equivalent of the English Knight of the Garter. The Royal Family occupied their stalls in St Giles' Cathedral, and Mark had been asked by his grandfather to be his page. 'Oh my!' said Sir Alec Douglas Home, former prime minister, and likewise a knight. 'Doesn't he look splendid!' Murray did not disagree as Mark and his grandfather and other knights were politely lined up in the Signet Library for the procession. Meanwhile, at an open window opposite, Mark's boiling sisters were announcing that it was simply Not Fair, and jostled one another because they were not getting to process.

But John had hardly nine months in which to enjoy the new house and the honour, as, apt to fall, he did so once more and now was badly hurt. He was moved to the Officers' Nursing Home in Belgrave Crescent. On a visit there, I had the eighteen-month-old Kirsty on my knee, a young person vigorous with new life. While she investigated her toys, he, disorientated, explored the lost loves of his childhood. From his mutterings, I recognised his mother, pausing at the door of her room as he, ready for school, was about to leave. She bade him work hard, and then goodbye, closing her door. There was Dr Reith, before his massed congregation, about to read the second lesson: 'Hear the Word of God ...', he commanded – and the rest was lost in incoherence. Next, Maggie Raeside, the nurse who had mothered the lonely lad – but now he told her he was not going out in the park. 'Too cold', he said, and rambled on to say something about Beta, the much older sister who, on leave from nursing in Edinburgh, had cared for him too. But now he was agitated: he had lost her. She had gone away. No wonder. In 1921, after a long illness, and largely estranged from her family, she died. John, aged 32, had driven to Glasgow, where occasionally she recognised 'her own dear wee Johnny'. In his diary, he had written: 'I prayed that I might be worthy of all the great love she had had for me, and which I had made little use of. She understands now how difficult it all was, and how very perplexed I was about it all.'

On 16 June 1971, we bade him farewell. George MacLeod conducted the funeral service in the Thistle Chapel in St Giles' Cathedral; and, after it, over lunch in the Queen's House, George was suggesting that John's wishes about no memorial service might be disregarded. There were further consultations; and then, a few weeks later, the Saltire flew from Westminster Abbey. The Earl of Wemyss and March, once also Lord High Commissioner to the General Assembly of the Church of Scotland, represented the Queen, and the Archbishop of Canterbury led the procession. Opposite us was arranged, it seemed, the BBC itself. And there was the BBC Symphony Orchestra, as in old times under the baton of Sir Adrian Boult. Murray read the first lesson from the Wisdom of Solomon; Charles Curran, Director General, read the second; and the Moderator of the General Assembly of the Church of Scotland, Dr Andrew Herron, preached.

Then the final Orlando Gibbons 'Amen' died into the strain of the one piper and the lament from Scotland: 'The Flowers o' the Forest'. It was as though that great gathering were together in that 'second simplicity where the music is not being played but is happening by itself'. The piper, in the full regalia of the Cameronians, John's old regiment, emerged from the sanctuary to play his way the length of the silent crowded chancel and then out at last by the west cloister door, where his notes merged with the roar of London continuing imperviously to go about its business.

Some years earlier, and in a spirit of reconciliation, John had visited us in the cottage which he had bought us in Duror of Appin on the western seaboard in Argyll. This was, for us, the lung from out of Glasgow city centre. As he and Muriel were preparing to leave, I handed him a bunch of corn marigolds, wild flowers that before the days of insecticides grew in abundance along the margins of corn fields. They were one of the few plants that he knew and could name. John was visibly affected by them, and, forgetting his assumed reluctance to exchange with Murray, spoke this time with a different kind of difficulty. 'I am inordinately fond of corn marigolds', he said, the rolled Rs carrying some of the tide of his feelings as he spoke. These flowers triggered some rare pearl of recollection which would have been his mother's attention during those 'halcyon holidays in Rothiemurchus' in the Cairngorm hills of the Scottish Highlands.

Throughout his life, John would make return visits to Rothiemurchus, not only to meet the boyhood memories, but also believing that there he might at last find his father – the father who throughout his young life had so steadfastly eluded him. He spoke of this natural – to him – expectation of his without difficulty. He would then go on to quote – with varying degrees of accuracy – the Old Testament story of the prophet Elijah and his follower Elisha: a story that resonated for him.

Behold, there appeared a chariot of fire, and horses of fire, and parted them both asunder; and Elijah went up by a whirlwind into heaven.

And Elisha saw it, and he cried, my father, my father, the chariot of Israel and the horsemen thereof. And he took off his own clothes and rent them in two pieces. And he saw him no more.

And he took the mantle of Elijah that fell from him and smote the waters, and said, Where is the Lord God of Elijah? And when he also had smitten the waters they parted hither and thither: and Elisha went over.[1]

In creating the BBC, John felt that he had taken up his father's mantle, and with it the conviction that for the BBC only the best was good enough. I grew up with that vision of his; and what he gave to Murray and me, and our four children, was the sense of life lived in a larger place.

It has always been clear that it had been among the Cairngorm hills that John had experienced those first stirrings to achieve, and from which sprang his vision for excellence in broadcasting, to which he clung until the very end. His other occupations, with however much of his own spirit he imbued them, he always experienced as intervals after which he might return to his vocation in the BBC.

And so it was back to Speyside that we took his ashes, to the old kirk of Rothiemurchus, where the graveyard lies in a hollow. Tall beech trees stand around to keep it hidden, so that, unlike his autobiography *Into the Wind*, all is still. There, joined by Muriel four years later, he can be left where he no longer has to strive to achieve, and has no need, in his own words, to be 'fully stretched'.

Malcolm Muggeridge, over the telephone to me, quoted this:

> Vex not his ghost: O! let him pass; he hates him
> That would upon the rack of this tough world
> Stretch him out longer.[2]

Peace at last – and only the Cairngorm hills to stretch before him.

His own words tell it best. In his autobiography, he wrote about how, over the radio, he heard the metrical version of the 23rd Psalm. It was sung in Westminster Abbey; and, because the occasion was the wedding of Princess Elizabeth, later to be Queen, it was broadcast all over the world:

> The Lord's my shepherd, I'll not want;
> He makes me down to lie
> In pastures green. He leadeth me
> The quiet waters by.

'The age-old song of Presbyterian Scotland,' he called it, 'the national anthem of its faith.' He went on, in *Into the Wind*:

I see my mother trace its lines for me to read. I hear my father's voice: 'John, can you say the 23rd Psalm yet?' I hear it sung at family worship in the manse; in the College Church in Glasgow; in the little highland conventicle of halcyon summer holidays. The Abbey of Westminster dissolves to Rothiemurchus.

Ite, missa est. [Go. It is done.] In the porch one's eyes would straightway lift to the everlasting hills that stood round about; to the purple expansions of the heather moors; to the forests of larch and spruce and pine; to the now-fed cataracts; to all the majesty and the beauty of the highland scene where first there came those fateful stirrings to achieve. So homeward to the gentler valley of the Spey. Here grassy knolls and silver birch; here whispering corn edged bright with yellow marigold; here softer flow of tributary stream. Green pastures and quiet waters. Out of the wind.[3]

NOTES

1. 2 Kings, chapter 2, verses 11, 12, 14.
2. Shakespeare, *King Lear*, Act V, Scene 3, line 316.
3. Reith, *Into the Wind*, p. 531.

Biographical References

Included are those who, for one reason or another, feature significantly, even if briefly, in the story. Those apparently omitted are described in the text.

Attlee, Clement (1883–1967)

His interest in social questions led him to become Parliamentary Secretary to Ramsay MacDonald and then Leader of the Labour Party in 1935. From 1942 to 1945, he was deputy prime minister in Winston Churchill's war cabinet. Thereafter, during his six years as prime minister, he carried out widespread nationalisation and ensured independence for India and Burma.

Auden, Wystan (1907–73)

He was born in New York, and his first book of poems was published by T. S. Eliot at Faber & Faber. His views were very left-wing, and he involved himself in the Spanish Civil War. He wrote the libretto for Benjamin Britten's *Ballad of Heroes*. His collection *Another Time* contained many of his most famous poems. In 1946, he took out American citizenship, returning to the UK to become professor of poetry at Oxford. *For the Time Being* and other anthologies brought him widespread recognition.

Baird, John Logie (1888–1946)

This television pioneer left his native Scotland to work in Hastings on the south coast of England, where he demonstrated the first image ever. The system he used was initially adopted by the BBC, but in 1937 it was superseded by Marconi's system.

Baldwin, Stanley (1867–1947)

He was Conservative prime minister from 1923 to 1926 and from 1935 to 1937, the Liberal coalition under Lloyd George intervening. His handling of the abdication of King Edward VIII was admired, but not his lack of response to the increasing Nazi threat.

Beaverbrook, Lord (1879–1964)

A Canadian, Max Aitken was a newspaper magnate and, under Lloyd George, Minister for Information. After he bought the *Daily Express*, it became the most widely read paper in the world. In the Second World War, he was in charge of aircraft production under Churchill.

Beecham, Sir Thomas (1879–1961)

The son of an industrial millionaire in St Helens, Lancashire, he became Principal Conductor of Covent Garden Opera. In 1946, he founded the Royal Philharmonic Orchestra, championing the works of Delius, Sibelius and Richard Strauss. He had a most disconcerting wit: 'I prefer Offenbach to Bach often', he remarked of a Third Programme concentration on Bach.

Betjeman, John (1904–84)

His father was a Dutch manufacturer; he was taught at school by T. S. Eliot and later influenced by Auden. He wrote a verse